How to Sell Your
Book Through
Public Speaking,
Interviews,
Signings,
Festivals,
Conferences,
and More

TALK UP YOUR BOOK

PATRICIA FRY

ALLWORTH PRESS
NEW YORK

D0829489

Allworth Press books may be purchased in bulk at special discounts for sales promotion, corporate gifts, fund-raising, or educational purposes. Special editions can also be created to specifications. For details, contact the Special Sales Department, Allworth Press, 307 West 36th Street, 11th Floor, New York, NY 10018 or info@skyhorsepublishing.com.

15 14 13 12 11 5 4 3 2 1

Published by Allworth Press, an imprint of Skyhorse Publishing, Inc. 307 West 36th Street, 11th Floor, New York, NY 10018.Allworth Press® is a registered trademark of Skyhorse Publishing, Inc.®, a Delaware corporation.
www.allworth.com

Library of Congress Cataloging-in-Publication Data

Fry, Patricia L., 1940-
Talk up your book : how to sell your book through public speaking, interviews, signings, festivals, conferences, and more / Patricia Fry.
    p. cm.

ISBN 978-1-58115-922-6 (pbk. : alk. paper)
1. Authorship--Marketing. 2. Books--Marketing. I. Title.
PN161.F7935 2012
002.068'8--dc23
                    2012023987

Printed in the United States of America

CONTENTS

Introduction

Experts agree that face-to-face interactions and public appearances are some of the most effective methods for authors to promote their books. Not only do we sell more books on the spot when we are personally engaged with one or more individuals, but we gain valuable exposure which can lead to additional sales.

I've written many articles on aspects of public speaking and one-on-one communication, dozens of them having appeared in *Toastmaster* magazine. While I don't claim to be the best speaker around, this is a topic I have studied, practiced, and taught for many years. I joined a Toastmasters club in 1992 and have been an enthusiastic supporter of the program ever since.

Even though I was born under Gemini, the communication sign, I'm not a natural public speaker. However, when I published my first local history book in 1983, I wrote into my marketing plan that I would "present speeches for historical society gatherings, at civic organization meetings, in schools and other venues" as a way to promote the book.

I had no problem getting speaking slots locally. This was the first comprehensive history ever written about our community, and residents were hungry to hear the stories and facts I had dredged up during my five years of research. I was never at a loss as to what to say in front of my audiences. Why? Because I wrote my speeches and read from them. This worked for several years. I seemed to be able to adequately entertain and inform my audiences this way. I always received favorable comments after my talks, and I sold books. People either didn't notice that I was reading from a prepared speech or they didn't care.

I realized years later that it was my rather conversational way of writing that helped me pull this off. I also memorized much of the speech content, so I managed to maintain eye contact with my audiences despite the fact that I was reading to them.

Over time, however, I grew dissatisfied with my presentations. I discovered that I felt a more satisfying connection with my audiences when I was spontaneous—when I told a story or shared information that wasn't in my script. I knew the material well and was quite good at relaying it in an interesting way, but I noticed that I was more comfortable during the question and answer sessions than while I was presenting a written or rehearsed speech. I instinctively knew that a more relaxed speaker is a more effective speaker.

During that time, I attended presentations by others. I was particularly taken by those who spoke eloquently without notes, and I wanted to be that kind of speaker. But I was afraid to let go of my written speech crutch. What if I forgot something or imparted information out of sequence?

As I became more discontented with my speech deliveries, I soon found myself declining speaking opportunities. I began to experience fear at the thought of going public again. When this happened, I knew I had two choices: become a public-speaking cripple and watch my books fail, or take on the challenge of improving my speaking skills.

Around that time, I happened to meet Barb, the president of a local professional speakers' Toastmasters club. (Who says things don't happen for a reason?) She urged me to visit her club. The very idea caused me to quake in my four-inch heels, my cowboy boots, or my aerobics shoes—whichever I was wearing at the time. No way would I subject myself to such critique as she described occurs during a Toastmasters meeting. At least, that was my decision until I took a good long look at my goals for the future. I was a writer. I wrote regularly for numbers of magazines. I had two books under my belt and I dreamed of writing many more. I'd already learned how valuable public speaking is in promoting and selling books. I absolutely had to get a grip on my growing fear.

One day when I was feeling particularly disappointed in myself and especially courageous, I called Barb and said in a weak but audible voice, "Okay, I want to come to a meeting."

I knew there were many Toastmasters clubs in the county. I chose a professional group because I wanted to do more than just an occasional speech at the club level. I genuinely wanted to become a more poised and effective speaker.

I must say that, again, while I am not the best of the best, I have come a long way. I have more confidence, I am willing to speak on the spur of the moment, I do not turn down opportunities to speak on behalf of my published books, and audience members seem to appreciate my style and the information and expertise I offer.

I am ever so grateful that I confronted my fears. I've been blessed with some incredible experiences as a public speaker, and I've had the opportunity to meet some amazing people throughout the world. In 2006, I was the first woman ever to be invited to give the keynote address at an annual Toastmasters convention in the Middle East. This was an all-expenses-paid gig in the fabulous emirate of Dubai. Talk about a challenge! I spoke before 800 people—the largest group I had faced at that point. The majority of them spoke English only as a second language as they were from the United Arab Emirates, Oman, Bahrain, Kuwait, Qatar, Jordan, Saudi Arabia, and Pakistan. Not only was it important, as a Toastmaster, that I speak well (and without my beloved notes!), but I had to be aware of cultural clashes in the terms and the gestures I used while speaking as well as during private conversations throughout my four-day stay.

To think, if I hadn't faced my fears, swallowed my pride, and began the journey toward improving my speaking skills fourteen years earlier, I would have missed this incredible experience.

Since coming out with my first self-published book nearly thirty years ago, I've added generously to the number and array of books published through my own publishing company, Matilija Press, as well as various traditional publishing companies. My books now number thirty-six, and most of them relate to publishing and book promotion. As a matter of course, for the last fifteen years, I've been speaking on publishing and book promotion as many as two dozen times each year to audiences of around fifteen to five hundred authors and hopeful authors. I've had the pleasure of speaking in many fascinating locales and meeting many amazing authors. I've been a presenter and workshop leader in California cities up and down the state as well as in Honolulu; Phoenix; Seattle; Dallas; Baltimore; Nashville; St. Louis; Atlanta; Wadesboro, North Carolina; White Plains, New York; Janesville, Wisconsin; and Anchorage, for example. I was an invited guest speaker for the prestigious Much Ado About Books in Jacksonville, Florida one year. I also present workshops and chat with folks at book festivals and signings. I am often interviewed for both on and off-line radio shows. I've been recorded and videotaped, and millions of my words have been noted during my talks.

Don't you know that none of this would have happened had I remained stuck in my self-created shell of fear? If you have a book to promote and you lack either the confidence, the skill, or both to get out and effectively talk about it, please keep reading. You are my audience for this book! If you are an author who is eager to speak on behalf of your book, keep reading. You, too, are my audience.

Through this book, I share with you some of the things I've observed, experienced, and learned about the various types of presentations authors can deliver and communication skills they can use in order to gain more exposure for their fiction and nonfiction books. You may recognize some of the experts and professionals who have assisted me with this book by revealing their experiences and offering great advice and tips.

Whether this is the first or the sixth book you'll read on public speaking and effective communication for authors, you will learn valuable lessons and gain important insights that you've never been exposed to before. So calm those noodle knees. Sit down with this book, buckle your seatbelt, and prepare for an amazing learning experience that could mean a huge increase in your book sales.

Personality Sells Books

Until fairly recently, it was rare to meet an author. You were familiar with the authors whose books you read either because they had celebrity status, they were high-profile authors, or they were well-known in their fields.

Now, you have enormous opportunities to learn volumes about the major (and minor) authors of books you read or might consider reading. You can visit the authors' websites. You are privy to their personal blogs and their Facebook, Twitter, and LinkedIn pages. You can visit their "author" pages at Amazon. com and their publishers' websites. You might also read about them in a variety of national and regional, online and print publications. You listen to author teleseminars and radio interviews, and you can even watch authors in action on TV as well as in webinars, book trailers, and other videos at their websites or on YouTube. Probably the most thrilling author experience is the face-to-face meeting at hometown book signings, book festivals, trade shows, conferences, and other author events held across the country each year.

What has inspired, motivated, or compelled you to buy particular books in recent months? If you're like me and millions of other readers, your purchases were author-driven. You either met the author or read something about her, heard her on the radio, saw a review of the book, stumbled upon the author's blog, or the book was recommended by a friend. I dare say that more books today are sold through personality than practically any other way.

If you can relate to this concept as a reader, it should follow that you understand it from the perspective of an author. The fact is that you and I are among the nearly seven million less celebrated authors who are competing with one another (as well as with the celebrity authors) for book sales in the United Sates and beyond. And competition is fierce. Every year around a million new books and ebooks are produced, and every year, thousands upon thousands of those newly published books fail. The latest statistics indicate that just under eighty percent of all books produced each year sell fewer than 100 copies, and their authors wonder why.

I say it is a lack of personality. Many authors are not willing or able to practice a hands-on approach when it comes to promoting their books. The intimacy these authors experienced with their books during the writing process fades once they face the overwhelming task of marketing. Yet, you should know that a sense of intimacy is at least as important to your project *after* publication as it was during the writing phase of the book—intimacy with your book and intimacy with your audience.

The first step toward a relationship with your audience is knowing who they are. You hear publishing experts tell you, and you read in books by professionals, that you must write for a specific target audience. Some of you still reject this concept. I meet authors every year who have discounted this advice, and whose books are struggling in the marketplace. That's why I devised a post-publication book proposal plan.

After these authors read my ebook, *The Author's Repair Kit: Heal Your Publishing Mistakes and Breathe New Life Into Your Book*, they may realize they are marketing to the wrong audience. With a little coaching, they soon begin actively addressing their true audience, thus experiencing greater bookselling success.

The second step in the process of developing a relationship with your readers is to go where they are. Meet and mingle with them whether it is in person or through some of this century's incredible technological innovations. Be advised that you probably won't be mobbed the first time you sit in a bookstore, pen in hand, behind your stack of books. Achieving celebrity status generally takes a lot of time spent in the limelight.

In most cases, your audience can be defined. They might be comprised of those who read mysteries, science fiction, or young adult novels. Your book might address avid cooks, other writers, educators, parents of preschoolers, dog owners, pilots, or people who are interested in World War I, fitness, home decorating, or self-help for adult victims of child abuse. A primary rule of successful authorship is to identify your audience early in the process of writing your book and keep them in mind throughout. When you truly understand who your audience is and concentrate on writing expressly for that audience, not only will your book have a stronger audience base, you will have begun the process of establishing a relationship with each and every one of them.

Some of you didn't create this sort of intimacy with your audiences while researching and writing your books, and many of you don't even know who your audience is. I can tell you this: It is NOT everyone. Your book has a target audience and, if you hope to approach them through live presentations, at book signings, and book festivals, through social media and so forth, you'll have to discern exactly who they are.

The wrong approach: "This is my book. I'm writing it for me—the way I want to write it—to satisfy my need to tell my story. Of course, millions of readers will care enough about me and my story to buy the book. It is, after all, a book for everyone whether they like to read or not."

The right (or at least a more sensible) approach: "I've done a lot of research and have determined that my target audience consists of readers of chick lit, horror, creative nonfiction, folks who adore cowboy humor, new and struggling authors, gardeners living in the Northwest, or parents of troubled teens—fill in the blank—and I'm keeping them in mind with every word I write. When I finish my book, I know just how to find and address my audience."

Sandra Beckwith is a former publicist who coaches authors to become their own publicists. She also publishes *Build Book Buzz*, an e-newsletter, and is the author of *Publicity for Nonprofits*. She agrees that we need to be thinking about our audience early on. She says, "It's crucial that you know as much as possible about the people you wrote the book for so that you know where they are—and, therefore, how to get your book title in front of them."

I write books and speak on publishing and book promotion. My audience consists mainly of writers who want to publish their works and authors at any stage of the writing/publishing/book promotion process. My audience for the book you are reading is comprised of authors and hopeful authors who want to know more about their book promotion opportunities and the techniques involved in addressing their audiences through effective one-on-one communication as well as live and broadcast appearances. In other words, they want to know how to use public speaking and communication skills to sell more books. This describes you, right?

So, what is the best way for you to compete with the big name authors as well as the other million or so new authors entering the competition for readers each year? After writing the book for your true audience, go out and promote it to them using your greatest asset: your personality.

What can personality do for book sales? As I alluded to earlier, people buy books by authors and celebrities they're familiar with. They also buy books from less celebrated authors whom they happen to meet, like, and trust. Even though authors are found practically everywhere today and everyone seems to know an author or six, readers still enjoy meeting authors face-to-face. They delight in listening to an author speak on the topic or genre of their interest. They are eager to learn from someone who seems credible in his or her field. They get a particular charge from hearing about the writer's life, and it thrills them to watch an author sign a copy of a book for them. There is just something about owning a book written by someone you know or have met. These are a few ways that personality sells books.

In fact, you probably bought this book from me personally at a book festival or after one of my presentations. See how that works?

Sure, you can (and should) promote your book online, by submitting stories and articles for publication in magazines and newsletters, through book reviews, by circulating press releases, by using your fabulous website, through your blog, and so forth. These activities help to introduce your book, your writing skills, your expertise, and, to some degree, your personality. It will behoove you to put some of yourself into your website and your Internet promotion through a personal way of communicating with your public, by posting candid photographs and video clips and by providing easy access to your contact information. Add to these efforts by initiating all manner of face-to-face appearances as well as radio/TV interviews, audio or video recordings posted at your site and others, and personalized social media techniques. Most authors can generate more immediate and residual book sales through personality than using practically any other method of book promotion.

This is my belief based on my own experiences and observations; but I decided to get some feedback from other authors. I was prepared to suggest that personality sells probably seventy-five percent of my own books. When I polled other authors, they came back with figures in the 85 to 90 percent range. Leon Cooper, author of several books on the war in the Pacific, said, "It's *all* personality."

Author and writing consultant Barbara Florio-Graham says, "People buy books for a couple of reasons, one of which is personal recommendation from a friend or a celebrity. The other reason that engages book-buyers is feeling they *know* the author."

Laura Dobbins is the publicity agent for novelist Lucinda Sue Crosby, author of *Francesca of Lost Nation*. She says, "While I do believe that to market a book you have to use every option available to get publicity, being a good speaker or a people-person is a plus."

Mark Levine, author of *The Fine Print of Self-Publishing* and CEO of Hillcrest Media Group, says, "As a general rule, the most success for an author comes when he or she is in a room live, at a book fair in a booth, and so forth."

Renay Daniels, author of *Ten Little Bulldogs*, a delightful picture book, has observed that, "Whenever I get one-on-one with people, I usually sell a book. They want to buy it because they sense my passion for creating it." She admits, "I used to dread public speaking, but now I look forward to it. It's fun to share—kind of like grownup show and tell."

I've met many formerly shy folks who, like Daniels, discovered only after starting the book promotion process that they actually enjoy addressing an audience and all of the attention they get as an author. It can become rather addicting. It's just my theory, but I believe the reason why most authors find it easier to stand before an audience when they're talking about their books is because of the passion they feel for their projects. The positive feedback from our readers spurs us on. If you want to experience this sort of recognition (and book sales), you must get out and meet your public.

What are some of your more personal selling options? They are more plentiful than you might think, and we cover most of them in this book. Herein, you'll learn about basic public speaking and how to get speaking opportunities locally and when you're out of town at civic club and association meetings, appropriate conferences, trade shows, galas and casual fundraising activities, and other events that members of your audience attend. We cover aspects of book signings and book festivals that you've never seen covered before. We talk about selling books during informal chance meetings and casual gatherings. We've even included the prospect of earning a few dollars teaching adult education college extension courses in your genre or on your topic and becoming a paid speaker at select conferences, on cruise ships, and so forth. We discuss speakers bureaus and associations and some of the various services designed to help you hone your communication and speaking skills. We coach you on successfully using radio and TV to sell books, and we talk about making your website and social media pages more personal through webinars, podcasts, and videocasts. Besides what I offer through my own experiences and research, you'll learn the mechanics and protocol of pursuing these various activities through the expertise of around two dozen other authors and leaders within the publishing/public speaking industries.

Most of them agree that authors should use a variety of promotional tactics and pay attention to those that work best in their specific situations. Peter Bowerman is the author of *The Well-Fed Author*. He says,

Assuming you're a good speaker and can do a compelling talk, I do think personal appearances are important, and can be very effective in selling books. People do respond more readily to authors in person, and being in front of a buyer can allow you to tailor your pitch to their situation, which can make it more fruitful. Plus, I like doing presentations because they're just fun. Not only do they get me out from behind the computer, they're richer than more impersonal web- and email-based interactions.

All that said, I wouldn't say that speaking in public is one of the best ways to sell books simply because 1) presentations are pretty labor-intensive, and 2) you can reach only so many people at any given event; and just because you pack a room, doesn't mean you'll sell a lot of books.

Bowerman continues,

One's marketing should emphasize those initiatives that can reach larger numbers of people (article marketing and securing reviews on "key influencer" sites, which are activities that can be done from home). Interaction for interaction, being in front of your buyer IS probably the best way to sell books, but again, the limited scope of such activities limits your yield.

Other authors maintain that meeting your public isn't as much about selling books on the spot as it is about exposure. Dallas Woodburn published her first book when she was in fifth grade and she's been speaking publicly about her books ever since. She says, "Your readers want to feel like they know you on a personal level. Public speaking is a chance for you to share yourself with your readers—your stories behind the book, snippets from your real life, insight into your writing life, and any future projects you have planned."

Children's book author Ned Rauch-Mannino agrees, and he adds,

> Communication is essential to promoting books, and practiced public speaking skills only enhance an author's ability to communicate. Every author should seek to develop a relationship with his or her readers. While social media and other online platforms present valuable opportunities to do so, face time is critical. It's more personal—you are better remembered. It is something that is valued by the reader, and should be by the author, too.

More and more authors engage in activities that require some level of personal communication. Bestselling novelist Margaret Brownley admits, "I never gave a speech before becoming a writer." But she quickly realized how important it is. She says, "It's a different world than when I first started to write. Nowadays, readers don't just want to read a book, they want a personal relationship with the author."

I can't stress enough that, while a single live presentation may not meet your grandest expectations in book sales, each and every time you speak to a group, the exposure could be invaluable in the short and the long term. Most of the authors I spoke with on this subject agreed. A few said that some of their best promotional opportunities came as a result of live presentations. This includes invitations to speak to larger groups and to be interviewed for regular or Internet radio.

Within these pages, we'll cover pretty much every book promotion activity that requires verbal communication, and many of them involve speaking to your readers and potential readers either one-on-one or in a group situation. So let's dive right in and explore the concept of how personality sells books.

What Can You Gain as an Author-Speaker?

What are the benefits of speaking in public? I think they are many and far-reaching. It's a way for you to communicate with your readers and attract and entice new readers for your book(s). Remember, readers are more apt to purchase books from authors they know, like, and trust. Thus, if your spoken message relates to your book and it contains information and/or a story that resonates with your audience, some of them will buy your book. Prolific fiction authors, who can produce a book every year or so, should delight in meeting their public. With each novel they sell to a satisfied customer, they recruit a new reader for past and future titles.

Public speaking affords good exposure for your nonfiction book, as well as for you as an author and as a professional in your field. People who benefit from your presentation are more apt to purchase the book you're promoting and any other book, course, service, or related item you have now or that you will produce in the future.

Rik Feeney is an author and the head of the Orlando Writers Group, which is part of the Florida Writers Association. He has observed that

> an author who speaks sells more books than an author who does not go out and speak. Getting your books up online is a good idea, but it requires a great deal of marketing effort to sell any copies. After a talk, you can sell your books in the back of the room. And more people are apt to buy them because they know more about you now. They've had a chance to meet you.

He adds this bit of wisdom: "Word of mouth is still king in marketing, and whose word is better than the authors?"

You'll notice references to the concept of *exposure* throughout this book. Too many authors discount or simply do not understand the potential for and the value of the exposure that can be generated from personal appearances and interactions. Pay close attention as you read through this book so you don't miss this important point.

Astute and aware authors can also gain a greater sense of professionalism when they begin to search out presentation opportunities. Before we discuss what goes into becoming an effective and personable public speaker, I'd like to stress the importance of your demeanor and your approach to obtaining the opportunities for this kind of exposure.

Don't save your best for that all-important presentation. There's sometimes a lot that goes into landing a speaking gig; if you make a less-than-excellent impression during the initial introduction, you might not get the assignment. Every email you send to the program director, bookseller, or conference organizer, for example, must be error-free and well articulated. Before booking you, the chairperson or radio host may want to hear your speaking style and voice via the telephone or see a video of you in action. This is another opportunity for you to put your best foot forward. I recommend making this a habit, because you never know where your next book-selling opportunity will come from. I urge my clients to always, always use their finest communication skills in every communiqué, whether written or spoken. I say to them, "You are a writer, let it show."

I sometimes receive email messages from people who want help publishing a book, and their spelling and grammar are absolutely atrocious. An occasional correspondent will apologize for his poorly composed email and promise that his manuscript is better. I won't even look at a manuscript from someone who can't (or won't bother to) write a coherent email. Instead of agreeing to consult with this hopeful author, I give what I believe is the best advice I can offer. I suggest that he take a writing course or that he solicit the help of a writer's critique group. This person is not ready to address a publisher or even an editor. There's much more work to be done in areas of writing and grammar.

I would venture to guess that anyone who is seeking good speakers and workshop leaders for their programs would delete any such emails they might receive. I certainly would not book this author. I urge you to make a good impression the first and every time.

Few inexperienced authors consider the far-reaching effects of their appearances beyond the presentation itself. Not only will you be in front of an audience of anywhere from two people to 200 (or more), you'll potentially reach thousands by placing announcements about your presentation in newspapers, magazines, newsletters, at your blog and website, at your social media sites, on related websites, and so forth. Then there is the follow-up publicity. Sometimes you can get the editors of your local newspaper, your alumni newsletter, your church bulletin, etc. to run something such as, "Jane Brown introduced her new book of inspirational quotes last night at the Kiwanis year-end meeting in downtown Seattle," or "Local author wows members of the Village Businessmen's Club on Saturday with tips from his new book, *Make Your Own Luck and Other Secrets to Success and Happiness.*" You can blog about this event and mention it on your social media pages afterward, as well.

What will all of this publicity get you? The possibilities are endless. In fact, I like to call them "probabilities" rather than possibilities. I can tell you this: You are more apt to fall into some sweet opportunities when you are out and about meeting your public than when you are sitting at home surfing the web, playing solitaire, watching TV, or taking a nap. (Read more about publicizing your appearances in chapter 10.)

Is Public Speaking for You?

Let's look at the scope of authors' attitudes and aptitudes when it comes to public speaking. Where do you fit in?

- There are authors who are absolute naturals in the public speaking realm but don't know how to find or recognize the opportunities, how to make the arrangements, or how to effectively pitch their books.
- Some authors hate the thought of standing before a group of people. They get noodle-knees just thinking about it. They don't mind speaking one-on-one with potential readers, but they lack the knack or confidence to attract or entertain an audience.
- Many, many authors are game speakers but have poor skills. While some are aware of their shortcomings, others simply don't get the concept of effective communication and carry with them numerous bad (and sometimes annoying) speaking habits.
- Then there are authors who have all of the right skills and savvy to pitch their programs and successfully promote themselves through public and not-so-public speaking. While some are exuberant, energetic entertainers, others may be effective in a more subtle manner. I've watched authors absolutely charm their audiences using a quiet, gentle approach. What matters is that they have a natural or even manufactured and practiced way of endearing an audience to them.

Speaking in front of a group isn't the only way authors can use their personality to sell books. So it is important to become a well-rounded communicator. I do hope that you will gain the courage and develop the skills to become an accomplished or adequate public speaker, however. A good way to begin the journey toward this goal is to seek out and accept any and all opportunities throughout your busy days to talk about your book. If you're a good promoter, you already tell everyone you meet about your book. And why do they buy it?

- Because it is on a topic or in a genre they are interested in.
- Because they met the author—you.
- Because they like you.
- Because they appreciate the personal introduction to your book.
- Because you offered to autograph it for them.

Once you become more comfortable having casual conversations with friends, co-workers, acquaintances, and even strangers about your book, maybe you will begin to take baby steps toward the public speaking realm. As we'll discuss in chapter 5, there is a process that can help you make the transition.

In the meantime, let's talk about what stops you from setting up speaking engagements on behalf of your book. For some, it is a fear of speaking. Bobbie Christmas is a book editor and author of *Write In Style* and other books for writers. She admits that she is a shy person by nature. She says, however,

> I had to overcome my shyness to get along in business situations. I'm fortunate that one-on-one I can be quite animated, but I had to learn to let that animation show when I'm in a group or in front of a group, as well. To help, I took classes and seminars on public speaking, and I practiced often. I tried Toastmasters, but their limiting nature and strict rules and methods did not allow for much creativity.

Christmas says,

> My public speaking education began in high school some
> fifty years ago. Determined to overcome my fear of speak-
> ing in front of the class, I grabbed the opportunity to take a
> public speaking course in high school. Decades later, I honed
> my speaking skills even more and learned how to give better
> seminars by taking classes at The Knowledge Shop, an adult
> learning center in metro Atlanta. There I learned from some of
> the leading consultants and speakers in the country, including
> Dottie Walters, the author of *Speak and Grow Rich*.

For those who are seeking help, she recommends, "Many colleges
have continuing education programs, some of which offer public
speaking courses, and most large cities also have adult education centers
that include such programs." She also suggests contacting the National
Speakers Association at www.nsaspeaker.org. (See the Resource List in
chapter 18.)

She makes this suggestion: "If authors are too shy or nervous to
speak casually in front of a crowd, perhaps the answer would be for
them to read from their books. This method works only if they can read
with expression, though, stopping now and then to make eye contact
with people in the audience."

Note: The topic of reading aloud from your book is somewhat controversial. While some experienced speakers advise this as a way to
share your story, others are adamant against it *unless* you have a good
reading voice and style. A story told generally comes across as more
natural than a story read. The fact is that, while reading seems like a
simple way to address an audience, it takes more skill than most people
realize. One reason is that most of us write in a different style than we
use to speak. I say, don't do it unless and until you have practiced for

hours, you've received meaningful feedback from people you can trust to be absolutely honest and you have watched yourself do a reading on videotape and are satisfied with the results. I further suggest that you attend author readings with a sharply critical eye while in the process of fine-tuning your reading skills. (Study the tips for reading to your audiences in chapter 9.)

Whether you choose to read from your book or present a speech, if this is a painful experience for you, Christmas offers this advice: "Fake it until you make it. You don't have to feel flamboyant or animated, as long as you act that way. I know. I had to fake it, and now I feel natural in front of a crowd."

For some authors, the fear they feel is beyond common stage fright. It is a feeling of inadequacy or a lack of self-confidence. If you don't like the way you look—want to lose weight, need some dental work done, or feel out-of-touch with today's styles for someone your age—maybe now is the time to make some positive changes. Perhaps you hate your speaking voice—you've been told it's too high-pitched or it lacks clarity. Maybe you have some annoying speech habits— you mumble or you speak in monotone. None of this should deter you from seeking out and communicating with your readers in small and large groups. These are not valid reasons for missing out on more sales than you can even imagine. You don't want to be one of those nearly eighty percent of authors who fail in the marketplace, do you?

Instead, make this the year that you facilitate the personal improvements that have been holding you back. Do you need additional motivation to see a dermatologist, lose weight, hire a voice coach, or simply use what you have going for you? Here are six of them.

Dana LaMon is blind. He is also a motivational speaker who earned the coveted title of World Champion of Public Speaking from Toastmasters International in 1992. I'm going to tell you later how important it is to maintain eye contact throughout your presentations and to be sensitive to audience feedback. Yet, LaMon became a world class speaker without benefit of this valuable sense.

I've had authors tell me that they can't go out and meet their public because of arthritis, diabetes, MS, or some other medical issue. Yet, Mike Schlappi rolls onto stages across the US in a wheelchair to expertly deliver his inspirational presentations several times a year. Judith Geppert entertains audiences even though she suffers from cerebral palsy. Amputees Daniel R. Davison and Brett Eastburn have also overcome their disabilities in order to share their inspirational and motivational messages with audiences everywhere.

Mary Ellen Warner is a storyteller and an author. She also has severe hearing loss. Yet she stands before audiences several times each year entertaining them with her humorous stories, and she enjoys every minute of it. Warner has also faced some challenges as a speaker. For example, I asked her how she handles the question and answer portion of her talks and workshops. She said, "I tell my audiences that I have a hearing loss and that if they have a question, to raise their hand and I'll come to them so I can read their lips."

I'm in perfectly good health for a woman my age, and I seldom turn down a speaking invitation. Once, however, I experienced a rare (for me) physical setback and all bets were off. That fall, I was scheduled to speak before a large group of journalists in New York City, and I was on the agenda to do a workshop for the annual Toastmasters Convention in Reno the following month. A few weeks prior to the first event, I broke my foot while snorkeling in the Caribbean. I was given a pair of crutches, put in a cast and told not to use that foot at all. I immediately cancelled my speaking engagements. I knew absolutely nothing about traveling with crutches or wheelchairs. Just getting around my home was difficult enough.

In recent years, I've traveled with my mother who is limited as to how far she can walk and often requires the use of a wheelchair at airports. I now know that, with some assistance, I probably could have kept my commitments and made the trips that year. LaMon, Davison, Eastburn, Schlappi, and Geppert travel and speak all the time despite permanent disabilities. I could have figured out a way to travel with my temporary injury. There were options that I wasn't able (or willing) to recognize at the time. Don't fall into that trap. If you want to experience successful authorship, you must be willing to make it happen no matter the inconvenience. Besides, there are perks to traveling with a disability. Those who need special assistance can board flights first.

Few of you reading this are dealing with such physical challenges. You simply don't feel comfortable in front of an audience. You're self-conscious, shy, or lack enough confidence to speak in public. This can change, however. Millions of people—many of them authors—have started where you are and have become quite comfortable and competent speakers. You just have to discover the right motivation.

Jerry Waxler, M.S. is the author of two books on writing, *The 4 Elements for Writers* and *Learn to Write Your Memoir in 4 Weeks*. He goes out and talks about his books every chance he gets, but he wasn't always an eager public speaker. He explains,

> When I got my degree in counseling psychology at the age of forty-nine, my supervisor told me that if I wanted to get clients, I was going to have to learn how to reach out to the public. I thought he was crazy. I hated public speaking so much that, when pressed to present in a classroom or in front of coworkers, I started to sweat and stammer, and my word

choice became so garbled and complex I didn't even understand myself. So I avoided speaking to groups and assumed I wasn't cut out for it. However, in order to survive, I realized I ought to at least try.

Someone suggested I visit a Toastmasters club. The first time I went, I sat out in the car to calm myself down enough to go in. On the break, I talked to an old-timer. I told him I was terrified and asked him if there was any hope for someone like me. He said that he started that way, too. He said that if I followed the Toastmasters program, it's like magic. He was right. A year later, I had overcome my fear enough to start teaching workshops to writers. I organized the handouts from my workshops and created books, and then gave more talks to church groups, memoir groups, and so on. Now, I can go into a room filled with people interested in my topic and am not intimidated at all. I look at it as a challenge and have learned to relax enough to crack jokes and have spontaneous interactions with audience members.

Waxler further comments:

Writers have three reasons for learning to speak in public. The first is the obvious one. They want to sell books. The second one is that by crafting your message and your handouts to effectively communicate with small groups, you are forming words and ideas that can help you organize your writing and bring it to life. The third reason has to do with emotions of courage and love. If you are afraid of people, you will hold back from them. When you gain confidence speaking to audiences, you will begin to look at people as friends and cheerleaders. This will increase your confidence in your writing.

According to Rauch-Mannino, author of *Fingertip Island*, a middle grade chapter book series,

> While not everyone needs to be or can be a "wow" speaker, readers and potential readers want to know who's behind the paper and the ink. They want deeper insight into the story, whether or not that insight concerns the giant talking clams or bathtubs falling from the sky. I advise those who are shy about public speaking to start local. Find venues you are familiar and comfortable with.

Victoria Cobb is a massage therapist and the author of *The Yin and Yang of it...a Simple Guide to Playing QiGong*. She finds live presentations the most effective way to meet her audience and gain customers and clients. She says, "Public speaking is the way I get my message out into the communities I want to target. As a massage therapist, I want clients, and many of those who hear my message come later for a massage. This is the easiest way to sell my book and sell my services."

Now, are you motivated to do what it takes to share your message and/or to introduce your book through your personality? Or will you allow your fears or your lack of confidence to sequester you to the background and sabotage your potential success? So important is the power of personality and persuasion that, without it, your book just might flounder.

Build Your Author's Platform
Through Public Speaking

You've probably heard the word *platform*. It is commonly used within publishing circles to indicate an author's following (who would buy a book by this author?), connections (who can he count on to help him reach his audience?), and way of attracting readers (the author's popularity, expertise and/or credibility in the topic or genre).

There are numerous ways to establish your author's platform and to build on it. Basically, it's a matter of becoming known in your field or genre. You are strides ahead of the competition if you enter into the publishing realm with a solid platform. One way to do this is through public speaking and other activities that put you in front of your audience.

Why build a platform before your book is a book? For one thing, this would go a long way toward impressing a publisher. Traditional publishers are interested in an author's marketing plan, and a solid platform can be a deal maker. If experience and exposure as a public speaker is part of that platform, all the better.

Additionally, no matter your publishing choice, once your book is launched, if you've established yourself as a speaker on your topic or in your genre, you already have a reputation and credentials. You know how to talk to people about your book, and there are at least a few people who trust your expertise in your field or appreciate your skill as a writer in your genre.

Conducting workshops and/or getting out and speaking on your topic before your book is a book will help immensely with name recognition. People are more willing to purchase your book if they already know who you are. If you also provide a signup sheet where you speak, you'll have a leg up when it comes to promoting your book. Depending on when you start the process, you could conceivably collect the names and contact information for hundreds of people who are interested in reading your book. You will have a following even before you have a book to sell.

Presumably, you are writing a book on a topic you know well. This is something you've studied for years. Perhaps it is related to your profession or a meaningful hobby. It might feature an insight that has changed your life and now you want to share it with the world. Perhaps you're writing your memoir, a novel, or compiling a collection of your poetry. Why not start now (no matter where you are in the process of outlining or writing your book) and develop a workshop designed to test your book idea? You could do this on your own or in tandem with a store or organization. This is a good way to find out if there is an audience for your book on quilting, photography, pet grooming, woodworking, memoir- or poetry-writing, family budgeting, bartering in tough times, aspects of fiction-writing, parenting techniques, vegan cooking, Internet marketing, overcoming depression, how to make money selling on eBay, or your system for living a happier healthier life, for example. Put together a pamphlet or booklet related to the theme of your planned book and hand it out or sell it to students.

If you're writing a novel or a children's book, consider greeting your public before your book is a book. This might be children or those who enjoy mysteries, fantasy adventure stories, historical novels, romance novels, or chick lit, for example. Teach some aspect of fiction-writing to adults or teens in your community or read some of your stories to groups of children. It's good practice, and it's a good way to build on your platform.

You wouldn't wait until the rains come to fix a leaky roof. Nor would you delay using sunscreen until sunset while outside on a hot day. Neither should you put off taking steps to establish your platform until after you become a published author.

Generate and Use Audience/Student Feedback

Another good reason for speaking and presenting workshops (where appropriate) before writing (or finishing) a book is to help you determine its viability. Is this book truly a good idea? Your proposed audiences will let you know. In fact, they may help you to write a more useful, effective, or entertaining book.

When you teach, you receive feedback that is usually worth paying attention to. If you can't attract people to your lose-weight-by-chewing-gum, wear-hats-for-greater-self-esteem, or sleep-on-stones-acupressure workshop, perhaps your planned book isn't such a good idea. You might want to tweak it to more appropriately fulfill your audience's needs/desires. If attendees don't respond well to your workshop material, you may want to rethink your book.

Waxler is a firm believer in the benefits of speaking for authors. He says,

> If you speak as well as write, you can communicate with the public through two mediums. Each method has its pros and cons, and together they provide a more powerful system of communication than either one alone. Writing gives you the

chance to sit by yourself and creatively form your message. Speaking gives you the opportunity to *see* how that message works.

As I suggest here, the earlier in the writing process that you discern whether or not your message works, the better chance you'll have of writing the right book for the right audience.

I started writing books for writers and authors only after doing a few writing workshops. Without realizing it, I had been establishing my platform as a professional writer for over twenty years by then. I was supporting myself by writing articles for magazines and I had two books to my credit. One was produced through a New York publishing house, and I established my own company to publish the second one. The self-published book was a highly popular local history, and I had become fairly well-known throughout our community. Not only were people constantly asking me questions about the early history, some came to me for writing advice.

Those I spoke with about writing seemed pleased with the information I passed along to them. In fact, I was surprised that I had so much to share. When you work day in and day out in your profession, you take your level of knowledge for granted. It's not until people begin quizzing you that you realize how much you know. It felt so good being able to help would-be writers that, at their urging, I decided to present a workshop on article-writing.

First, I sat down with a steno pad and pen and began listing topics I could cover in my workshop. I dug up articles and borrowed library books on writing, which I scanned for additional ideas. This mainly served to jog my memory related to my own freelance writing experiences. Once I felt confident that I had enough material to present, I applied at a local art center for space, determined what to charge and began advertising through fliers posted at bookstores and libraries. I submitted press releases to local arts councils and community-wide newspapers. I also called everyone I knew who was interested in writing. I filled my first two workshops rather quickly.

Students helped me to expand my teachings by voicing their questions and personal concerns about article-writing. I incorporated their comments into future workshops. This was my first lesson in the importance of audience feedback. Folks, listen to your audience. Not only can they help you to better serve them with regard to your planned programs, their feedback can give you ideas for new articles and books, as well. I can't even begin to count the number of articles, blog posts, and book chapters that have resulted from student, audience, and client feedback over the years. At least four of my books were motivated by my readers and clients. Some of my online courses also resulted from audience and client feedback.

It didn't occur to me at the time to create a prototype of a book for the article-writing workshops, but I provided plenty of handouts. It was from those handouts and the workshop outline that I created my first book for writers, *A Writer's Guide to Article-Writing* (Matilija Press, 2000).

I know many other authors who wrote their books after becoming known in their fields. Most were like me; they were just going about their business, making a living, enjoying life, and, because of something a customer, student, or client said, they decided to write a book related to the theme of their work or interest.

As you can see, a platform is not difficult to establish. In fact, you may already have many elements of your platform in place. If you haven't been out meeting your potential readers in person—by presenting workshops, teaching classes, giving demonstrations, and speaking—you could be missing a key aspect of your all-important platform.

Put Your Platform to Work

While public speaking is a good introduction into a book on your topic, a book is also a valid introduction into the world of public speaking. Program chairpersons, conference directors, and radio/TV show hosts, for example, are more apt to invite a published author to speak on a topic than someone without a book. Owners of stores and businesses of all kinds will more likely agree to have you speak to their customers if it is in conjunction with a book signing. But the fact that you have speaking experience may be even more important in landing speaking gigs. So by doing some speaking before your book is a book, you are also gaining the experience you will need when you're ready to promote your book through speaking engagements. Besides, you'll have collected some dynamite topics to offer program directors.

I've had clients in both categories—those who published a book and then began going out and talking about it and those who had been speaking previous to their books being published. The authors who had bothered to establish a platform by teaching the concept of their books, or by entertaining or inspiring audiences before publication, were definitely ahead of the game when it came to promotion and book sales.

Author Carol Sanford is an innovator and consultant to business leaders and the author of several published works, including *The Responsible Business: Reimagining Sustainability and Success*. She speaks on average about two dozen times per year. She says, "I cannot say enough about how important it is to build a platform so that people know you and respect your work and ideas." She suggests starting to establish yourself within your topic or genre at least six months before a book is released in order to have your platform in place. She reminds us that "public speaking is only part of the process." She says, "I built my book up on Twitter for six months before it was released."

According to Sanford,

> Publishers have told me that there are two things they want from an author: first, a huge list of contacts that matter—that is, people who have valued you, but who also have connections. They want you to have accomplished something with regard to what you are writing about and, hopefully, be recognized for it.

She says,

> Sure, establish your platform by speaking, but also by keeping the names of people who attend and are willing to be contacted, by having respect in your field from people who matter, and by doing work and creating in the world in ways that it are valued and recognized. Platform means you have respected access through many doors that will help you when you have something worth offering.

Way too many hopeful authors (that is, writers who dream of becoming published authors) don't see the big picture. If they haven't taken the time to study the publishing industry before getting involved, they believe that their books will sell easily through bookstores. They don't realize that book promotion will take their full attention, loads of creativity, tons of energy, and sometimes a little (or a lot of) money. They enter into publishing without a following. They are not known or are little-known in their fields. It did not occur to them to start implementing a marketing plan before their book was a book, and that's generally because they didn't know that promotion would be up to the author.

One of my jobs—something I've taken upon myself to do—is to inform hopeful authors of their responsibilities as published authors.

Part of that is to urge them to educate themselves about the publishing industry, just like they would if they were entering into any other industry or profession. Avoid this step and failure could be the next stop on your publishing journey.

If you have a book in the works or in mind, start now establishing your platform through live presentations directed toward your book's audience. This is an enormously wise step to take on behalf of your ultimate success as an author. Study the industry as soon as possible by reading *Publish Your Book, Proven Strategies and Resources for the Enterprising Author* (Allworth Press, 2012).

Locate and Create Speaking
Opportunities

As a published author, you'll soon learn that it's up to you to reach out to distributors, booksellers, newspaper reporters and columnists, book reviewers, Internet and traditional radio show hosts, and those seeking to fill speaking slots. Without some effort on your part, you will be overlooked by those people you need to connect with most. So how do authors get noticed? They go out in search of opportunities for exposure. Why should you pursue speaking opportunities? It's a darn good way to become known and to sell books.

I sold three dozen copies of my book, *The Right Way to Write, Publish and Sell Your Book,* after speaking to a group of writers in Nashville the year it came out. That same year, I sold ten books after presenting a workshop at a writer's conference in Baltimore, fifteen from the SPAWN booth at the Los Angeles Times Festival of Book, fifteen at the Wisconsin Women's Writers Conference, ten at a workshop in Atlanta, and around thirty at local events where I spoke. At the same time, I sold about fifty of my other titles at these events. That's 166 books I would not have sold if I hadn't appeared personally on behalf of my books. In the process, I became acquainted with over a 150 new customers who might buy any subsequent books I'll write on the topic of writing and publishing. (In fact, some of them did!)

Let's not discount the exposure. I like to look at exposure as another layer of bookselling. What do I mean by layers of bookselling? There are the immediate sales you make at an event, for example. Those are tangible, real-time sales. There are also residual sales from people who will go home and order the book cheaper from Amazon.com, those who will purchase the book at a later time when they run across it in a bookstore or see it at your website, and those who will tell others about it. Then there are those people you meet who will bring you some sort of opportunity—often, the opportunity to speak.

Think about it: While I sold 166 books that year on the spot through author events, the exposure level for my books and myself was much higher. I actually connected personally with around 1,500 people. That's how many people I met in person, who heard me speak, who picked up my books and handled them, who registered on my sign-up sheets, and/or who walked away with my brochure or a catalog featuring my books and services. So besides the 150 (or so) people who made the decision at those events to purchase my books, there may have been over a thousand others who became aware of me, my books, and my work. Add to this number those who read the promo related to each of my speaking gigs, those who considered attending and didn't, those who read about the success of the events after the fact either in newspapers, newsletters, or online. Then there is word of mouth. It is possible that my name and the titles of my books came before an additional thousand or more people through publicity before and after the actual event.

A few of those estimated 2,500 or so signed up for my online courses. Some of them now follow my blog. Many recognize my name when they see it in an article in a publication they read or when they become aware that I have a new book out. A handful of those people have contacted me seeking assistance with their projects. Many of my editorial and consulting clients come to me as a result of my live presentations. My travel expenses that year were around $2,500. My known profit resulting from those events was over $12,000.

As you can see, it is beneficial for authors to wear a coat of many colors—to offer additional items and services related to the theme of their books. But don't worry about adding to your repertoire just yet. You have your hands full learning the book promotion ropes. Just remember this passage in this book once you get a flow going with your speaking programs and book sales. At that time, you might consider other commodities you could offer your public. This might be additional novels, a spin-off book related to your nonfiction title, an accompanying workbook, audio tapes of your presentations, consultation services in your area of expertise, audio books, your own seminars or workshops, webinars, online courses, and so forth.

For now, let's consider your potential for selling books through live presentations, teleseminars, online and traditional radio shows, book signings, book festivals, etc. during one year. Multiply that figure by the number of years you plan to actively promote your book. Add in all of the other promotional activities you pursue—maintaining a fabulous website, blogging, involvement in social media, submitting articles or stories to numerous appropriate publications, getting book reviews, selling book excerpts, placing your books in appropriate stores, and so forth. Each activity builds on and depends on the others in order to generate the sort of exposure that leads to impressive sales. It all works together.

Omit the personal appearances aspect of your promotional plan, and your book could end up at the bottom of the competition heap.

I can't tell you how many times I've met authors or hopeful authors at speaking events who know me by name because they've read some of my articles on book promotion or publishing, for example. People sign up for my workshops because they know me through my affiliation with SPAWN (Small Publishers, Artists, and Writers Network), because they've heard one of my radio interviews, because they've bought one of my books, or because they follow my daily blog.

I met a woman at a writer's conference in North Carolina a few years ago who said she carries a recording of one of my workshops presented at the San Diego State University Writers Conference in her car and listens to it frequently. She said she signed up for the conference that year primarily to hear me speak.

A gentleman came up to me at a writer's conference in Alaska and said he is a SPAWN member and that he gets a lot out of the monthly *SPAWN Market Update* that I write, and he follows my blog. He said he was most pleased to get this opportunity to hear me speak.

Are you beginning to see how important it is to reach out to your public using a wide variety of mediums and methods? Sure, you can probably get some speaking gigs without having done much prior promotion and without a platform, but those opportunities will be much more successful if you have laid some groundwork first. You will find it easier to get speaking opportunities, and you will attract a larger audience where you are known.

It's hard work to locate and to create opportunities for the right kind of exposure. Most authors are in constant research mode. After thirty years experience as a public speaker, I still spend a lot of time searching for good speaking gigs. However, sometimes I fall into a sweet speaking deal with little effort on my part. It happens occasionally that someone reads one of my articles, they've heard me speak, they stumble across my website, or they read a review of one of my books and they contact me with an invitation to speak before their group or at a writer's conference. Word of mouth has also landed me invitations to speak. Writers who heard me speak at one club meeting or event may tell those at another club about me.

So you see, there are two main ways to get speaking opportunities: You can go out in search of them or you can grab the opportunities that unexpectedly come your way. If program chairpersons and radio show hosts are not filling your email box with invitations, perhaps you aren't getting out enough and you're not reaching out enough. Here are some ideas to help you enter into the competition as a sought-after author/ speaker:

- Create some purposeful and/or entertaining programs or demonstrations related to the theme or genre of your book.
- Present your programs in safe zones (friendly territory), among family members, at your local Toastmasters club meeting, before your writer's group, in front of your fellow business or civic club members. These are good opportunities for you to work the bugs out of your presentations. Solicit candid comments from your friends/peers and take them to heart.
- Find out where your readers congregate or do business and what types of activities and meetings they frequent. Then contact the program chairpersons and ask to be invited to speak. If this is a place of business, convince the manager to invite customers in for a demonstration/talk, refreshments, and a book signing.
- Read what your target audience reads and pursue speaking slots at some of the events mentioned.
- Read local newspapers to discover where other authors are speaking. Contact the program directors or organizers for those programs. Most newspapers have a community calendar section.

- Do an Internet search in order to locate pending events, book clubs, and organization meetings for those folks who are interested in your book's topic or genre.

- Visit the websites your readers visit. Whether your book is for gardeners, fishermen, or artists; people who love cats, cooking, or home decorating; or folks who enjoy horse stories, romance, novels, or historical fiction, stay abreast of the industry, subject, or genre via the Internet. When you find a site of interest, look for event announcements listed on the press/media page, at the blog site, and in the forum.

- Likewise, visit the websites of other authors of books similar to yours. Check their press/media and appearances pages. Even if these authors live in other states, you'll get some ideas to pursue in your home state.

Start Speaking Locally

I generally advise authors to start their speaking journey in familiar territory. Get a list of local groups and organizations that meet regularly in your city/county. You may find a list in the front pages of your phone book. Or check with the local Chamber of Commerce. Some city websites list local clubs and organizations.

If you belong to a club or organization or know people who do, use these connections to get your toes wet as a public speaker. Did you notice I used the term *connections* again? This is an example of the type of connections you need to recognize, acknowledge, and pursue. Contact the program chair for your college alumni organization, your businesswomen's club, and your church auxiliary and arrange to speak about your appropriate book. Call on your co-worker who belongs to a couple of civic organizations, your cousin who heads up a book club, the principal of your children's school, your friend who is a librarian, and the neighbor who is a supporter of a local Boys and Girls Club. If your book is appropriate to the group, ask your contact to recommend you as a presenter.

There could be numerous other speaking opportunities close at hand. It is up to you to locate them. Study your local newspaper regularly for listings of clubs and organizations as well as announcements of special events occurring at the women's center, schools, senior facilities, animal shelter, Moose Lodge, library, city hall, churches, etc. Depending on the topic of your nonfiction book or the theme of your novel, you might arrange to speak to nurses, vegetarians, horse owners, adoptive parents, real estate brokers, homeowners, educators, adult victims of child abuse, daycare workers, pet owners, or a general audience.

I suggest starting your speaking career by arranging to talk at pre-scheduled meetings. Find out where clubs and organizations are meeting and when. Do a little research to discover the types of programs they feature and which organization meetings are open to guest speakers. Once you become familiar with speaking before readymade groups who are accustomed to hearing a speaker every Thursday, for example, then consider organizing some local presentations through established groups that don't typically have guest speakers. From there, you can get more creative. With the assistance of store managers, librarians, corporate or church leaders, or teachers, for example, you might devise programs at appropriate venues and invite the public.

Your book topic might be conducive to some rather unique venues and presentations. An author of a poetry book might participate in poetry slams and/or read her poetry at local coffeehouses, natural food restaurants, and retreat centers. You could talk about your animal/pet-related book at feed stores, pet shops, animal shelters, vegan restaurants, wildlife preserves, kennels, catteries, animal rehabilitation centers, parks, forest service properties, campgrounds, stables, and more. What if your novel or children's book features a bird? Why not arrange to speak anywhere there is an aviary—botanical gardens, exquisite spa properties, pet stores, bird rescue facilities, during a bird watching tour, private aviaries, zoos, the studio of an artist who specializes in drawing birds, and/or Audubon Society events and activities.

In 2009, Leslie Korenko produced the first of two historical books related to Kelleys Island, Ohio. She advises authors, whether their book is of local interest only or not, "Definitely start local, even for children's books and fiction. Many libraries, schools, and organizations are hungry for interesting speakers. Beside, you have an *in* with local groups. After all, you *are* a local author." She admits, however, that finding venues can be challenging. So she borrowed an idea from a successful businessman. She explains, "I heard an insurance salesman say that he can pick up any newspaper on any day and find three potential sales. Using the same approach, I scan newspapers for locations where other authors or speakers are appearing and for organizations that fit my book's topic, and I contact them."

Author, Dallas Woodburn says,

> When I published my first book, *There's a Huge Pimple on My Nose*, the teachers in my elementary school asked me to speak to their classes about how I published my book. Naturally shy and more comfortable expressing myself with pen and paper, I was hesitant at first to speak in front of a group. Thankfully, the teachers were so encouraging that I swallowed my nerves and said "yes." The students' response was incredibly positive and I was asked to speak to other classes throughout the school district. I am very grateful for those teachers' support. Not only did they bolster my

confidence in my writing, they also nurtured my self-confidence in my speaking abilities. Now, in addition to writing, I find great joy in public speaking. Over the years, I have spoken at numerous events including the Jack London Writers Camp, the Cal Lutheran Authors Faire, and the Santa Barbara Book Festival, in addition to more than a hundred schools, youth groups, and community organizations.

I started Write On! For Literacy in 2001 to encourage kids to discover joy, confidence, a means of self-expression, and connection to others through reading and writing. I also hold an annual Holiday Book Drive to collect and distribute new books to disadvantaged kids. More than 12,000 books have been donated to date. Often I coordinate my talks with book drive efforts—schools will collect books for the drive and present them to me after my talk. Speaking is a wonderful way to give back and encourage the next generation while also spreading the word about your books!

Rauch-Mannino also speaks to school children. Like Woodburn, he had connections. He explains, "Reaching out to teachers I already knew was a natural step. I think that 'warm calling' is so important to those first book sales." He points out, however,

As an author, I need to demonstrate the value I bring to the classroom, which extends well beyond selling a few books. My book series *Fingertip Island* examines key themes for developing children, including self-confidence, imagination, forgiveness, rising above influence, and responding to bullying. Educators find these themes attractive since they're delivered in an exciting, appealing story. My book is relevant.

Without relevance, I doubt I would have had so much success with schools, despite whatever relationship I owned.

Begin your journey as a public speaker on behalf of your important or entertaining book. Arrange to speak or provide a demonstration at an appropriate venue. It might be the nursery down the street, a local gym or spa, the lobby of a busy veterinarian's office, a gift shop or toy store, a video store, a busy bistro, or the home of a friend or a local celebrity. Use your imagination and then make it happen.

Design an Intriguing Pitch Letter

How do you start the process of getting speaking engagements when you have no speaking experience? See, that's a very good reason why you should be getting some speaking experience even before your book is a book. (Refer to chapter 2.)

But, wait a minute. You may not have experience, but you certainly have something to talk about. You are an author. You are an expert in at least one thing—writing and publishing your book. If your book is fiction, you might also be considered credible as a mystery writer, children's book author, or a writer of young adult fantasies, for example. You will certainly be thought of as an authority on the topic of your nonfiction book whether it is a memoir or a book on accounting, making remedies from herbs, using a Kindle, baking without sugar, popular country singers from the 1970s, or health and fitness. Basically you're going to:

- Do some research to locate the right venue and audience for your presentation. If it is a club or organization that typically schedules speakers, discern what type of programs they generally present, who has spoken there previously, and their time slot allowance.

- Find the name and contact information of the program chair or event planner and/or study the submission guidelines and follow them (as in the case of a conference, which we'll discuss further in chapter 12.)
- Call (if appropriate) and introduce yourself and your program. Or email the chairperson with an informal proposal.

Sample Pitch Letters

There aren't many strict rules for writing a pitch letter. Basically, you're going to introduce yourself and your program and request that you be considered as a speaker/presenter/workshop leader. Here are a few examples:

Dear (name of program chairperson):

I'm the author of *Boot Scootin' Ballads, The Story of Country Music* (WindPiper Press, 2012) and I'd like an invitation to speak to your group during one of your Thursday meetings.

I think your members and guests will enjoy my presentation which includes a little cowboy singing history, a little music (I play the harmonica), and a fast-paced trivia game I've devised for those who enjoy Western culture.

My program will fit nicely into your forty-five-minute time slot.

Please contact me at the email address or phone number below for additional information and references. Learn more about me and my book here http://www.xxxxxxx.com.

Sincerely,

Douglas Strangle

xxx@xxxx.com

xxx-xxx-xxxx

Dear (name of program chairperson):

Your fellow member, Sharon Easel, suggested I contact you about speaking to your group. I've just launched a new book featuring twelve therapy pets and their stories of amazing heroics. One of the animals is my own and, if allowed, I will bring him for a demonstration.

I am a board member and volunteer for the state-wide Pet Therapy Association, and I've been presenting workshops and educational programs throughout the US for the last six years. My most recent presentations were for the Winchester Ladies Auxiliary Annual Banquet, the local branch of Dog Trainers International, the Jersey Dog Trials Organization monthly meeting, and the Main Street Kiwanis Club.

Please contact me to discuss the type of presentation most appropriate for your members. Most often, it is a general introduction into pet therapy sprinkled with stories from my book.

> Sandra Salinas
> xxx-xxx-xxxx
> http://www.xxxxx.com

Or for fiction, try this,

Dear (gift and bookstore owner):

I'm the author of *Slaughter Alley*, a mystery set in the late 1920s in Philadelphia. I'd love to arrange a presentation in your store. My programs are unique in that I typically dress in period clothing while sharing the story, introducing the characters, and providing some of the interesting back story related to my book. I can do a thirty minute talk or I can speak for forty-five minutes with a Q and A session.

I've earned my Advanced Toastmaster Silver and I'm the president of the local branch of the Mystery Writers of America. I'm accustomed to speaking before groups of from five to 105 people and audiences seem to respond well to my humorous way of presenting.

You can count on me to widely promote my program to the 150-or-so locals in my address book, on my Facebook and Twitter pages, and at my blog and website, and I'll bring in some posters and fliers you can post and distribute. I know a reporter at the *Daily Bulletin*. Perhaps we can get some newspaper coverage for the event.

There were twenty-five people in attendance at a similar presentation at the Kirk County Library a few months ago, and we attracted thirty when I spoke at the Raven's Nest Bookstore.

I can provide a list of references at your request. In the meantime, I look forward to hearing from you.

> Sincerely,
> Petra Dristan
> http://www.xxxxxxx.com
> xxx-xxx-xxxx

I'm sure that some of you are wondering what to say if you haven't had much speaking experience yet. First, I would urge you to get that experience even if it is in casual settings among friends, at your Toastmasters club meeting, and/or before your writer's group. You'll be better prepared, you'll have more confidence, and you won't be fibbing when you say that your audiences seem to enjoy your presentations.

When You Get the Call to Speak

Your pitch email (or phone call) is more apt to get a response than not. That response will generally be one of the following:

1. "Yes, we would love to hear your story. Can you speak this Friday at noon?"

2. "Sounds interesting. Please send a proposal, including a synopsis of your presentation, a bio, and a few references."

3. "Let me get back to you on this—we have a full schedule for the year. Can I call you if we have a cancellation?"

4. "I like your theme, but our members are not too interested in programs where they are asked to participate. Can you do a straight educational program?"

5. "It sounds great—how much do you charge?"

6. "I've never had a program like this in my store. But the idea is intriguing. Let's talk."

If your request is accepted, you may be asked to send a bio and flesh out your program description for the organization, club or business newsletter, and the local newspaper. If they don't plan to put something in the paper, do it yourself. (For more on how to publicize your presentation, read chapter 10.)

Stay in close communication with your contact person from day one. Determine between you who will handle which portions of the publicity and which of you will arrange for a microphone, projector, table to showcase your books, and other necessities you require. Make sure they follow through. There are crackerjack program chairpersons who are on top of all the arrangements, and then there are those who can't get their act together. It is up to you, the author, to ensure that everything gets done.

How important is publicity to a successful program? It's vital. I've spoken with many an author who sat alone at a book signing because communication with the bookseller or other business owner broke down.

I attended a book signing for a friend a few years ago. The only people who showed up were me, a couple of friends who accompanied me, and one other person the author had personally invited. She expected the store owner to put posters in the windows, submit press releases to local newspapers, and, perhaps, spread the word to customers. But none of this occurred, and my friend sat alone with her stack of books.

When she talked to me about it later, she said, "Well, I won't be doing book signings anymore. This is not a good way to sell books."

I told her, "Oh yes it can be, if you take charge of the publicity." (Read more about promoting your appearances in chapter 10 and how to have a more successful book signing in chapter 11.)

It is easy to get discouraged after an embarrassingly unsuccessful event. But I maintain that even an event that seems to have bombed brings gifts. There are, perhaps, more lessons to learn from those activities we view as having failed than those we see as successes. Take this position when you experience a presentation disappointment and you will realize greater success more often in the future. Evaluate the situation, discern what did and what didn't work, devise a new working plan for the next opportunity, and put it into action the first chance you get. In other words, get back up on that horse, but do so with greater understanding, additional knowledge, a better plan, and a renewed sense of positive enthusiasm.

Margaret Brownley, author of several inspirational romance novels—some of them having achieved *New York Times* bestseller status—plans speaking engagements to correspond with book releases. She says, "This gives me the most impact for time spent. I've spoken at writer's clubs and conferences. Since I write inspirational novels, I'm often asked to speak to church groups. I've also spoken at libraries, high schools, senior citizen centers, and service organizations. I even gave a workshop on a cruise ship once." (Read more about how she managed that gig in chapter 17.)

So how important are workshops and other presentations to an author's bottom line? Brownley reminds authors that you can't always judge success by the number of books sold. She says, "Sometimes it's the exposure that counts. Some appearances lead to newspaper or radio interviews and other speaking engagements. In recent years, I've noticed that online sales spike after one of my appearances. People will order books online after the event because they might be cheaper or they want an ebook."

Whether your book is fiction or nonfiction, a children's, young adult, scientific, how-to, self-help, mystery, romance, or a book of poetry, you can get more recognition as an author and make more sales if you will venture out of your writing room and greet your public. Waxler agrees. He says, "My whole business model combines speaking with book publishing. I sell most of my books at my speaking engagements."

Most of us who edged into the world of authorship without formal training as a speaker or leader, for example, have had much to learn and many obstacles to overcome. Here's one of my early challenges— maybe some of you can relate.

As I mentioned in the Introduction to this book, there was a period when I refused to accept speaking opportunities. During that time, when someone called and invited me to talk about my latest book at their club meeting, I would think about it for only a few seconds before responding. Usually, I would say no. Well, it was a safe answer. I wasn't comfortable speaking in public anymore. What if I messed up? I reasoned with myself that it was the right answer. However, later, I often regretted my snap decision.

Eventually, I decided to handle things differently. My new plan was that when someone called and asked me to do something outside of my comfort zone, I'd say, "I'll think about it and call you back." Invariably, I'd talk myself out of it and end up missing a worthwhile activity or an interesting event. Obviously, that wasn't the solution to my decision-making problem, either. So I developed a new tactic. This one took some courage. It also took some getting used to. But it worked and I am so happy that I challenged myself to follow through.

The next time someone called to ask me to speak (or to attend a writer's group meeting or to help organize a group), I said, "Yes." Then I figured out a way to do it. Instead of focusing on the negative possibilities and my perceived short-comings—rather than dread failure—I began a self-improvement regimen. I started using positive self-talk. I joined a Toastmasters club and worked hard at improving my public-speaking skills.

Now, when I say yes to a speaking invitation, I spend my days preparing for a positive outcome rather than dreading failure. Consequently, book sales are up, I'm getting more client work, and I'm having a lot of fun traveling all over the place.

I learned my lesson: Make snap decisions based on your fears and insecurities and you could miss out on some exciting adventures and great book-selling opportunities. That's why I just say *yes*.

Set Up Your Own Speaking Events

Some authors design and coordinate their own workshops. I've organized and presented writing workshops in private homes, at the local art center, in libraries, at a church, in the conference room at various businesses, at a recreation center, in bookstores, at senior centers, and in the banquet room at a high-end restaurant. You could do something similar around the theme or genre of your book—recycling, traveling, quilting, fitness, cupcake-baking, beachcombing, using the iPad, or some aspect of writing fiction, for example. Secure space at a community center, public or private boarding school, hotel, monastery, bed-and-breakfast, or a private foundation facility, for example.

What's the difference between *seeking* speaking opportunities and *setting up* speaking opportunities? In the former scenario, you are filling a slot in someone else's program agenda. In the latter, you are creating the program, securing the place, and handling all of the organizational details yourself.

Simply lead your own workshop or organize a conference including other experts who can teach on aspects of your topic. Do this completely on your own or share the pressure by partnering with someone who has great connections, ideas, and energy.

I have presented workshops quite successfully on my own as well as with other authors and writers. Once, I called on a local poet to teach a poetry segment for a writing/publishing workshop I conducted for a group of homeschooled children. I also invited someone who does page layout to come in and work with the group to design the cover and the text for a book of their writings and drawings, which we actually published.

In light of the perceived gridlock on today's information highways—everyone is teaching something—one must be pretty clever when creating a program or workshop. Carol Sanford offers this advice to authors: "Make sure you have something unique to offer. No one will come to your workshops or talks unless you have something they have not heard. You need deep content, not just an idea."

We generally learn a lot when we first launch out to conduct workshops or seminars. It sometimes takes a while to discover what works and what doesn't. This was the case with Mary Ellen Warner. She says, "In the first few workshops I presented on how to organize your papers, I overwhelmed students with information. As my skills improved, I learned that less was better and that stories worked best of all. I began to use stories to help show what I meant and I used fewer black and white details."

Why develop and present workshops on your own when you can just go out and speak at ready-made venues? There are many benefits. Some people would rather attend a workshop than just listen to a speaker. If you choose a venue that is familiar and comfortable to your audience, you will more likely attract some of them. Plus, you are in charge, which means you can charge. In fact, you may have to if there is a fee for using the facility.

Here's is an example of how hard work developing your own workshops can pay off.

Peter Bowerman is a sought-after speaker. He helped establish his popularity as a presenter by conducting his own workshops for writers. He says, however, that the challenges are many.

Probably the biggest one was that I'd be handling all the logistics myself. I'd set the date, rent the hotel meeting room, send out the promo, try to get some media coverage, etc. If I was lucky, I'd get twenty to twenty-five folks and could make a few bucks. Obviously, local events (i.e., no travel expenses) were best, but even those were pretty labor-intensive. As for out-of-town events, if I wasn't able to get the media interested (often the case), I'd occasionally deliver a seminar to four or five people, and barely break even, or not at all.

Is it worth your time to develop your own workshops? If you are new to the world of public speaking, a workshop is a great icebreaker. This is a good way to become familiar with your audience and their needs/desires (which is why I suggest presenting workshops even before your book is a book). It can be a feeder program if you offer services and other products. You will gain experience and exposure as a speaker/ teacher, and you have something to add to your resumé.

What does it take to set up your own event? Whether you plan a small workshop for a dozen people in the backroom of a local gymnasium or a conference for 100, the steps are pretty much the same. In the latter scenario, however, you may have more people involved, so more follow-up is required. Basically, you need to decide on a theme for your event, find a suitable location, set a date, and promote, promote, promote. (Chapter 10 will give you some ideas for publicity.)

Many authors create programs around the topic of their books and present them in corporate, university, institution, or public and private school settings. Some of the programs are connected to charities, which makes them more attractive to some organizers and customers.

Karen Lee Stevens, founder of All for Animals, takes her program and her children's book, *Animals Have Feelings, Too!* into local schools.

Karen says,

All the proceeds from the sale of our book goes directly to All for Animals, so that we can offer humane education and literacy programs to children in the community. Because of the organization's nonprofit status, we were able to seek grant funding to publish our children's book (the funds we received from a local foundation paid the entire cost of illustrations and printing). The grant has helped us in two major ways: 1) We can give away copies of our book to low-income school children, and 2) we can use the book as a fundraising tool by approaching businesses to be corporate sponsors. Sponsors will purchase a large quantity of books (thirty, forty, or fifty books at a time), which we then give away to school children who attend our humane education presentations.

Take Your Book and Your Program Out of Town

Once you begin to feel fairly comfortable speaking to relatively small groups of people in your hometown and within your comfort zone, consider doing as Bowerman did and branch out into other geographic areas. But be forewarned that it's more difficult to attract an audience where you are not as well-known.

Bowerman admits that, "Doing it all oneself can be a frustrating, though exceptionally character-building experience." But he says, "Now, I rarely do those types of events anymore. The only out-of-town events are if someone's willing to pay me to come (expenses and some sort of honorarium). Or, if I'm going to be in an area anyway, I might set something up, BUT only with the help of a local organizer."

For example, some of the programs he conducted attracted the interest of local writers' group leaders, and they began inviting him to speak when he was in town. He describes an event he did recently in Ohio while there visiting family for the holidays: "I got in touch with the head of a local writers group, and he bent over backwards to help. He got me on TV locally the day before the event, and we had thirty-plus folks show up. The evening was a hit and I sold about $350 worth of product (for which there is a high-profit margin since I self-publish)." He also believes that he generated a lot of goodwill. He says, "No doubt I'll pick up some coaching business from it, so all in all, it was a great outing."

There are a couple of ways to do some test marketing. The next time you plan an out-of-town trip, incorporate at least one signing or speaking engagement into your itinerary along the way. Or do as I did with my local history book and schedule a mini-book tour throughout a 100 to 300-mile radius of your city.

I stopped at museums, libraries, and bookstores all along my route and was successful in placing around forty-five books on consignment, and I sold a few to libraries. I planned ahead to do some presentations in libraries and bookstores, where I sold a few copies to members of the community who attended. Some of the bookstore and museum gift shop managers purchased additional books after my visit, but I had to prompt orders. I contacted them when I planned a radio or newspaper interview that would be broadcast or run locally in their area or when one of my articles was scheduled for publication in a local (to them) magazine or newspaper. At these times, I suggested that they order extra copies in case my promotional efforts brought in customers.

Because I currently focus mostly on my books for authors, when I plan a trip now, I check to see if any writer's groups are meeting nearby during my stay. You can do the same with regard to groups associated with the theme of your book. Be advised, however, that most groups schedule speakers three months to a year in advance. So plan ahead. Plan far enough ahead so that your publicity efforts are effective, as well. (Read more about publicity for your speaking engagements in chapter ten.) Here are some tips for setting up speaking engagements while traveling:

- Use local connections. Ask someone you know to introduce you to a Kiwanis member in another city, for example, or recommend you as a speaker for the Red Hat Ladies monthly luncheon, the camera club, or an alumni group.
- If you don't have a personal connection, make a connection via the Internet. Most club and organization program chairpersons are hungry for good programs. Business leaders and institution directors are eager to present programs that might bring in more customers/patrons, and organizers for fundraising activities want to book speakers who will attract a good crowd.
- Be creative in your quest for speaking opportunities. Arrange to present a program in that city's library museum, art gallery, dance studio, popular coffeehouse, bicycle shop, gym, country club spa, craft shop, health food store, flower shop, lobby of a popular bed and breakfast, candle shop, etc.
- Be prepared to send a copy of your book for review, an outline or at least a description of your presentation, and possibly references from other program chairpersons.
- Follow up with your contact person frequently so that you don't fall between the cracks during the planning stages, so that you are well-informed as to their expectations (and vice versa), and so that you can plan adequately for the event.

So how do some authors get speaking gigs, and where are they speaking? C. Hope Clark, author and founder of Funds for Writers, pitches to conferences in states she likes to visit in much the same way she would pitch to an agent, publisher, or magazine editor. She says she locates opportunities by reading writing magazines and checking www.shawguides.com. She says, "I also Google states I'd like to visit, to locate appropriate venues."

She offers this:

> When my mystery comes out, I will contact bookstores and tourism locations in the area where my story is set. I've had a restaurant I frequent offer to host a book signing. I have a friend with a connection at a college who wants me to sign at the bookstore. I have connections in the writing industry, so why not use them? I'm writing a piece for *The Writer* about contests and I'm using my novel as an example of how to capitalize on contests. I'm writing a chapter for *Writer's Market* and I'll mention the novel in that piece, as well. It's called leveraging: using your strengths—all of them—to capitalize on your latest project.

It may be more difficult to entice members of communities outside of your hometown to attend your scheduled programs. If you're just starting out and haven't established a strong platform yet, they don't know you. They aren't familiar with your book. They don't even know anyone who knows you. So how are you going to lure them out of their homes or away from their weekend or evening activities? It will take a lot of publicity. Here are some ideas:

- Plan a festive evening—or, where appropriate, one that promises surprises or intrigue. I can tell you from experience that I would be more likely to attend something that hints of an interesting affair rather than a straight "author will speak" event. If I see a program billed as a "gala festival of fun," "fundraiser" (for a favorite charity), an evening that promises something special/ extra—a celebrity guest, for example—I will contact one of my girlfriends and off we go.

- Offer a free gift to all who come or something else of value to your audience. This might be a free Tarot card reading, audio book, or brownie cookbook to the first five people to respond, for example. I sometimes offer a few free manuscript evaluations for authors.

- Land an interview with a local newspaper reporter. In order to manage this, you will have to come up with a tantalizing hook. Read more about this tactic in chapter ten.

- Have the event included in the newspaper calendar of events. Your local contact might be able to help with that.

- Try to get on a talk show that airs during heavy commute periods throughout the day the week prior to the event.

- Create posters for the store window and see if you can recruit someone to post them at other key places where your audience members shop and/or hang out.

(Learn more about publicity for your speaking engagements in chapter 10.)

Gear Up for Back-of-the-Room Sales

While I encourage you to consider exposure as one of the greatest benefits to your live presentations, certainly, you'll want to sell as many books on the spot as you can. In fact, on-the-spot sales are the most reliable sales you can make. Sometimes you have to work a little at making the sale, however.

Potential customers might say they don't have the cash with them or they left their checkbooks at home and they'll order the book from your website later. Some people prefer purchasing books through Amazon.com or they promise to stop in at a bookstore and pick up a copy. But I can tell you that even those who appear to be most interested in purchasing your book, receiving your free report, asking you a few questions via email, etc., very often neglect to follow through.

That's why I recommend taking the upper hand. Get that person's name and contact information so you can follow up with them. Offer little enticements to get those sales that you may not get otherwise. Give a discount and/or a bonus gift if they purchase the book on the spot; and make sure that you accept all means of payment—cash, checks, and a variety of credit cards. You've probably heard how important it is that the vendor (that's you) make it as easy and attractive as possible for customers to buy from you. This is absolutely true.

Prior to your presentation, and with the chairperson's permission, set up a display of books, preferably in the room where you will be speaking. You'll hear the term, "back-of-the-room sales," indicating that the speaker goes to a table at the back of the room after the presentation where he or she greets members of their audience, discusses the book with them, and sells copies.

According to novelist Raven West, however, your books should never be in the back of the room. "Whenever possible, they should be up front with you in a very prominent display, not just an ordinary stack. Purchase some book display stands; you can find them at craft stores where they sell decorative plates." She also suggests this, "Distribute copies of your book to a few members of your audience. Have them feel it and make it theirs. Some will hand it back to you; others will feel guilty and buy it. Point to your books throughout your presentation, especially when you're talking about your characters."

Here are some additional tips for making those back-of-the-room sales:

- Make sure it is okay to sell books at this venue. The bylaws of some nonprofit organizations may prohibit book sales on the premises. Bookstore managers generally want to sell your books and make that forty percent profit. (Read more about book signings at bookstores in chapter eleven.) Librarians may suggest that you donate a percentage of book sales to the Friends of the Library.

- Mention your book during your presentation. In fact, take a copy to the lectern with you and even display it, if appropriate. While it is important to let attendees know that you are the author of a book related to the story or information you are sharing, do not turn your presentation into a commercial. You are there to give your audience something of value—to educate, teach, inspire, motivate, and/or entertain them. (Read more about creating presentation topics related to your book in chapter 9.)

- Give brief instructions for purchasing books. Before you finish your presentation, quickly explain that you'll respond to questions and that you have books to sell at the back of the room or out in the hallway (if there will be another speaker after you). If you're in a bookstore, customers will have to make the purchase through the cashier and then bring the book to you for an autograph. Some conference organizers involve a local bookstore through which all book sales are made. In this case, you would direct audience members to the on-premises bookstore. Make sure they each have a copy of your brochure or a promotional postcard with the title and cover image of the book for easy identification once they visit the bookstore, or in case they want to order it later.

- Bring plenty of books, as well as promotional brochures, book-marks, etc. I generally hand these materials to attendees as they enter the room or place them at each seat before the session starts. Leave extras on a table near the entrance for those who come in late or want additional copies.

- If you'll be selling your own books, bring change and either credit card slips or a way to charge credit cards. There are smartphone apps now that allow you to run credit cards for payment.
- Offer a discount or a special gift to those who purchase the book now. But also provide information about how they can purchase books later.

It's a wise author who stays on top of the details of an event and who is prepared to take charge of a situation that may be going south. But these are lessons most of us learn with experience. Let the anecdotes and information in this book keep you from allowing some of these things to occur on your watch.

Bobbie Christmas tells about the worst thing that happened to her at an event, as far as bookselling opportunities. She says,

> The conference organizers set up a book-signing room separate from the area where the seminars and other events took place. Absolutely nothing was done to draw readers from those rooms into the book-signing room. To make matters worse, the book-signing took place in the morning, *before* most of the authors had given any seminars or readings. Attendees had no knowledge of any of the authors or their books until after the authors spoke, but the books were not offered for sale after the presentations, only before. I think I sold one book that day. Most authors sold nothing.

Christmas continues, "Do people go home and order a book later? Not in my experience. If you don't close the sale at the time you have the prospect in front of you, your chances of ever making that sale take a nosedive."

This is a good argument for collecting names, email addresses, business cards, etc. from the people you meet at presentations, signings, book festivals, and other live events. Don't let them vacate the premises without leaving their mark. This is especially important for anyone who has expressed even a slight interest in your book.

How many books should you bring to an event? If you expect a showing of thirty people, you might conceivably be able to sell between five and eighteen books. For an audience of twelve or fifteen, plan to make somewhere between three and eight sales. Certainly, there are a wide range of exceptions, so bring more books than you expect to sell. You might sell thirty-five copies of your gift book or local history book to nineteen people during an engagement around the holidays. Or you might walk out of the meeting hall having sold zero books. This may not be a reflection on you or the quality of your book.

For the most part, if you appropriately entertain and/or inform the right audience, unless they are children without pocket money or transients just getting in out of the cold, you will typically sell a non-fiction book to around ten or twenty percent of attendees who are there because of a keen interest in your topic. You might sell that many copies or more of your historical novel set in the Deep South during the 1870s to a group of DAR members (Daughters of the American Revolution).

Again, let me remind you that the number of books sold on the spot is not the only measure of a successful event. Your public appearances will be much more enjoyable for all (including you) if you keep this in mind.

I like to take a friend along to my presentations, or I'll initiate the help of an audience member to handle sales at the back of the room while I respond to questions and listen to authors' stories. Life is so much easier at these events when you are not trying to juggle money, make change, fill out credit card slips, sign books, and answer questions all by yourself.

Which brings us to a problem that comes up in these situations fairly often. Have you met the Attention Hog? This is the man or woman who demands more than his/her fair share of your attention either during your talk or afterward. And he often walks away without purchasing even one book. I was asked recently how to handle these people without being rude. My inclination is to say, "Why should you be concerned about your rude behavior when the individual is obviously being rude?"

Spend any time doing presentations and you will meet a heckler or two and a few Attention Hogs. The more controversial your book topic, the greater your chances of attracting these folks. I've had to deal with just a few potentially disruptive people over time. Generally, they are well-meaning. They're just passionate about their projects and hell-bent on gleaning as much information as they can from the opportunity in front of them. How do you deal with someone who tries to monopolize the program? Be giving—to a point. If you have to move on, be gentle but firm. Always offer something to replace what you are taking away. In other words, if you must limit the time this individual wants to take and if you believe you can be of some help to him, invite him to join you for coffee after the event. Encourage him to call you or promise to email him with some resources. I like to be generous, but I realize I also have to be practical. In a group situation, I must be cognizant of everyone who wants some of my attention. Further, my time is worth something. In many, many cases, the questions someone wants me to answer are all addressed effectively in one of my books, and I will direct them toward that book.

Authors, it's a fine line we walk. While we want to be there for our customers and potential customers, we must also take care of ourselves. It's all about boundaries. There is nothing wrong with setting and enforcing boundaries. Here's my formula for handling the Attention Hog:

- Acknowledge the individual.
- Listen to him or her.
- Respond as best you can to one or two questions—when you are the speaker, take only three to five minutes with this person (unless the rest of the audience is getting involved and expressing great interest in the topic).
- Before moving on, if the situation seems to warrant it, offer to spend additional time with this person after the program. Or ask him to contact you via email so you have time to gather some resources for him.
- If he is standing in front of you at your signing table in the back of the room or at a book festival, and he continues to vie for your attention while others are waiting to have books signed or to speak to you, you may have to ask him to step aside. I typically give this sort of attention hog a specific suggestion (email me with your question and I'll take the time to gather some resources). I might wish him luck with his project and then I look around him or make eye contact with someone next to him and begin engaging that person.

I had someone call me one weekend after a story appeared in the local newspaper featuring an event I hosted with regard to my book on how to present a Hawaiian luau on the mainland. The reporter had included a few things from the book about how to roast a whole pig and this woman called to ask questions about the process. I was happy to respond, believing all the while that she had purchased a copy of the book. In fact, I referred to specific pages in the book as we talked and I thought this woman was following along. But she just kept asking more questions. After talking to her for a good thirty minutes, I asked, "Do you have a copy of the book there with you?"

She said, "No, I just read the article in the paper and wanted more information." At that point, I suggested that she consider purchasing the book. I told her where it was for sale, I thanked her for her interest and ended the conversation.

I guess this story wouldn't gall anyone but an author with books to sell. We go to great lengths to create useful (or entertaining) books. While we are certainly willing to freely give what we can, we do not appreciate people loaning out our books, nor do we like someone taking our time to pick our brains when they have no intention of purchasing the book. I believe in drawing lines and setting boundaries. If we don't take ourselves and our work seriously, no one else will.

How to Prepare for a Speaking Engagement

While it appears that you are a guest when you land a speaking gig, it is important that you take charge. Know what to expect—the approximate number of people who will attend, the audience's interest or aptitude related to your topic or genre, your time allotment, the layout of the place, and so forth. Will there be a microphone and/or a lectern? Will you be presenting from a raised platform (podium)? Will you be standing or seated? Will you be able to use a PowerPoint projector? Is there a projector and screen on site or will you need to supply these? What does the agenda involve? It's important to know all of this before the event, but sometimes the information you get isn't absolutely correct.

You arrive at the venue only to discover that someone has borrowed the PowerPoint projector, there isn't a working microphone, after all, or way more or way fewer people have shown up. You may begin speaking and discover that your carefully organized speech isn't quite right for the audience that is waiting for you.

Jerry Waxler understands the importance of preparation and the possibility that things could go south. He says,

The concept of speech preparation suggests one of the most important reasons why writers should speak in public. When you are preparing to speak to a group, you are forced to create a sort of hypothetical image of who they are and what you will tell them. This exercise of imagining what you want to say to a particular imaginary group will not only improve your public speaking skills, it will also improve your writing. Why? Because in an abstract sense, this is the skill at the heart of good writing. Writers must sit alone and try to imagine how to communicate with their unseen audience. Every time I book a public talk, I develop the knack of speaking to that imagined group. Then, when I actually stand in front of them, I can learn from their reaction how closely my imagined communication matched reality.

Yes, it is imperative that you prepare for your presentations, but don't be so attached to your cleverly strung words that you can't deviate from them. If the audience expresses an interest in something you cover or a story you share, it's okay to focus on that for as long as your audience is interested and for as long as makes sense in light of what you were invited to or have promised to teach or share.

You may be prepared to talk about the condition of the real estate market in your region, but discover that your audience is more interested in learning how to "stage," showcase, or photograph their property so it is more appealing to buyers. You might go in expecting to share entrepreneurial rags to riches stories from your book, when your audience would rather hear your business success tips in the new millennium. So the companion rule to being prepared is to also be flexible.

Recently, I was asked by a friend to speak at a senior center. The program director told me that the residents were not interested in publishing. She said they weren't interested in writing programs, nor did she think they wanted to hear about my journey as a writer. Further, she told me they certainly would not participate in the program—so it was no use setting up quizzes, Q & A sessions, or anything like that. I was at a loss as to what to say to this audience. Finally, I came up with an idea. I made a few notes—readjusted the notes several times—and off I went to greet the group of seniors.

I started out talking about what goes on behind the scenes of the books they read. I thought it was a decent topic—most people aren't aware of the passion and toil that goes into a book or the challenges of getting that book to the public. I was pleased with my topic, but I noticed that I wasn't getting much response from the group as I spoke. I was told ahead of time that some of the residents would go to sleep and only a few would be interested no matter what I talked about.

Well, early on in my talk, I shared an anecdote from my own writing life. Suddenly, I noticed an expression of interest coming from the audience. A little while later, I got a question about my career as a writer. In a few moments, I realized that I was the attraction—me and my world as a writer. Audience members asked questions and they sat on the edges of their seats, wheelchairs, and walkers waiting to hear my answers. As I looked out over the audience, I noticed that several people were smiling, and no one was sleeping.

I was having so much fun sharing tidbits and insights into the writing life that I took the notes I'd prepared, quipped about how the best laid plans (and speeches) of mice and men sometimes go awry. Then I tore up my speech notes, tossed them up and let them rain down over me. I'm a rather animated speaker, at times, and I'm sure members of this audience wondered what I would do next. It seemed that they didn't want to miss anything, as they remained attentive throughout my off-the-cuff presentation.

I wrapped up my talk at the appropriate time so the residents could go to lunch, but I noticed something odd. No one was leaving. They remained in their chairs, walkers, and wheelchairs fixated on me as if hoping I would continue. Finally, I walked over and sat down among them, where several of them continued to chat with me.

What were the tangible results of that presentation? I sold one book—to a staff member. One resident is working on his memoir and has contacted me about coaching him through the process. Even more significantly, I learned something about the value of winging it if one is inspired to do so. I was reminded that intuition is an essential part of a public speaker's toolbox.

Another time, I arrived at a book festival where I was supposed to speak for twenty minutes on publishing. I planned to present a condensed version of my "Two Steps to Publishing Success" program. I prepared notes for a talk appropriate for a small, intimate group seated around me in a room. Yes, I broke one of my cardinal rules by assuming this would be the case rather than communicating with someone to find out for sure. As it turned out, there would be several speakers that day and we were required to stand in the middle of the barricaded street and speak to whoever happened to be sitting at the tables off to the side—most of them were there to eat lunch or to rest their feet, oblivious to the fact that someone was speaking. We had use of a microphone, but the commotion all around the speakers was distracting, to say the least. It was a challenge to compete with the noise associated with the book festival in progress.

As I observed the first few speakers struggle in this environment, I realized that my planned talk was inappropriate for this setting. So I quickly created new notes focused on a list of what I believe are the ten best book promotion ideas—those that every author should pursue. I figured that this presentation—with bullet points and brief comments—was more well-suited to this situation. I was right. I found out later that there were a few people who came to the event just to hear me. They visited my booth after the little talk and bought books, too.

Prepare, But Be Flexible

So, while preparation is crucial in public speaking, it is also important to be flexible.

Author Dallas Woodburn agrees. She says, "I have learned that my best talks happen when I really take the time to plan ahead and keep in great contact with the person planning the event, whether that is the teacher of the classroom or the organizer of the book festival." She advises other author-speakers,

> Be grateful. Let the organizer know how much you are looking forward to the event. Ask if there is anything specific they would like you to cover, and make sure you know how much time you will have. When I speak in classrooms, I send ahead a flyer with information about my book drive and writing camps, and also a flyer with information about ordering copies of my books. And I make sure the teacher has links to my website and YouTube videos in case he or she would like to share them with the class before I come. Audiences are more receptive when they know about you and are excited to meet you. The teacher or book festival coordinator is the one who can build that enthusiasm in the days and even weeks before your talk begins.

Woodburn cautions, however,

> You can do all the preparation in the world and a talk still might not go as you planned. Maybe you organize a speaking

event at a bookstore and only three people show up. Maybe you spend an hour leading a writing workshop for a classroom and not a single student buys your book at the end. Both of those things have happened to me more than once! But, no matter how big or small your audience is, no matter how many books you sell or don't sell, try to focus on the people you *do* reach. Every person you speak to is another person who knows about you and your books and what you do. Maybe they don't buy your book that day, but they go online and find it later. Maybe they tell their friends how much they loved your talk and how impressed they were by you. Maybe something you said sticks with them and inspires them when they feel down or discouraged. You never know when that might come back in the future or what it might lead to.

As part of this concept, let me add that it is also important that you maintain a demeanor appropriate to your presentation. You might be disturbed by the fact that you've had to shift gears. You might be upset with the organizers for dropping the ball or with yourself for not double checking the event details. You may even be in a bad mood because of any number of things. However, if you expect to sell books, make a lasting impression on your audience, and fulfill your obligation as a presenter at this event, you'll have to shake it off and maybe even do a little play acting.

If you typically approach your presentations with obvious enthusiasm and an upbeat and friendly manner—if this is the sort of demeanor that is appropriate when you represent your book—you need to devise a way to manufacture this stance if it isn't in place that day. Some speakers use meditation, others use prayer, and some just have the amazing ability to control their attitude/demeanor using willpower or some other power they possess. Whatever your choice of attitude adjustment methods, do *not* allow yourself to wallow in a negative mental or emotional place while in front of your audience.

Here are a few methods to use in preparing for the unexpected.

- Communicate clearly with the organizer and stay in close contact with him or her. You want to be sure they are taking care of promotion and other promised details. Also, as Woodburn suggests, create a rapport with the program director, organizer, or bookstore manager and this individual may become one of your best advocates. Provide interesting information, facts, and materials. You want him or her to be so taken with you and your book that they will talk up your program at meetings, to customers, and so forth. This is one way to make sure you attract a decent crowd.
- Arrive on site early and check everything out before the program starts.
- Set up your book display, brochures, bookmarks etc.
- Bring extra handouts.
- Have plenty of books to sell—always keep backup copies in your car.
- Bring a bottle of water and hydrate well before speaking.
- Have a solid speech plan, but know your presentation so well that you can deviate from it if needed.

This brings us to another point that many orators ignore—audience feedback. All the while you are speaking, the audience is responding either by expressing interest or not. You are there, not to deliver the material you want to share, not to impress someone with what you know, but to enlighten, teach, inform, and/or entertain your audience. Watch the members of your audience—each and every one of them—to determine if what you are delivering is in alignment with what they seem to want.

Are the majority of audience members paying attention? If they are sitting on the edges of their seats, leaning slightly forward, smiling, nodding in agreement with your comments, taking notes, and/or asking questions, these are signs that they are interested in what you're presenting. If, on the other hand, several of them are sitting back in their chairs with their arms folded across their chests, they have a frown or a puzzled look on their faces, they are chatting among themselves, or they are reading something unrelated to your program, you may not be getting through to them. Also, pay attention to where their eyes are. If they are not making eye contact with you, but are gazing around the room, you can be sure that you are not holding their interest.

Before evaluating your audience, take into consideration their level of weariness. If this is one of the last sessions at a jam-packed four-day conference, for example, they're going to be flat exhausted.

There are things you can do to capture the attention of your audience. Learn more about this in chapters six and eight.

Write a More Effective Speech

As I alluded to in an earlier chapter, an effective written speech will read differently than a chapter in a book. We use different terminology and techniques when speaking than we do when writing something that will be read. That's one reason why the process of reading aloud to audiences from our books sometimes falls flat. The exception is young children's books, which are generally written to be read aloud, and books by authors who have a friendly, conversational style of writing.

Not everyone does. In fact, some professionals recommend that authors read their books out loud during the self-editing process as a method of catching problems in the text. If you stumble across words and phrases when reading it aloud, possibly there is something wrong with the flow or the choice of words in that section.

Most speakers write their speeches (or hire speechwriters). So a speech often starts out as a written document. I write my speeches. But first, I type out (or jot down) an outline—noting the points I want to make and establishing the focus of the presentation.

Accomplished speakers suggest that you include no more than three key points in your delivery. Beginning speakers with a lot of knowledge in their area of interest often try to cover too much when they speak. A nonfiction author might choose the topic from one chapter in his book or even from under one heading within a chapter. For example, let's say you've written a book on business management. If you are speaking to a group of businesswomen, you might present three tips for successfully managing the males in your office, how to use intuition in the daily execution of your business, or three things your customers/clients want from you and how to provide them. (Read more about how to create presentations from your nonfiction and fiction books in chapter nine.)

Basically, your speech will have a beginning, middle, and end. Does this sound familiar? Yes, it will be structured similarly to your book, your short stories, your articles, your blog posts. Depending on your audience and your topic, you could begin with an introduction, so folks will know what to expect during your presentation. Or you might start with a shocking fact or provocative statement designed to capture the attention of your audience. For example, if you are going to talk about how to get it right when writing about crime scenes, you might say, "Seventy-five percent of fiction authors are liars." Then go on to describe the high percentage of mistakes found in fiction murder mysteries. Perhaps you are speaking about natural and inexpensive beauty aids. You could start out by asking, "What do beet juice, castor oil, oatmeal, and petroleum jelly have in common?"

Avoid starting your presentation by thanking all of those who have made your stay so lovely and commenting on the great weather. Unless you can use this sort of beginning to edge into a dramatic or intriguing opening, save it. Attempt, instead, to capture the audience's attention from word one.

So create a beginning that will either explain the program or grab everyone's attention. Then ease into the middle of the talk. This is where the bulk of your story or your information is shared. Make sure it is presented in a crisp, clear, concise, succinct, and fascinating way. Do not inundate your audience with too many facts or too much information. Strive to entertain and/or inform within the confines of the topic you promised to explore.

Then end it. I like to bring my talks full circle. In the case of the presentation I suggested above, I might end by saying, "Don't be a liar. Refer to my new book, *Write a More Believable Novel: Crime Scene Tips From the Experts.*" (Read how to rehearse a speech in chapter 7.)

Improve and Maintain Your Speaker's Voice

You hear a variety of speaking voices throughout the course of a day. While some are pleasing to the ear, others are irritating. While some are strong and clear, others are weak and strained. Some women speak in breathless tones; their use of breath actually sabotaging the clarity of their messages.

Most of us are not born with vocal dysfunction. You develop poor (and good) speech habits over the years. I know children who mumble and do not enunciate well. They talk as if they have mush in their mouths. I've met kids (and adults) who speak too loudly, too high pitched, or through clenched teeth. I've heard children who sound like they are abusing their vocal chords in the way they are using them.

When I look at these children, I wonder about their career futures. If I was the parent, I would encourage a mumbling child to speak up. I would coach a screecher to use more normal tones. I would then ask school officials to provide speech therapy for my child early on, or I'd hire a speech therapist myself. Those of you born in the 1950s or before will remember your parents, grandparents, and teachers constantly reminding you to stand up straight, to speak up, to avoid using slang in conversation, to use correct grammar, etc. It doesn't appear that parents or teachers have the time to do this sort of coaching these days. Not only that, but modern technology is encouraging some of these poor speaking habits with the acceptance of an abbreviated style of communication used in texting, for example.

Unfortunately, most of these children do not get help with speech delivery and voice problems. Parents and siblings become accustomed to the child's way of conversing. They learn to understand the child and to tolerate the speech habits or the annoying voice and soon do not see the speech pattern as a problem. Thus, it may continue into adulthood.

If you have grown up with poor enunciation skills or an unpleasant voice, there may still be something you can do. The first step is to recognize that you could use help.

I heard an author being interviewed on the radio recently who had a tendency to speak clearly at the start of his sentences, but his final several words seemed to lack breath and they sort of evaporated into a muted gravelly tone.

On my last flight, I listened to an airline hostess who had a perfectly good voice, until the last few words of her sentences. She ended her sentences on a rather shrill note. Her voice would rise and become quietly but annoyingly, piercing.

Most airline hostesses, receptionists, telemarketers, and some inexperienced public speakers talk too fast. Understanding fast talkers can be a problem for many people, especially as we age. I am certain that, as we get older, we don't hear as quickly as we used to. If you have a tendency to speak fast—try slowing down when you are before an audience or speaking to a potential customer one-on-one. But don't allow your sentences to drag on, either. Speak too fast and you'll lose listeners. They'll get tired of trying to understand you. Speak too slowly and your audience will lose interest in what you're saying.

We've all heard revival preachers speak—in person, on TV, or in movies. They tend to shout out their messages with booming voices. Some speakers adapt this style. I heard one a year or so ago who spoke in a relatively small room using a regular tone for the most part. But occasionally, he would blast his strong, rich voice out over the group in an attempt to emphasize a point. This speaker certainly used vocal variety and expressed emotion during his presentation. This is all good. But his volume should have been checked according to the size room he was working.

A common problem is a strained speaking voice. A voice that is forced through the throat can sound and feel strained. I know a woman who seems to purposely strain her voice as she speaks. It sounds as though if she were to back off of her vocal chords just a little, there would be a nice, feminine voice in there somewhere. Instead, it is forced sounding and raspy. I'm sure therapy would help. It is important that we learn to speak from the diaphragm instead of through the throat if we want to project a more pleasant vocal tone.

Think about your voice, how it sounds and how you create the sounds. There are definitely times when you are using it properly—this is evident by the clear, strong sound of your voice and the fact that you can speak for extended periods of time without tiring. Now compare this with those times when you get tired after chatting with friends or speaking before an audience for a relatively brief period. During these times, pay attention to how your voice sounds and what it feels like as you speak. No doubt, you'll discover that you are speaking through a tight throat and your voice sounds and feels strained.

When you become aware of the differences, you should be able to make some conscious shifts in how you use your voice.

You're accustomed to the sound of your voice. So are your friends and coworkers. But you will hear it differently if you listen to a recording of yourself. That's where I would start. Listen to yourself speak. I suggest letting the recorder run while you chat with a friend. You can also record yourself actually delivering a speech in front of an audience. I suggest doing both. Also ask fellow Toastmasters to critique your voice and offer suggestions.

Contact a voice coach. A speaking voice coach is best, but if there isn't one in your area, you might learn some techniques from a singing or drama coach. Breathing exercises facilitated by a knowledgeable voice coach can help with all manner of voice and enunciation problems. Just remember that your voice does make an impression, and you want it to make a good one.

A few years ago, I read an interesting article by marketing and writing coach and professional speaker Catherine Franz. The subject was "Voice Care for Coaches and Speakers." Here are some of the highlights:

- Drink warm or hot beverages before a performance, not cold ones.

- Avoid caffeinated drinks and acidic beverages.
- Avoid anything with mint or menthol.
- Take Black Currant Pastilles (a throat lozenge) twenty-four hours before speaking—also recommended after flying.
- Use Throat Coat Tea. It contains licorice root and is used to enhance throat and upper respiratory tract health.
- Avoid shouting, excess talking, and even extended whispering prior to a performance.
- Avoid stress before a performance.

I suggest that, if you do public speaking gigs to promote your books or your business, or if you frequently suffer with throat problems and/or laryngitis, read this article. It has a lot to offer in either situation. (http://www.selfgrowth.com/articles/voice_care_for_coaches_and_speakers.html)

I had a long conversation with a voice coach prior to my appearance at the Alaska Writers Guild Writers Conference in Anchorage, where I was to present two ninety-minute keynote speeches and a three-hour workshop within a three-day period. I was concerned about the strain on my vocal chords. I told the voice coach that I sometimes come away from a presentation followed by a weekend book festival with a hoarse voice, and I didn't want to lose my voice before I fulfilled my speaking obligations in Alaska.

She gave me several exercises to try. Two things stick with me. She said to hum just before starting to speak. She said that humming tends to relax the throat. I know what it feels like when I am straining my voice and what it feels like when I am using it correctly. But sometimes it is hard to back off from the strain and adopt the more comfortable, pleasing, and less tiring method of speaking. If I hum, I will start out using my more comfortable voice, and I can more often than not maintain it.

The second thing that I planned to try if I ran into a problem in Alaska was, if my voice got strained and I felt laryngitis coming on, to rub Preparation H on my throat. No kidding. I followed up that suggestion with some online research and discovered that this is quite valid advice. Do not take Preparation H internally.

Even an experienced speaker sometimes needs assistance with his or her speaking voice. As a gymnastics coach for thirty years, Rik Feeney spent a lot of time in front of large groups of athletes and their parents. He says, "I learned to project my voice across a ten thousand square-foot gym while giving instructions." He now speaks in smaller venues and has had to retrain his robust voice to conform to his new audiences—readers and potential readers for his books on a variety of topics. He says, "I certainly could be better, so lately, I have been doing vocal exercises from a book and CD titled *Love Your Voice* by renowned voice coach Roger Love."

Feeney offers this visual,

> Every day, I pop the CD into my car stereo and cruise around central Florida bellowing out the various vocal exercises that Love claims will make my voice thicker, stronger, more resonant. I do think my voice is getting stronger and that the exercises are adding a bit more in range and tone. One reason I am doing vocal exercises, I plan to do some audio CDs of my books and other materials and I want to make sure I sound the best I can.

As an author, you understand the importance of careful preparation. You prepare an outline before you write your book. You prepare a pitch for a publisher and maybe a book proposal. You create a marketing plan. Preparing for your presentations is every bit as important. So don't neglect this aspect of your speaking pursuits.

It's Time to Face Your Audience

It doesn't take long for an aware, alert presenter to understand the importance of connecting with an audience. We spoke earlier about the value of knowing something about your audience before you plan your presentation. When you face them, you'll learn even more about their aptitude and attitude with regard to your topic and you. You'll discover this partially by observing them and partly by communicating with them.

Rauch-Mannino pays close attention to his audiences. He says,

> Before the event, I consider the audience. I research those who are likely to attend, if necessary, and place myself behind their perspective. I want to have an idea of why they are listening to me, what they want to hear, how to keep them entertained, and what to avoid. Having had experience with dynamic audiences helps, too. Given the range of ages, backgrounds, interests, and so on, I feel as if I've been before every type of audience. So the preparation comes from thinking about my own prior experiences as much as it does new research.

During the engagement, I find it important to keep a keen eye on audience members. I gauge how the most attentive and least interested listeners appear, and I make subtle changes to my presentation when I feel it is appropriate. A seamless reaction and adjustment can make the difference between a few listeners really absorbing what you're saying and the entire audience enjoying the engagement.

In some cases, you know what your audience needs, but that isn't necessarily what they want, so you must attempt to hand-feed the information to them in a palatable way. Sometimes members of my audiences seem to balk at the idea of hiring an editor for their manuscripts before sending them to a publisher, or they simply do not want to write a book proposal. I can see their eyes glaze over and their minds snap shut when I start talking to them about book promotion. I so believe that they need to hear and consider these things if they want a successful publishing outcome, however, that I work hard at finding ways to present this material so they will accept it. I use a combination of tactics to entice them to hear me—among them, statistics and anecdotes. Statistics provide shock value and a reality check. Anecdotes can be entertaining, but they also help audience members relate to the message in a more personal way.

If I see faces light up with regard to a particular topic I've touched on, I might use it to make the point I want them to walk away with. If I see a swell of interest when I mention that many publishers today go to blog sites in search of books to publish, for example, I will provide additional information and anecdotes on this concept.

Some audience members are just stoic. It is hard to read whether you are getting through to them or not. When people nod off, however, that's a good clue that your talk may be bogging down. Don't let that fluster you—instead, look around the room for perspective. What is the demeanor of the others in the audience? If everyone looks confused or bored, definitely change gears. Add something of interest, share an anecdote, or involve the audience, for example. Perhaps you have a quiz or an exercise planned, or you want to invite audience members to share something about their projects. This might be the time to do it. Ask a provocative question. Offer a challenge.

However, before changing your entire approach, evaluate the overall demeanor and level of attention of the audience. If some are expressing interest in what you're saying, shift your focus from the slumbering person to the one who is most animated and seems to be the most in love with you and your presentation. Sure, you want to sweep the room, locking eyes with each and every individual several times throughout the presentation. But it's confidence-building and encouraging when you spend more time glancing at those who are nodding in agreement with what you have to say—who are leaning forward in their chairs, who are smiling.

Another sign that audience members are interested in what you've said is when you see them furiously writing or typing notes.

Nancy Barnes speaks to audiences on the topic of memoir-writing and publishing. She says,

> As a retired schoolteacher, I can still act like one (we all can!), and I find that audiences always respond to tried-and-true classroom tricks. Just ask them to raise their hands. Young and old—they love it! Before the presentation, I distribute (branded) booklets with the PowerPoint slides and a place to take notes. I get everyone talking by having them "pair-share" and swap ideas, answers, or stories with the person sitting next to them. Conduct mini-surveys. Ask for five volunteers

to stand up and tell the class. . . whatever. If I have a small enough group, I will find a way to get people out of their seats, if only for three minutes, and have them form small groups. In the end, the only thing that matters is that people get to speak. It changes the dynamic from you, the boring lecturer, to you, the exciting facilitator, and they will always remember that you showed them a good time.

The Confidence Factor

Even frequent speakers sometimes feel a lack of confidence when they face an audience. Every speaker handles his or her butterflies differently. One excellent method of organizing those butterflies is to have a great opening line memorized perfectly. The first words you utter (or bellow) should come across clear, crisp, and with impact. Make this a confidence-building moment.

You could do as some professionals suggest and imagine everyone in the room naked. All that does for me is make me giggle. I guess a giggle does take the edge off. In fact, I learned a long time ago, when I was a young mother and the president of the Juanamaria Grammar School PTA, that laughter can settle the nerves of a speaker. I discovered quite by chance that if I could get a chuckle from the audience before I started the meeting, I became more relaxed. Still, before I begin to speak, I'll either purposefully or subconsciously do or say something to break the ice in the room by initiating a response from the audience. That response often involves laughter.

Speaking professionals recommend *not* starting a speech with a joke. I can see the logic in that. An opening joke that falls flat can be disastrous. Not only can it affect the audience's opinion of you, but it can shake your confidence. I don't tell jokes. I simply sometimes make an off-handed comment that the audience can relate to and that causes them to smile or, as I said, chuckle. However, this won't work for every speaker. It is a personality thing, and it's never staged or rehearsed.

Before I started my keynote speech at the conference in Alaska, I announced with glee that I had seen a moose that morning—something quite common to Alaskans, but certainly not something you experience along the coast of California. Not really funny—but an ice-breaker, nonetheless. An ice-breaker, after all, is a way to build rapport with your audience. At least some of them got a kick out of my delight at seeing my first moose.

As far as attitude: Instead of imagining all of those poor people in front of you without clothes, try viewing them as students. If you shake in your boots at the thought of standing before certain groups of people, here's something that might help. Whether you're teaching something— sharing your knowledge and expertise—or talking about your memoir, remember that you know more about your topic than anyone else in the room. Now if that isn't a confidence booster, I don't know what is.

Sure, it's likely that other people have had experience in your topic. But none of them is in the same place that you are. No one can tell the same stories that you can. No one has had the exact experiences nor have they done all of the very same research as you have.

I remember watching a program on TV years ago where a bodybuilder challenged anyone to stand up under his workout routine. Time after time, strong, muscular men came forward to take on his challenge and failed. Why? Because, while they were in good shape, they had not practiced the exact routine in the exact same way as the challenger had. Thus, they had not built the muscle bulk and stamina required to perform this specific routine.

So you need to know that when you stand up before a group, while others in the audience might be familiar with the subject, might have had experience in the topic, may be well-versed in aspects of the subject, no one knows it the way you do. No one has had the exact same experiences, conducted the exact same research, gained the same amount of knowledge, nor do they have the same interest level. You are unique. You have something unique to share. Do not buy into that trick your mind will play on you by trying to make you believe your audience is more knowledgeable or savvy than you are. Just as you could learn from some of them, each and every one of them can learn from you. So go in with the attitude that you know more about your topic in the way you plan to present it than anyone else in the room.

This brings me to one more issue I'd like to touch on. It is important to look at these presentations you give not necessarily as a total bookselling opportunity or even an opportunity for exposure, but also as a learning experience. I've been writing for publication for close to forty years. I have thirty-six published books to my credit. I've been writing, speaking and teaching about publishing and book promotion for around thirty years, and I always, *always* learn something new when I venture out to speak or participate in a book festival. So, while you are preparing yourself to speak on behalf of your book and you are facing audiences locally and afar, always keep an open mind and be willing to learn.

Nonfiction authors of self-help, how-to, and informational books are in a particularly good spot to learn about new trends in their subject and news items related to the topic of their books, etc. Whether your book features techniques for changing cat behavior, origami for the beginner, the art of bookbinding, cross-country ski tours, vegetarianism for overweight dogs, bookkeeping tricks and tips, medical miracles, or butterfly-watching, when you meet and greet your readers and peers, you're bound to learn something new, discover a new resource, or hear a unique story that you can use in future books, articles, and speeches.

Comfort Control—Yours and Theirs

Even with these techniques and perspectives in place, you might still get a case of noodle knees before speaking. Sometimes even seasoned speakers get a few butterflies before going on stage. Do you know what this means? It means that you are alive and that you want to do a good job. If you don't feel a twinge of nerves before stepping up to the mic, it could be that you are either deceased or you really don't care about your audience.

Every speaker has a unique way of handling his nervousness before a presentation. Some prefer silence prior to a performance. They arrive through the back door at the last minute and remain in seclusion until the moment they are announced. Others get hyped up for their talks by mingling and chatting with audience members before going on stage. I know authors who do a silent meditation during the introduction. Others might stretch a little to get a sense of calm or shake their bodies and jump up and down in a ritual to shake off any stress-causing potential interferences. I suppose there are also authors who say a little prayer before taking center stage. I say, do whatever works for you.

Leslie Korenko found her level of comfort as a speaker the hard way. She says,

> I learned never to stand behind the lectern because I clench the sides and stare straight ahead, then I seize up and find myself reading from my notes. It is awful to experience and uncomfortable to watch. I feel more relaxed standing or leaning against a table. But when I get excited about something, I move around. I scan the audience when I speak—people always comment that it seemed like I was speaking to them personally. That way you can watch for questions or confused looks or even sleepy heads.

Your main goal as a presenter is to inform, teach, educate, entertain, and, if appropriate and if you can manage it, dazzle 'em. When you agree to speak, you owe something to your audience. You've taken on a responsibility. You have an obligation to fulfill. No matter what the organizer tells you about your audience—their interests, their proficiency level, etc.—you may still want to check with them to make sure you are on the right track with your presentation.

Will you stand during your presentation or sit down? Will you use a microphone, or does your voice project well enough in the size room you'll be using? If you are part of a panel discussion, will you stand when it is your turn to speak? I generally do, and I appreciate it when other speakers do when I'm a member of an audience.

I even recommend that authors dress for professional confidence and stand (or, at least, sit up straight) when giving an interview over the phone. Your voice will carry better if you are standing. You are in better command of the room when you are standing.

Once you reach your comfort level, it's time to consider your audience. You want them to be comfortable and enjoy their time with you.

When I'm conducting a ninety-minute or longer workshop for writers or authors, I'll generally introduce myself and my planned program and then ask attendees to introduce themselves and their writing projects. When your audience consists of twenty-five or more people, this isn't practical. When I'm addressing fifty to 100 or more people, I might ask for volunteers to respond to questions related to their involvement with my topic or for a show of hands of people who are writing a book proposal, who have never written one, or who would like to learn how to write one. Let's say your talk covers issues of divorce. Ask how many people in the audience are divorced, how many have amicable relationships with their former spouses, how many would like to get along better with their exes, etc. Someone who is teaching a skill might ask questions designed to get a sense about audience members' level of proficiency in this skill.

An additional tactic for putting an audience at ease, especially for longer presentations, would surely include breaks during which audience members can stand, stretch, get a glass of water, etc.

Change the pace now and then when presenting a longer program. There are a number of methods you can use, but those I find most effective rely on audience involvement. Give an assignment or ask for audience feedback or questions, for example. I've seen speakers break up the monotony of their presentation by bringing in someone to teach a specific skill for fifteen minutes, have an actor read a portion of his book, showing a film, or using a PowerPoint program to offer a few minutes of entertainment.

To Use or Not to Use Props

This question is pondered by many an author. I sometimes like to use props in order to give my talk variety. It can also help me to stay focused on my material. Some authors use PowerPoint presentations. Others, such as Barbara Florio-Graham, would rather speak directly to their audiences without interference or a crutch. She says, "I never use PowerPoint because I feel it is important to face your audience and interact directly with them."

I, personally, find a PowerPoint presentation quite useful in many situations. If it is a long program, it helps mix things up for the audience so they don't get weary. It aids you in staying on track during your speech. It's a nice "crutch" when you have to prepare something on short notice.

PowerPoint presentations do not have to be made up of charts, key phrases, and statistics. They can be sprinkled with photographs, drawings, and cartoons. It can be a wonderful addition to a presentation when your book is visual—a travel memoir, for example, or a history book illustrated with old photos. I've used PowerPoint technology to show photographs during a talk about my trip to Dubai and I've used one to promote the Ojai, California history book. I've also made my conference presentations more interesting, poignant, and impactful by my choice of PowerPoint slides. What fun I had one year locating cartoon drawings to illustrate various points I wanted to make during a workshop. I even included comical slides showing how I perceived my workshop students before the conference—all fresh and eager to learn—and at the end of the two-day event—exhausted, bleary-eyed, and obviously a tad overwhelmed.

When using a PowerPoint program, be sure to practice it so you can present it flawlessly without giving too much of your attention to the visual program and without turning your back on your audience.

Local history author Leslie Korenko always uses a PowerPoint presentation to illustrate her talks. She says,

> My lead to each topic is a slide with an interesting picture on it. For example, my talk on historical Kelleys Island (Ohio) deals with maps and early settlers. Then there are sections on historic houses, churches, schools, etc. Each slide has a line of description and maybe some statistics, but its main purpose is to cue me into the story behind the slides in that section. I personalize the segment by saying, "Oh, did you know . . ." or "If you look closely, you will see . . ." I also have a timeline handout, so if anyone puts me on the spot with a "When did . . ." question, I can respond.

Korenko suggests this for authors who are hesitant to use a Power-Point projector. "Setting up a slide show is much easier than you think.

If you have pictures, you have a slide show." She suggests, "Think back to the best presentations you have attended. Those that impressed me were colorful, entertaining, enthusiastic, and interesting. And many of those were accented by a slide show." She cautions, however, "I don't like to use slides with a lot of text because, when people are reading, they are not listening. I like slides with pictures because people can look at a picture and still listen."

She advises, "The best investment I made was an inexpensive remote slide advancer/laser pointer. This makes advancing the slides seamless, and it eliminated all those trips to the computer, blocking people's views of the slides."

As for using other types of props, Korenko says,

Make sure they are located within easy reach, but also that they don't interfere with your presentation or distract people from listening. Keep them simple and out of sight or people will wonder what they are for instead of listening to you. Most important, adapt your style to whatever makes you feel comfortable. Because if you are comfortable, you will put your audience at ease.

The Question and Answer Session

Not all presentations have a question and answer session, but many do. There are two basic ways to handle the Q & A. Some authors allow questions throughout their presentations. This can actually help you to direct your speech. It's sort of the lazy man's way of presenting a program. You prepare an opening, offer a few ideas, and then invite audience members to ask questions. You could conceivably fill an hour time slot by responding to questions on your topic. But I'd avoid depending on this style of speaking. You can't always count on your audience to feed you enough questions. On the other hand, using this method, you'll be sure to respond to what audience members want to know.

Raven West uses this approach. She says,

> You can always prepare certain key points you want to make, I just find it a lot easier to go with the flow and concentrate more on the question and answer session than rely on a set of structured notes. Sometimes the conversation can go off in a totally different direction from what you had planned, and if you're not comfortable with improv, you run the risk of totally losing it. When you're the guest speaker, it is your job and responsibility to give your audience something they can take with them—something that they didn't have when they arrived. That could be a new idea or something new about you or your books. Whatever it is, you want to leave them with a good feeling and not disappoint them.

Yes, there are a variety of methods for dealing with audience questions. You can use them to drive your speech, as West does, allow questions throughout your presentation, or even ask audience members to write their questions on slips of paper and respond at the end of the session. This works well for a larger group.

I often ask that questions be held until I've delivered the material I think audience members need to hear. I promise them a generous helping of time in which to ask their burning questions after my presentation.

Leslie Korenko handles her question and answer periods this way: "I delay answering questions that others might not be interested in until the end." This is a good point. There are always those who want to get into a long discussion about something personal that may not be of interest or relevant to others. Korenko says, "I say, 'Can I answer that later? Remind me later.' I might tell them, 'The library made it clear that I only have so much time to do the presentation, but I can help you out afterwards.' This is a good way to limit someone monopolizing everyone's time."

Some audience members are just too timid to ask their questions in a public forum, and they will come up to you afterward for a private conversation.

What if you don't know the answer to the question? Mary Ellen Warner suggests that author-speakers be humble and honest. She says, "Don't pretend to know the answer to a question when you don't. I sometimes get odd questions. If it is something I don't know, I say, 'That's really interesting, does anyone have an answer for us?'"

If I don't have the answer at my fingertips, I ask that person to email me after I return home and I will locate the answer for him or her.

You Can't Plan for Every Possibility

No matter how heads-up you are in preparing for your presentations, there's always something that can go wrong—but "wrong" may not be the right word to use. If we consider every change or departure from plans as something wrong, that could put a negative shroud over the program. When this happens, you tend to go into repair mode—rescue mode. Instead, consider it simply a departure from the script. Deal with it—find ways to make things work. Make it appear to others that this was the original plan.

You might arrive and discover that the projector doesn't work, no one can find the extension cord, or the mic isn't operating. I've had to adjust to smaller (or larger) rooms than originally reserved. There have been times when the program coordinator became ill or was called out of town and I had to start over with someone new. I once conducted my workshop over the sound of a basketball game in progress on the other side of the wall. I've even had my presentations inter-rupted by inconsiderate servers or event coordinators who wanted to make an announcement or ask a question. On one occasion, the person in charge forgot I was coming to conduct a workshop and neglected to turn off the alarm system. Of course, it set to screeching when I unlocked the door. After the police got things quieted down, we just drove to a nearby home of one of the attendees and I conducted the workshop there.

How does one prepare for the unexpected? Always have a backup plan. If the projector absolutely, unequivocally refuses to work, speak without slides. Pull some of your clever quizzes or a trivia game out of your back pocket. Ask audience members to gather in small groups and write a play or a poem. Share a scene from your story. Build it up to a near climax and then ask audience members to write the conclusion. Or simply recite a list of tips related to your topic or genre generously interspersed with anecdotes and examples.

I once watched an older woman speak on novel-writing. I don't know if she had forgotten her props or if her PowerPoint slide show was damaged, but she used the most delightfully crude signs to illustrate the points in her program. It was as if she had arrived at the conference site too late to visit an office store, so she found a few cardboard boxes behind the building, borrowed some scissors and crayons or markers from a local restaurant or a playroom on the premises, and created these signs. She held the signs up for emphasis at certain points during her session—usually rather awkwardly and not exactly in sync with the pace of her talk. It was one of the most charming presentations I've watched at a conference. Not everyone would be able to pull it off, though. This was a case of a personality-driven presentation and I still don't know if it was planned or not.

While preparation is highly important for a speaker, flexibility is equally vital. Here are a couple of examples of an authors making lemonade out of what could have been potentially thought of as lemons:

Leslie Korenko learned the hard way that, at least in her area, speaking during the summer is pretty much a waste of time, unless the weather is bad.

She says, "Even I would like to be outside on a nice day. Saturday mornings are bad. I've found that evenings produce the best audiences." She talks about one challenging presentation she experienced. She says, "It was a Saturday morning on the first sunny day of spring. One person showed up. I asked the librarian to invite anyone who was at the library that day to join me and one more person came in. So I walked through the library and asked for everyone's attention. I invited them to a FREE lecture with gorgeous slides of Kelleys Island (you cannot be timid in promoting yourself). Eight people dropped what they were doing and came in. I sold three books!"

Rik Feeney once found himself without space for his presentation and had to improvise. He says, "At Vermont College, the meeting room was unavailable and I ended up giving my talk to the group while they sat on the stairs going up to the third floor."

So how does an author-speaker prepare for the unexpected? Take a cue from Korenko and Feeney. The next time you are scheduled to speak, make well-defined plans. Follow-up to make sure that everyone else involved is handling things on their end. Then give a little (not too much) thought to what you would do in a variety of scenarios. For example, what if no one shows up, the power goes out, the organizer arrives late, you have unexpected distractions to deal with, etc? Plan thoroughly and then have a few backup plans for "just in case." This is an especially helpful exercise if you aren't typically flexible in your thinking.

Timing Is Almost Everything

The timing of a speech is so important that a major part of the Toastmasters program revolves around this issue. When you are on an agenda to speak, you can tell if the speaker ahead of you has had Toastmasters training or not by how prompt he or she is in starting and ending their presentation.

So often, per the event coordinator's instructions, I write, organize, and rehearse a forty-five minute talk with a question and answer period. But when I get to the event site, I discover that I have only thirty minutes total. It is rare when programs run according to schedule and that can certainly mess up a speaker. This is why it is important that you know your material so well that you can be spontaneous if required.

How is it that program agendas can change so dramatically? The event might start late or get off track at some point. A business meeting scheduled prior to the talk may run overtime because of a hot issue members want to discuss. Other speakers will talk past their time slots, leaving you with less time to deliver your presentation.

What is a speaker to do? If your speech is part of a crowded agenda that includes other speakers, offer to signal the speaker in front of you when his time is almost up.

I also do my best to keep myself on schedule—which is highly important to me and should be to you when you're speaking. If I can't see a clock from where I stand, I take off my watch, lay it on the lectern or a nearby table and glance down at it occasionally to make sure I am on track.

Barbara Florio-Graham believes in precise timing, as well. She says,

I always prepare careful notes on cards with flags to indicate timing so I know if I have time to digress (in which case, I will include an extra card of a different color), or if I need to press on in order to cover everything. I like to prepare hand-outs with details I want to remember. I arrive well ahead of time to check the room set-up, lectern, microphone, and fill my mug with water. Then I chat with people as they arrive. When I take the stage, I feel as though I'm talking to friends, not a hostile audience, and it also helps me make eye contact with individuals as I speak.

Mary Ellen Warner likes to arrive early for her presentations, as well. And she believes it is important to be "on" from the moment she arrives. She says, "Have you ever been waiting for the entertainment and the speaker comes in looking frazzled? This is not a great start!" She suggests, "Be ready to perform when you turn off the key in the car!"

Warner describes her arrival: "I am the entertainment from the time I pull into the parking lot. Sometimes I am walking into an event and the person walking near me is on the way to the same event. I reach out to him or her and then I already have a friend in the audience. I make sure to connect with that person when I am up front!"

I hope that we've hit upon the points that resonate with you in this chapter. So much of what constitutes success as a presenter is tied into perspective and attitude. It's the old adage of seeing the glass half full instead of half empty—viewing changes as challenges rather than problems—perceiving occurrences beyond your control as something different instead of something wrong. It all boils down to preparation and your level of flexibility as well as your mindset.

Public Speaking Tips for Authors

Obviously, speaking is one of your planned book promotion activities. You no doubt hope to speak before large and small groups of people as a way to gain exposure for your book. Please, before you launch out on the speaking circuit, heed the following advice:

1. Join a local Toastmasters club and actively participate for at least a year. You will benefit in ways that you can't even imagine. You'll become a more accomplished and confident speaker as well as a more effective communicator. Go to www.toastmasters.org for a list of clubs near you.

    Author and storyteller Mary Ellen Warner is one of thousands of advocates for Toastmasters. She speaks to groups regularly and says, "My Toastmaster journey has been life-changing." She advises other authors, "The best thing an author with a book to promote can do for themselves is to join and fully participate in the Toastmasters International Program. I have witnessed hundreds of fellow Toastmasters become outstanding communicators."

    Carol Dean Schreiner is a professional speaker and the author of four books. She agrees and says,

I suggest each author-speaker join a local Toastmasters club to learn how to convey their thoughts verbally. It is one thing to write and another thing altogether to speak and to be interviewed. At each Toastmasters meeting, every speech is evaluated verbally and in writing, providing the speaker a world of ways to improve.

Waxler is also a fan of the Toastmasters program. He says,

I found that the group experience helped me not only by imparting tips about public speaking but also by giving me a social context for the knowledge. This group of aspiring public speakers that met every two weeks made a perfect representative audience for me while I was learning. Toastmasters is a gentle, compassionate teaching organization and a support system all built into one.

Toastmasters isn't for everyone. Instead, you can get speaker training through adult education courses at your local college or another organization in your area. Check the resources in chapter eighteen. Also do an Internet search using keywords, "speaker training" and your city, for example.

2. **Volunteer for opportunities to speak.** Take leadership of a project at work or for a charity. Tour around and educate citizens on a political issue or speak at fund-raisers for the local library expansion or a new community arts program, for example. Practice, practice, practice.

3. **Attend other speakers' programs.** If you are observant and alert, you will learn volumes about public speaking by listening and watching. How do audiences respond to other speakers? What would you do differently to put the audience at ease, make this

a more pleasant and informative experience for the audience, get your point across to this audience, etc?

Margaret Brownley says that she didn't join any organizations or hire a coach in order to learn about public speaking. She says, "Prior to speaking, I listened to speakers and took notes. I paid attention to what worked, what didn't—what kept my attention. I also noted stage presence. For my first speech, I shared the stage witvh a friend and we took turns speaking. It really helped and gave me the confidence to fly solo."

4. **Get involved with a storytelling group.** This is a particularly enjoyable way to improve your speaking skills. You'll also get some training and practice in using vocal variety. I especially recommend this to authors of children's books, novels, and books of poetry. If you're not naturally animated and if you don't have good use of vocal variety, a storytelling group could be most valuable in helping you to develop a more interesting and effective way of presenting to children. Poetry should be read with the same emotion and passion that went into writing it. If you don't have natural skills you can use when sharing your poems, a storytelling group could greatly assist you with this.

    Many novelists and nonfiction book authors also use natural or learned storytelling techniques to entertain their audiences. Lucinda Sue Crosby grew up learning storytelling skills and she uses them when talking to groups about her novel, *Francesca of Lost Nation*. She says,

    > My presentations are very well-received and I believe I ace them through a combination of passion for my story, familiarity with the subject, honed storytelling skills (after years of acting/singing classes and stage, TV, and film appearances), and, most importantly, the

blessing of people surrounding me in my youth who were amazing conversationalists, all of whom could put you inside any tale they chose to tell.

5.   **Hire a voice coach.** If you have a voice that doesn't carry well or that is unpleasant to the ear, a voice coach might be able to help. Perhaps when you speak out, your voice becomes easily strained or you tend to speak in monotone. Maybe you've developed a habit that makes it difficult for audiences to understand you— you mumble or speak too fast, for example. If people often ask you to repeat yourself or if you recognize a problem with your delivery or your voice, start working with a voice coach early in your introduction to public speaking. I can tell you from experience that there's a lot to learn if you are to develop a better, richer, and more far-reaching speaking voice. But it is worth the effort. Give yourself plenty of time to learn the techniques and apply them before launching out on your speaking tour. Find voice coaches listed under "music teachers" in your local Yellow Pages. Sometimes a singing teacher or drama coach can help.

According to Warner, who has had to overcome challenges of hearing loss, "I would recommend a voice coach for anyone who mumbles or someone with a breathless voice or a little girl's voice."

How do you know when you need a voice coach? Warner says, "Pay attention to what happens when you tell your story. Does your audience smile, nod, laugh, cry, or do they look at their watches?"

I happen to be a fan of vocal therapy. I've seen (heard) the difference a voice coach has made with a couple of my friends. But the most glaring improvement I noticed was with a radio personality. I listened to this person for years. Suddenly, I began to notice something different. She was more pleasing to listen to. I couldn't put my finger on what had changed until one day I read that she had taken some time out to work with a voice coach. That was it. Her voice had a richer quality. I could actually listen to her for longer periods without getting annoyed.

Waxler points out, however, that a voice coach is not for everyone. He says,

> When I started at Toastmasters, I thought a coach could help me get over my initial clumsiness. I found a professor of drama at a local college. He was a great guy, and clearly wanted to help, but I didn't feel like the experience was worthwhile. I did not understand how to apply his lessons to the experience of speaking in front of an audience. A more effective system for me was to ask questions during the coffee breaks at Toastmasters. The short spontaneous interchanges incrementally added to my overall understanding and gradually helped me improve.

(For more about improving and maintaining your speaking voice, study chapter 5.)

6. **Find a mentor**—someone who's speaking abilities you admire. Ask him or her to help you change a bad speaking habit, strengthen or give more quality to your speaking voice, plan and organize your speeches, rehearse and/or deliver a more professional presentation. Some Toastmasters clubs and other speakers' organizations have mentor programs.

Sandra Beckwith solicited the help of friends before she actively pursued speaking engagements. She says,

> Public speaking requires knowledge about how the process works and skill as a speaker. It takes practice. And feedback. And more practice and feedback. When I was first starting out as a speaker, I asked people I trusted to be honest, to attend my early sessions and critique my content and delivery. Their input made a big difference.

While we each have a unique way of speaking and we don't want to be carbon copies of each other, there are some public speaking rules that always (or almost always) apply. First, let me share with you some of the most common and most obnoxious mistakes people make when attempting to speak in public:

Public Speaking Rule Breakers

- Many speakers let their voices trail off at the end of every sentence. The audience can hear the first part of their sentences, but they have no idea what pearls of wisdom might be lost in the whispers at the end. Sometimes this speaker will deliver complete sentences inaudibly while looking down— obviously not interested at that moment in engaging the audience. I'm sure you've all witnessed this behavior. Sometimes speakers on stage or during a conversation will speak inaudibly when verbalizing an afterthought or adding what could be considered an addendum or postscript to his original statement. He must believe that what he's saying isn't very important or he wouldn't be muffling the words. Then I would say, if it isn't important don't say it at all. If you want to say it, speak up.

- Speakers with poor reading skills stand up and read from their books. Few speakers can read out loud in a way that is entertaining and pleasing to hear. If you are not skilled at reading something aloud, don't do it. (Read more about this issue in chapter 9.)

- Mumbling is not cool. Inexperienced speakers will often speak at conversation level, not giving any thought or consideration to the people in the back of the room or those who may be hard of hearing. Some years ago, I sat in on a panel discussion at a workshop. The panelists chose to sit instead of stand to address the standing-room-only crowd, which I thought was rude. One man, whenever it was his turn to speak, rested his elbows on the table and folded his hands in front of his mouth during the entire time that he was speaking. He listened with his hands flat on the table, but when he spoke, up came those hands to cover his mouth, which muffled the words he was speaking. Many people rely on a form or a level of lip-reading in order to catch all that is being said. This man was preventing some members of his audience from benefiting from his wisdom, and he was probably completely unaware of this habit he had developed.

- Inexperienced or thoughtless speakers leave members of the audience out. When an audience member asks a question, it is rarely heard in the back of the room. I've seen many expert speakers respond to questions by engaging in a one-on-one conversation with this person while the rest of the audience is left wondering. Speakers, I urge you to repeat the audience questions so everyone is on the same page. Then respond to the question so that everyone in the room can hear your response.

- Some speakers choose to sit down on the job. In a very small, intimate group or when the audience is sitting in a circle of chairs or on the floor, for example, speaking while seated is generally okay. If you have a room containing six rows of chairs or more, however, you really should express respect for those in the back of the room by standing so that you can be seen as well as heard.

- Even some professional speakers (and radio personalities) still use too many filler words. It takes practice, but you can rid your vocabulary (especially while speaking in public) of those filler words such as, "uh," "ah," "um," "er." Also avoid connecting sentences by overusing "and." An important function of a Toastmasters club is helping members recognize to what extent they are using filler words so they can begin to eliminate them from their everyday conversation as well as their public speaking engagements. Most members of Toastmasters have seen some miraculous turn-arounds when it comes to the use of filler words. Someone will come into the group using "um" after every three or four words he speaks. With practice, however, this person soon delivers complete sentences without ever interrupting the flow with a filler word.

- Many speakers have trouble staying within the time allotment. Most programs or presentations are carefully organized. Each segment is designed to fit into a specific time slot. I've seen speakers completely disregard their time constraints and foul up an entire evening's program. Not cool. Learn to fit your speeches into specific time slots. This is another aspect of public speaking that Toastmasters teaches.

Public Speaking Tips

Speak out. Practice speaking up and speaking out. Whether addressing a large audience or a small group, always speak so that you can be heard even in the back of the room. Keep those folks in mind throughout your speech. Speakers often heed the advice of their audience and speak up at first. But if not prodded, they soon fall back into their old routine of quiet talking, mumbling, or dropping their voices at the end of their sentences. You'll hear the speaker ask in a strong voice, "Can you hear me?" When everyone assures him that they can, he then ratchets his voice back down to his conversational tone.

In order to make it easier on yourself as a speaker, if there are empty seats, invite those sitting in the back to fill some of the seats toward the front of the room. But most will not budge. They choose their seats according to their level of comfort. Some sit close to the door in case they don't want to stay. At conferences, some people bounce from one session to another in order to pick up a few ideas and the free handouts from each. Some people don't want to sit close to others, don't like people sitting behind them, or just want to spread out without infringing on others or vice versa. So, while you can try to rearrange audience members, just know that some will not comply.

Make eye contact. Move your attention around the room as you speak, making eye contact with each person throughout your presentation.

I like to make frequent eye contact with those in the audience who are responding to what I'm saying. Some will smile. Others will nod in agreement and, perhaps, frantically jot down some notes. These people energize me and keep my enthusiasm level up throughout my presentation. I avoid focusing on those with blank stares, those who are chatting with their neighbors while I'm speaking, those who are nodding off, or those who are sitting back appearing a bit smug—as if what I'm talking about is of no importance to them. When you make eye contact with audience members, you are getting some feedback. Some of it is positive and some might be rather disturbing, even confidence-shattering.

Sure, you want to know that you are reaching at least the majority of your audience with your message. If you see the blank stares and it appears to you that people are not interested or are not getting it, start asking questions. You'll learn a lot about how you're coming across if you allow your audience to respond to some pointed questions.

In the meantime, don't shortchange the entire audience by reacting to the negative vibes you might pick up from a few people. Always focus on the positive. You will often discover that what you perceived as disinterest or indifference—even arrogance—may have been erroneous. I've had these people come up to me after the program or speak up during the question and answer session expressing keen interest in the material I was presenting. Some of them even bought my book or hired me to edit their manuscripts.

I remember a gentleman in one of my sessions a few years ago who seemed indifferent to the material I presented. He sat in the back row with two other men. They talked among themselves several times. He didn't take notes. His eyes kind of wandered around the room. But he didn't leave. After the program, he came up to me and introduced himself as the president of the organization. He said, "You're amazing. You gave us more value in one presentation than our speakers did throughout the entire conference last year."

Don't apologize. Avoid sabotaging your presentation by making excuses for not being well-prepared or for poor speaking skills. Stand tall, appear self-assured, and you will gain the confidence of the audience.

I've heard speakers stand before an audience and actually say, "My voice tends to drop off at the end of my sentences, so forgive me if you can't hear everything I say." "Sorry I've been busy and haven't had much time to prepare. Just bear with me, will ya?" Or "I've been flying all night and don't have much energy today. I hope you don't expect much of me." No, no, no. Never indicate to the audience that you do not plan to give them your very best performance.

Sure, if you have a cute story as to why you rushed into the meeting hall at the last minute, tell it. Or if there is an important message or lesson in something you feel you should apologize for, perhaps you should share it. What I'm trying to prevent you from doing is to give audience members the impression that you are not going to give them your all—that there is something more important to you than this presentation. You certainly don't want to negate any credibility you have with this audience.

What if, after you're introduced, you say to the audience, "Well, I don't really know that much about the topic of my book. I'm just one of many who have written about it, but I'm not the authority. I will tell you what I know, but you should take it with a grain of salt. Joe Schmo knows a heck of a lot more about it and I always recommend his books." Sure it seems ridiculous that someone would sabotage themselves like this, but you would be surprised at how little some author-speakers know about promoting themselves and their books, human psychology, and even communication.

Use vocal variety. Make your talks more enjoyable by using an assortment of vocal tones and pitches rather than speaking in monotone. If you need help developing vocal variety, practice reading to a child. Use your highest and lowest voice and everything in between. I've mentioned joining a storytelling group a few times already. Please consider this if you need help with vocal variety and if you are going to read publicly to children or tell stories related to your novel.

Eliminate non-words. Inexperienced speakers generally use so many filler words that Toastmasters actually have an "ah counter" at every meeting. This person counts the number of filler words each member uses throughout the course of the meeting. Filler words include uh, ah, um, er, and so forth. You can start eliminating filler words by paying close attention to your speech during your daily communication. Listen to yourself (and others) during conversations. Practice speaking without inserting those fillers between thoughts and sentences. This is a habit you can definitely break.

As they do in each Toastmasters meeting, ask a friend to tally the number of filler words you use while rehearsing a speech or during a casual conversation. The numbers may shock you. Once you are aware of your filler word habit, you will be more motivated to make some changes.

Improve poor speaking habits. Rid your vocabulary of stagnant verbiage. Break yourself of those mundane phrases you like to repeat, such as, "yada, yada, yada" or "know what I mean?"

Be prepared. You will be more at ease if you know what to expect. Find out if there will be a lectern or microphone, for example. How many people do they expect? How will the room be set up? Also, have your props or notes organized so there will be no annoying fumbling during your presentation. Know your material well enough so that you are prepared for any interruption, agenda change, etc. that could, and often will, occur.

As Dallas Woodburn points out, you should "relax and enjoy the process. Be yourself and have fun." An important step in mastering this is to master your speech jitters, which typically result from lack of confidence. Don't you know that you will have enormously more confidence when you are more well-prepared?

I know two speakers who have had the power go off during their presentations due to storms. One was in the midst of a PowerPoint program. With the use of candles, flashlights, and battery-operated lanterns, both of these shows went on, only without the digital props.

Rik Feeney tells the story of a sudden power outage due to a hurricane during one of his seminars. He quips, "The first thing I did when the power went out was get out my flashlight and make hand pictures on the wall to illustrate my ideas. Unfortunately, there are only so many things in publishing you can illustrate with a shadow bunny." He offers this advice:

> Actually, my theory is that if you really know your subject, you don't need a PowerPoint presentation or even notes. I constantly work to stay abreast of current trends in publishing, take notes, write blogs, attend other talks, read industry publications, and write books and reports on publishing topics just so I can be prepared at a moment's notice to do a talk. I walked into a conference once (Florida Heritage Book Festival) where a speaker backed out at the last minute. With only five minutes' notice, I was able to go in and put on a talk that blew their socks off. Once their socks and shoes were back on, I got the hearty applause many speakers cherish.

You may never experience this sort of interruption while speaking, but you should prepare so well that you could carry on expertly should anything like this happen.

Brian Jud is an author and popular seminar leader. He believes in being prepared. He shares this:

> I don't really know why my best presentations were so much better than the flops. I wish I knew. It's not that I practiced more, or the size of the audience, or what is at stake. At times, things just click. I can sense a connection with the audience,

and I may become a little more engaged and relaxed. Sometimes my stories go over better or my humorous comments get a good reaction, and other times they fall flat. All I can say is that speakers should prepare for every presentation and give each their best shot. Do not fall into the trap of "winging it" because you think you know your facts. If you sense a negative reaction, do not let it get to you, but try a different approach. Know your material so well that you can adjust your presentation in midstream if necessary to the personality of the audience. Do not be afraid of trying new material; in fact it is good to update your content with the latest information.

Write your own introduction. You know what you want your audience to know about you before you speak and what information you will share during your presentation. So doesn't it make sense that you would write your own introduction? If you don't, the person in charge of introducing you might get it wrong. I've had MCs introduce me based on the back cover info of a book I produced three years earlier. This might not include the fact that I am now the author of thirty-six books or that I am now the executive director of SPAWN rather than the president, etc. If you want the intro to be correct and to include only certain information, take charge. Find out who will be introducing you and email them your introduction. Also carry a copy of it with you to the event in case it was misplaced.

Know your audience. Gear your speech to the needs and interests of this particular audience. When I talk about the local history, I give a completely different talk to students at local elementary schools or a visiting tour group than I do when addressing civic organization or historical society members. When I speak to a group of writers who may or may not decide to publish anything they write, I put a very different slant on my talk than I do when my audience is comprised of published authors.

A standard rule in preparation is to learn as much as you can about your audience from the program coordinator. This is an excellent place to start. However, I can't tell you how many times I've discovered while in the process of speaking to a group that they do not actually resemble the demographic given to me. That's why I also pay close attention to the promo going out to the public or organization members. This will give me a clue as to who would be attracted to this program, to this slate of speakers, etc. Once I stand before my audience, I almost always ask a few questions before I get too deep into my planned presentation. Let's say that I have prepared a speech on writing a book proposal. I'll ask for a show of hands representing those who are in the process of writing a book, those who have a book they are pitching to publishers, and those who have a published book. If the majority of audience members already have a published book, then I might spend some time talking about the post-publication book proposal—something I have devised to help authors with faltering books determine their true target audience.

Perhaps your book covers do-it-yourself home remodeling and you've planned a presentation for homeowners who want to remodel their kitchens. Only, after quizzing the audience, you discover that most of them are renters, so your original talk wouldn't actually apply to this audience. What to do? This is when your professionalism, or lack thereof will become apparent. Can you shift gears and share ideas for making a kitchen more user-friendly? This would not involve tearing down walls, building new cabinets, putting in flooring, and such. Instead, it might cover storage ideas, how to create a new look in your kitchen without spending a lot of money, tips for choosing the right countertop kitchen appliances, and how to give your old kitchen a fresh and modern look simply by using paint and wall covering creatively.

Dress to stand out, but not to distract from your presentation. If you're a man, you'll most likely wear a suit and tie or slacks/jeans and an open-neck shirt. Unless you have a statement to make related to the theme of your book, I would avoid faded jeans and a tee shirt. For women it might be a suit, dress, skirt and top, or slacks and a sweater. Just keep it neat (fitted, crisp, and pressed). Be tasteful (no low cut tops, too short skirt, or too tight skirts/slacks). I've seen authors dress in costume related to the theme of their books—a WWII bomber jacket, 1950s vintage outfit, Victorian dress and bonnet, overalls, an apron, and so forth.

Anyone can get up in front of an audience and speak. How well you do it is what counts. Consider each and every one of the points above when you next take the stage.

Basic Podium Protocol

Perhaps you've noticed that there is a correct and incorrect podium protocol. This is something, I'm sad to say, that escapes many program coordinators and masters of ceremonies. You may want to teach this etiquette to the MCs you meet during your speaking tours. For example, the number one rule is: Never leave the podium area (or stage) empty. Here's how it goes:

1. The master of ceremonies introduces the speaker and waits for her to join him at the microphone.
2. The speaker greets the MC and shakes his hand. The MC either turns and leaves the stage or he steps behind the speaker and walks off stage. The MC never crosses in front of the speaker.

3. As the MC exits the stage, the speaker very breifly thanks him for the introduction and then begins to address her audience.
4. When the speaker concludes, she nods toward the MC indicating the end of her program (or she might say, "Mr. MC..." to get his attention, or even "Mr. MC, I return the program to you.")
5. The MC then joins the speaker on the podium and shakes her hand. The speaker either turns and walks off stage or she steps behind the MC to leave the stage going in the opposite direction.

Particularly for a major presentation before a large group of people, I recommend that the speaker go over this protocol with the MC or coordinator prior to the program. Rehearse it a time or two. This will give your entrance and your performance a greater sense of professionalism and you are providing a valuable service to the leaders of the organization by showing them the proper way to enter and exit a stage.

How Does an Author Rehearse for a Speech?

Speakers use different methods for preparing a speech. I write my speeches and then revise, revise, revise.

I read the speech several times in order to familiarize myself with the material and the organization of it. I especially want to be sharp when it comes to the examples and anecdotes I'll be using. I also run through it twice or more in order to check the timing. If I go over my time allotment while practicing, I start cutting out areas that drag.

When I am comfortable with the organization of a speech and the scope of the material, I break it down into outline form and practice it again and again.

Eventually, I reduce the speech outline to notes. Sometimes I just note each new topic. But I generally find it more helpful if I use the opening few words of key sentences on my note card(s). Most experts recommend that you create and memorize a dynamite speech opening.

Timing, they say, is everything. And it is important when speaking. So, when I rehearse or practice the key elements of a speech, I pay close attention to pace and pauses. If you're involved in or interested in speaking in public, surely you listen intently to other speakers. One thing you may notice in other presentations and your own is how well (or how poorly) pace and pauses are used for emphasis and impact.

If you would like to know more about timing, just watch some of the most popular TV sitcoms and even some of the more brilliant commercials. Pay attention to how the various jokes and skits are executed. Those that really work do so because of precise timing.

Beatrice Wood was a world-known ceramic artist and a colorful local figure who lived to be 105 years old. I went to her home one day to interview her for an article. I arrived a little early, and Ms. Wood left me waiting on the front porch until precisely the appointed time. She told me, as she graciously ushered me into her home, that she was watching an old rerun of *Laurel and Hardy*. She said she watched them every day at that time. She remarked that she was fascinated by their incredible sense of timing. That was my introduction to this concept. Now I began to understand what makes a joke or a story work and what doesn't. It's all in the timing and, I dare say, the pacing.

So how do author-speakers (and professional speakers) rehearse for their presentations? Speaking for myself, I do not typically memorize my speeches—the exception being an hour-or-so-long keynote address for a large group. Then, I have a unique way of rehearsing.

I learn my speeches while walking. I've tried rehearsing in my office, while driving in the car, etc. But I don't seem to be able to concentrate well enough to learn a speech unless I am walking alone. I walk every day, anyway. I might as well get double-duty out of this time commitment.

I start out carrying the written speech with me on my walks. When I am familiar enough with it, I reduce it to an outline and I practice it that way for several days. Eventually, I rehearse the speech while walking without any notes.

At that point, I also rehearse portions of it at night in bed before I fall asleep. I might even stand before my three cats and recite the speech to them. It's also a good idea to rehearse in front of a mirror and/or have someone video tape you giving the speech.

When I do actually memorize a speech, I am not attached to every single word and sentence. My concern is with the timing and organization. The words might be different each time I practice the speech—and the actual presentation might not closely resemble the original walking speech. But I make sure that I know the material well enough that I cover it all adequately and expertly.

Over the years, I've developed quite a few speeches. I probably have over a dozen different presentations I've given related to the local history book. My presentations around the topics of my publishing and book promotion books must number forty or more. Some of them are on the same topic, only with different slants, in different lengths, and geared toward authors at different stages of writing and publishing.

I recommend that, as soon as you know you will be speaking as a way to sell and get exposure for your book, start outlining a variety of presentations you can do. For a how-to or informational book, you should develop at least two or three—maybe more—presentations you can give on the spur of the moment. Key in on various topics your audience might be interested in and then flesh them out. For fiction, you might hone a presentation around one of the stories or scenes in your book, some of your characters and how you created them, some of your techniques in writing the book, and your back-story—your experiences while writing this book and getting it published.

Remember that you are more apt to be invited back by conference and club leaders when you have a wide variety of speech topics you can present. (Read more about creating presentations from your book in chapter 9.)

Leslie Korenko rehearses her speeches before she goes public with them. She says,

> I pretend that I'm doing the actual presentation. I click the slides and talk the talk. Standing is best when doing the rehearsal. It makes for more natural hand motions and you can track the number of times you have to look at the slides. I suggest doing a dress rehearsal in front of someone. They often spot problems that you can't see. If I keep stumbling or forgetting something important, then my presentation needs to be tweaked—perhaps add another slide, maybe add some text on the slide to prompt me, or include an important statistic.

Korenko has one ritual that she always does just prior to her live presentations. She explains, "After I set up my slideshow and test it, check the sound, and put on a welcome slide, I change into my high heels. That puts me into professional mode. I stand a little straighter and speak a little more slowly. It's like I step out of my regular persona and transform into the professional speaker I want to be."

Mary Ellen Warner doesn't get that much out of rehearsals. She says, "When rehearsing at home, your talk sometimes seems flat. I need the reactions of my audience to bring my presentations to life."

C. Hope Clark doesn't memorize her speeches. She says,

> I like to appear as though I'm speaking to the audience, not reciting or preaching to them. So I make sure I know my

material. I often use a bulleted list with quotes or cites written out verbatim. I read the info dozens and dozens of times prior to the presentation. I also don't prepare the speech itself until the week I intend to present it, so it remains fresh in my head.

Using notes can be useful but awkward. Sometimes it can be downright inconvenient. This is why it is so important to know your material well. Clark tells this story: "I spoke at a conference for a dinner meeting as a motivational speaker and they unexpectedly lowered the lights. I have a touch of night blindness. There I stood in front of 250 people squinting at my notes, frustrated, and continually losing my place."

It is difficult to think of everything, but I'm sure that Hope Clark will ask about lighting from now on when she goes out to speak. Many auditoriums have lecterns that are equipped with little lights for the speaker. Or you can bring your own.

We humans seem to learn a lot of things in life the hard way. Clark, for example, learned to speak more extemporaneously after a horrifying experience during a speaking class. She says, "I unexpectedly had my notes taken away from me and I choked big time. I've learned since to wing it as much as possible."

So there you have it. Hopefully, we've raised your awareness about the importance of public speaking for authors. We've given you some guidance with regard to locating and landing speaking engagements. We've provided some tips for preparing your presentations and expertly delivering them. Before we move forward with ideas for establishing rapport with your audiences, here are a few encouraging words from two of our experts.

Peter Bowerman offers this:

> I'd urge those who consider themselves shy or introverted to not let that stop them. I read a great piece of advice about public speaking once that went something like this: "While having good nuts-'n-bolts speaking techniques down is always a good thing, the two most important attributes of all good speakers are 1) they're experts on their subject, and 2) they love sharing it with others." If you were passionate enough about a subject to write a book on it, certainly you could get up in front of a few people (who came, remember, to hear you!) and talk about it.

Dallas Woodburn adds, "As writers, communication is what we do—though we are often most comfortable using the written word as opposed to the spoken word. But I have found in my personal experience that public speaking skills are essential for successful book promotion."

Let me interject here that, if your book is a nonfiction how-to, informational, reference, or self-help book, your readers also want to learn from you. Meeting your readers in person under positive circumstances will go a long way toward building trust and credibility in your field.

Establish a Greater Rapport with Your Audience

As a speaker, you may not develop a good connection with each audience member. There are personalities to consider. While some personalities meld nicely together, others just grate on one another. And things can change momentarily. A word, a gesture, a look, or the expressing of an unpopular opinion can make the difference between an audience member who is with you and one who has a problem with you.

You might remind him of an uncle or a boss he hates. He doesn't like the message in your opening statement. You put him off when he tried to ask you a question in the hallway. He heard someone else say that you are not friendly or helpful.

However, if your reputation as a credible and/or entertaining speaker precedes you and if audience members have been primed to expect a great performance brimming with good information, most of them will be in your corner. You will have a head start toward developing rapport with your audience. But, there are things you can do to help create a stronger link with your audiences.

First, speak their language. This is one reason why it is important to know your audience—are they a group of engineers, mostly serious artists, staunch businessmen and women, ranchers, young parents, troubled teens, avid craftspeople, city leaders, church members, or disabled seniors? Your approach and, probably, your message to each of these groups—even on the same topic—would differ. You'll need to ascertain whether members of this audience hope to learn something from you, want to challenge your viewpoint, are simply curious, are passionate about the subject, are on a fact-finding mission for their own purposes, or are among your loyal followers. You may want to adjust your demeanor, your material, and your presentation methods accordingly.

Most audiences are made up of people who are either mildly or wildly interested in the subject of the presentation they are attending. Some who attend an informational talk on a topic of interest are hoping for new ideas. Some want their own beliefs on the subject validated. Others are somewhere in the middle. Then there are those who attend your presentation because it is part of their monthly club meeting routine or, at a conference, your topic sounded slightly more interesting than the other sessions scheduled in this time slot.

Typically, you'll look out over the audience and see people assuming many postures from relaxed to stiff and everything in between. Unless you have a thunderous voice, you'll probably notice at least one person in your audience taking a little snooze from time to time. Perhaps he's getting your message subliminally.

So how do you develop rapport or a relationship with your audience? Start by reaching out. A good way to do this is to introduce yourself. In some cases, you've been introduced and maybe your bio is printed on a program that was handed out to audience members. But there is nothing quite so personal and bonding as the speaker or teacher sharing something about him or herself. Sure, you might want to give a little information about your credentials and relevant achievements (generally done during the formal introduction), but also share an anecdote or two revealing how you came to write your book or some of the stumbling blocks you've faced in your profession, for example.

Your main objective is to establish a connection with your audience that you can work from throughout your program. Let them know, for example, that you were once unpublished or struggling to become an author just like they are. Share the fact that you were once afraid to speak in public or that you dropped out of school for a time and almost missed your opportunity for success. People want to know that you *get* them—that you can speak to their situation with empathy. Someone who is homeless or about to become homeless is more apt to listen to a speaker who has experienced homelessness and is now successful, than one who was born into a wealthy family. The people in your audience will be more inclined to listen intently to your message and accept it if they sense that you actually understand their situation.

When dialoguing with your audience, and even when delivering your presentation, try putting yourself in each audience member's place while also maintaining your authority. It's sometimes a fine line for speakers to walk, but a good balance between vulnerability and authoritativeness can, in many cases, serve as a bond.

Help Audience Members Form a Bond

You want to make a connection with your audience, and you want them to connect with one another. If they sit apart from each other, they are individuals either for or against you. Yes, against you. Some people come to your presentation with a chip on their shoulder and they are daring you to knock it off. In other words, "Tell me something I don't know and that I can actually believe."

Note: I find that this is rare. It happens and I think it is important to mention. But, unless your book and your talk cover something quite controversial, you'll find most of your audience members congenial, alert, and eager to hear what you have to share.

I suggest that you try to bring audience members who are spread all over the room closer together. Invite them to come forward and take some of the seats toward the front, for example. Some will and some won't. A few people will move one row closer. Others won't budge.

Even if audience members sit apart, you can still pull them together and create an atmosphere of camaraderie, which will greatly enhance your presentation. Here are a few ideas:

- For a smaller group, ask them each to introduce themselves and their projects related to the theme of your talk or their interest or experience in the topic.

- Ask what they've come to learn from the session. Some might reveal a problem they're having. This would provide the opportunity to encourage audience input. Ask, "Has anyone else had this happen? What did you do to resolve the issue?" If someone asks a question or expresses a desire for additional resources or information, respond, but also consider soliciting comments from the audience. People will begin to connect. I've seen it happen so often.

- If there is time, at some point in the program, assign an exercise that requires audience members to come together in groups— something that depends on teamwork. Try to make it fun.

- Present a challenge to audience members at large—something that requires discussion among the entire group—again, something light, so you get them laughing together.

- Once audience members have revealed something about themselves with relationship to the theme of your talk, mention it a time or two throughout your presentation. Say, for example, "Just as Sonny said earlier, 'some cats are more train-able than others.' Does anyone have a cat as stubborn as the one he described?" or "Angie told us that she plants her sweet peas in December—does anyone else have success doing this?" This will endear the individual to you and, again, help to create a connection between him or her and the rest of the group.

As I alluded to earlier, laughter is a great connecting factor. Maybe you could ask audience members what was the most humorous experience they ever had within the realm of your topic—accounting, gardening, parenting, overcoming depression, preparing a meal, becoming more fit, photographing animals, or writing a novel, for example. As an icebreaker, share yours first.

I also recommend using emotion as a bonding agent. Audience members who experience something rather emotional together have a greater sense of camaraderie. Your audience will pick up on your energy (whether it is friendly, warm, and genuine or phony, distant, and defensive). Tell the tender back-story that inspired your novel or children's book, or talk a little about the abuse you endured as a child, and the audience will come together with feelings of compassion for you, a greater sense of understanding, or even admiration.

Use your creativity and ingenuity to connect in a positive way with your audience, and you (and your audience) will experience a more successful presentation.

I like to use suspense and shock when I speak. Even though my presentations focus on the business of writing, publishing, and book promotion, I try to find ways to surprise my audience members. I'll spew startling facts, using an accelerated tone in my voice and a demeanor to match. I'll ask a provocative question that requires a shocking response and milk the moment for as long as audience members seem keenly eager.

I might say, for example, "Nearly eighty percent of all books published today fail. And do you know why?" Certainly, authors at any stage of their project are going to want to know the secret to being one of the successful twenty percent; and they want to know now! Only some of them are afraid they are not going to like the answer. So they're apprehensive and eager all at the same time. I might go so far as to draw an imaginary line through the audience showing what eighty percent of this group looks like. In a room of fifty people, I might say, "Okay, you nine people represent authors with books that are selling somewhere between 101 and maybe 1,000 per year. One of you is selling more than that every year—somewhere between 1,000 and a million, perhaps. The rest of you represent those authors who have failed."

Mary Ellen Warner has learned some important techniques for developing a rapport with her audiences. She says,

> The blessing of my hearing loss is that I focus on the person in front of me. I am not able to communicate (speak or listen) unless I give my full attention to people's faces. When I am in front of the audience, I continually make eye contact with people. I am an expert at speech reading (eyebrows tell full stories!) along with body language.
>
> My skills have had years to improve since my progressive hearing loss developed overnight more than thirty years ago." But it took time to perfect her techniques. Warner started out speaking on her expertise related to home and office organizing. She says, "My first organizing workshops left my poor audiences glassy eyed with too much information. Now I am

much better at recognizing when I need to switch gears. It's a matter of practicing before an audience and paying attention to them. It doesn't really take thirty years!

Warner offers this tip for creating the opportunity for greater audience rapport. She says,

> I never use the lectern or allow a table between me and the audience. A Toastmaster friend once invited me to share my story about volunteering to help shelter animals at his Optimists breakfast club. Did I need the lectern? "Of course not!" Later, he told me that many of their invited speakers stand at the lectern, read their information, and torture the group during breakfast!

This brings up another important point. While we've all been aptly entertained by presenters who stood behind lecterns, this isn't appropriate for every speaker. Someone who is rather short in stature, whose voice doesn't carry well, who drones on without much vocal variety, or who uses the lectern as a barrier between him/herself and the audience, for example, should probably avoid using one. As Warner has discovered, you can connect more successfully with your audience if you are closer to them. You create more interest if you move around and use gestures rather than homestead one square-foot section at the front of the room.

I generally trade off between using a lectern and moving around in the front of the room. Why? I'm not sure—it's spontaneous and subconscious. I like the freedom to emphasize or highlight what I am saying. Sometimes this is best done when I am standing comfortably at the lectern, while other times I feel a need to move around the room and gesture while I'm talking. I will also walk into the audience to field questions—always trying to face the entire audience and repeating the question before responding.

How to Reach the Most Reluctant Student

I've had some humbling experiences as a speaker. In fact, I've come to realize something that will help me and my audiences in future presentations. If you promote your book through speaking engagements, my realization might help you, too.

Here's what I've learned: There are some things that people don't want to know. They may come to you with questions on the subject of your expertise. They may attend your presentations on that topic, but they don't want to hear what you have to say, especially if it means they are required to step outside their comfort zone. If someone is seeking an easy way to achieve something, he does not want to be given a complicated how-to list. Some people do not want to be told the proper or even the most reasonable way to succeed if it means he might have to change his mindset or his approach.

Think about it: there are some messages that we just don't want to hear. Here are a few: "You should visit the dentist/doctor regularly," "Exercise is good for you," "You need to go on a diet," or "When are you going to quit smoking?"

Along the same lines, I'm discovering that some new authors do not want to know how to write a book proposal. Others are completely closed to the idea of promoting their books. They don't want to read about it and they don't want to hear about it.

While I was in Hawaii some years ago giving a couple of workshops for the Honolulu Branch of the National Pen Women's Writers Conference, a gentleman named Jim came up to me and asked how to go about getting his book published. I gave him some basic information and suggested that he purchase my book, *The Right Way* to *Write, Publish and Sell Your Book*. (Revised edition now published under the title, *Publish Your Book, Proven Strategies and Resources for Enterprising Authors*.) He poo pooed my information and my suggestion and he asked me again, "How do I go about getting my book published?"

I explained the basics again and handed him a copy of my book. "All of the questions you have are answered in this book," I replied.

He promptly put it down and said, "But all I want to know is how to publish this one book."

Finally, it occurred to me that Jim, an attorney, by the way, was seeking a quick and easy avenue to producing a book. He didn't care about traditional channels or what comes after publication. He didn't want to know about options. He didn't want qualified, appropriate guidance. He wanted to learn the easy way to publishing success. He wanted to hear what he wanted to hear—he did not, necessarily, want to hear truth. He did not care about tried and true methods. He wanted to buck the system without even taking the time to understand the system. He wanted magic that does not exist.

He was obviously unreasonable in his goal, but I might have been able to help him if I'd taken more time to understand his plight. What did he really want, and was it something I could give him? If there had been time, I might have listened more intently to Jim and, perhaps, found a way to connect with him—to relate to his reality rather than trying to force mine on him. Once I comprehended his reality, I may have been able to lead him toward the information he needed presented in a way he could accept it.

I may have been able to help this hopeful author if I'd had the wherewithal and the sensitivity to reel myself in, get off of my professional platform, and try to understand where he was coming from. I should have stopped and put myself in his place for a moment.

Jim wasn't ready to hear the whole truth of the publishing process; he needed information and facts that he could comprehend now. I could have given that to him. In a few days, weeks, months, or even years, when he has gathered more information and had more experiences within this field, he may be ready to hear what he couldn't hear before.

Lately, I've had audiences sprinkled with people like Jim. That is partly because of my workshop topics. I've been speaking often about how to write a book proposal. While people genuinely want to learn how to write a book proposal, some of them don't like what I have to tell them. They resist my message and my instructions because this is not what they want to hear. They are looking for the easy and quick way to create a book proposal. They don't necessarily want to understand the psychology behind a good book proposal and all of the steps to developing a successful one. And, after the session, these people don't buy my book, which is designed to guide them through the process they must understand in order to succeed.

As a speaker, I can sometimes feel the resistance of some audience members. I'm aware of their reluctance to buy into the rather intimidating process of writing a book proposal, promoting a book, or thoroughly studying your publishing options before selecting one. When you have only an hour to teach and share, there is no time to build a sense of camaraderie with audience members. Or is there? I've been thinking about this and wonder if maybe it is actually more important and effective to spend the time building a rapport with the audience than to just throw unfamiliar facts, information, and processes at them for an hour.

Should I teach what I know as proficiently as I can and hope that at least some of the students get it, or should I risk short-changing some students in order to help more students? What happens to the students who are ready to gobble up the material if I cater to those who need to be hand-fed? Good handouts will help. But I also realize that it is important to establish a balance in my workshops so that everyone walks away with something of value. Of course, this is something that you should take into consideration when you speak or conduct workshops on the subject of your book, too.

Here are some of my thoughts with regard to the book proposal workshops—and these concepts could certainly be applied to other topics. Perhaps the audience would pay more attention to me if they knew that I once avoided writing book proposals. It's true. I used to cringe at the thought of tackling something so seemingly foreign. When someone said "book proposal" to me, I covered my ears, closed my eyes and started chanting as loudly as I could, "La La La La." The very idea of preparing a book proposal was way too overwhelming for me to even consider.

This may surprise an audience, and it would certainly be a step toward establishing a sense of rapport—a connection—a commonality. Maybe it is important to let your audience know that you have had the same fears, desires, concerns that they are experiencing and then tell them how you managed to overcome the roadblocks. In most cases, this is absolutely legitimate. Most of us who write a how-to or other nonfiction book were probably once incompetent or lacking in the area of our expertise. Novelists all had to start someplace. They didn't always know how to develop a believable character.

After my blast of insight, I attended a local writer's conference, and sat in on a book promotion workshop. To my surprise, the workshop leader (I'll call her Julie) didn't even attempt to teach book promotion techniques. What she did was convey a concept around the book promotion theme by sharing personal stories revealing the things she learned as she progressed along the book promotion trail with her first book.

It was a totally different approach than I use when I talk about book promotion, but, because there was a lesson at every promotional turn for her, it seemed to be highly effective. The audience loved her warm style and the wisdom she shared.

My book promotion presentations are hard-hitting, give-me-the-facts-ma'am, well-researched programs reinforced by an incredible amount of experience and education. It's much different than the one Julie presented. While my workshops are very well-received by the majority of attendees, I learned something useful from Julie's presentation. As a result, I have softened my approach to presenting my material since then. While I believe I communicate my information in a user-friendly manner, I realized that I could probably lighten up—perhaps not take my material quite so seriously.

Yes, I had some things to think about before I presented my next workshop. First, I came up with a more provocative title. I attempted to entertain more while teaching. I became vulnerable and admitted my former shortcomings in order to connect with my audience. I reminded myself that some writers are not ready to shift into professional mode, even though they say they want to be published. Some of them just aren't ready for the facts—the truth that they need to know in order to survive in the competitive and shark-infested waters of publishing.

When someone attends a workshop or a speech on a nonfiction topic, he or she is generally saying, "I have a problem." And they've come to you for solutions. The trouble is, they don't always embrace your solutions—so you have to somehow convince those audience members that what you are offering is valid. For some attendees, this means sugarcoating the truth and using more gentle means to entice those students to open up enough to at least consider what you're teaching.

As for me, instead of focusing on the myriad of things that generally comprise my book proposal course, I now select just a few ideas that will help my audience. I flesh out those ideas and gently massage them until the students become comfortable with the concept or the process. Rather than attempting to teach students everything that I think they need to know about writing a book proposal, I might simply discuss the reason for the book proposal, the purposes the various sections serve, to whom and how, and tips for completing each section. I offer anecdotes demonstrating or illustrating (rather than telling) the benefits of writing a book proposal. I also provide handouts with some of the more advanced information these students will eventually need.

I've come to realize that speaking is not like writing. In an article or a book, you must provide the hard facts and the solutions succinctly—driving home the points and offering up the necessary material. In writing, the reader looks to you as an authority, but in speaking, he wants an ally. In person, he wants nurturing and hand-holding. He wants a friend. If the student doesn't like you or he doesn't like what you're saying, even if it is the gospel truth, guess what? He won't learn anything, and he won't buy your book, either.

Teaching is not an exact science—especially, when you're facing a group of adults who are at different knowledge levels and resistance levels in your particular field. For this reason, it makes sense to head for the middle ground—to address those folks who are somewhere between the highly experienced and the uninformed. It is okay if you endeavor to enlighten and educate audience members to an unknown and undetermined degree of understanding rather than attempting to teach them everything you think they need to know. That's probably a more realistic goal to accomplish within the typical hour-long time span, anyway.

Successful public speaking, like any other opportunity for interaction with people, is not something you can absolutely depend on to always go exactly the way you expect. Sometimes your fears around a particular event are happily quelled. Other times, your confidence is shattered. You never know what kind of audience you'll be facing, whether you'll be lavished with positive attention or heckled or intimidated in some way. Things happen, personalities clash, expectations are not always met.

Jerry Waxler has experienced some disappointments which he handled in some interesting ways. He says that you can't always accurately peg the attitude of some audience members. Here's his story:

> I have had audience members who seem distant during the talk, don't contribute much, and then, as they are leaving, they come up to me and offer the most amazing heartfelt thanks. In fact, I have had so many of these experiences, that I have come to believe that the quietest audience members might be my biggest fans. They only seemed distant because they are taking it all in.

Waxler recalls a time when he inadvertently developed a rapport among the audience. He explains,

> I was invited to speak at a senior expo, where around fifty vendors were at tables pitching services to seniors. The area where I gave my talk about memoir-writing was in the corner of the meeting room. I had a good turnout, but everyone had to gather close in order to hear me. Even then, the room was so noisy, I had to shout to be heard. After my talk, the group gave me a standing ovation. I think in a way the noise brought us closer in more than just a physical way.

He adds,

> When I was first developing my material, I offered workshops for free, and I never knew how many people would show up. Always an optimist, I often made thirty copies for

an event where only a few people turned up. In one series of free workshops, the manager of a small church gave me the key and I let myself in. Some weeks, only one or two people showed up, and we ended up doing more of a coaching session than a class. Once, I was the only one in the building. I decided to take a stand and not let this discourage me; so I gave the talk to an empty room. I loved the practice, not only of giving my talk, but also of rising above the disappointment. I left the room feeling victorious.

Now that was something a seasoned actor might do. I've come to realize that, once you begin dabbling in public speaking as a way to get to know your readers, you actually do adopt a slightly (or majorly) different persona. We tend to become mini-actors. We take ourselves more seriously and even find ourselves delighting in the attention that we get prior to and almost always after a presentation.

I think it is a good trait to take ourselves seriously, but first, we must take our audiences seriously—our readers. Remember, we're there for them, not for our ego-thrill. Sure, you may discover that you love being before a group, but always remember, you're there for your audience.

Now go out and schmooze with that audience and be prepared to sell carloads of books.

What's an Author to Say?

Okay, so you've joined a Toastmasters club (or you're taking speaker training through your adult education program or a private educational center) and you're becoming more comfortable as a speaker. You've contacted a few program directors for local organizations about giving a presentation. You may have even set up a speaking engagement. Now what? What will you talk about?

First, find out something about the organization or group you'll be speaking for and then learn something about your audience. How much time will you have to speak? Your subject matter, slant, and way of delivery all depend on the circumstances and the audience you'll be facing.

You have more options and possibilities when you have more time to speak. While some people prefer brief time slots in which to speak, I crave the hour-long or even two-hour-long opportunities. I can give and teach so much more when I have more time. I also sell more books when I have more time to spend with an audience. It just takes longer to convince some people of the value in your book.

You should be able to design a speech on nearly any topic to fit just about any time slot. You'll also want to come up with a variety of topics and slants for an assortment of audiences. Here are some ideas for your next speaking engagement:

- Talk about what prompted you to become a writer or to write this particular book. This works well for any kind of book—nonfiction, fiction, a children's book, memoir, a book of poetry, etc.
- Talk off the cuff about your experiences while writing and publishing this book. Non-authors, especially those who love to read, are often fascinated by the writer's life and what it takes to actually bring a book from concept to the hands of the readers. Make sure to use a lot of interesting anecdotes.
- If it is a novel or children's book, share parts of the story and read a few sections. (Read from your book only if you have practiced reading out loud and are very good at it.) Some experts advise authors against reading to their audiences.

Novelist Margaret Brownely is one of them. She says,

> I don't feel comfortable reading from my books. Personally, I want to hear a novelist speak not read. Unless you are a gifted reader who is able to hold an audience's attention, I would avoid reading. My speech philosophy is this: don't waste an audience's time. Give them something of value—either knowledge or information—that they can carry home with them. Reading from a novel, no matter how well-written, would not, in my estimation, meet this criterion.

- Ask audience members to help present your story. Give them parts to act out. Bring props (hats, smoking pipe, kitchen utensils, stuffed animal, a cape and cane, etc.).
- Give a demonstration. Maybe your book features handmade kites. Actually show how to create one. Involve the audience.
- Present an experiment or a lesson related to the theme of your book.

- Talk about something new that has come to your attention since you completed your book—a new theory, process, or concept. Maybe one of the characters in your novel is bipolar or autistic. If this audience has an interest in these issues, announce a new finding and be sure to provide anecdotes and resources where appropriate.
- Talk about some of your experiences as a published author. Here's another fun topic that might intrigue most audiences.

Still can't think of anything to talk about? Here are some ideas that work for me and my colleagues. Mary Ellen Warner uses humorous stories to entertain her audiences. She says, "My stories are all true . . . told with exaggeration, of course. Most are my own stories from life experiences; some come from people I meet. I often capture ideas from the questions asked after my presentations. Really, I see stories everywhere!"

Peter Bowerman began speaking in 2000 after self-publishing his book on starting a commercial writing business. He says,

> Since I write how-to books, it was a natural evolution to do how-to talks on my subject. Given the nature of my books (I've since produced a book on profitable self-publishing), I primarily do workshop-type speaking.
>
> And since my workshop sessions are just encapsulated versions of my books, I end up selling far more books than most speakers (i.e., a novelist who has a few fiction titles and is doing a talk on some aspect of fiction writing).

Here are a few ideas for using your book to create speech ideas:

- Break your nonfiction book down into potential subjects. Use your table of contents to help define the main subjects, and then divide each topic into subtopics. For example, in order to promote my publishing books, I speak a lot about book promotion. I might break this topic down into ten presentations, such as things you must do in order to promote your book, book promotion for the timid author, how to get book reviews, how to sell books at book festivals, how to get speaking engagements around the theme of your book, how to use your blog to promote your book, article-writing as a way to promote your book, using social media as a promotional tool, and so forth.

- Share some of the stories from your memoir, slice-of-life stories book, children's book, or novel. In order to promote my book of cat stories to an audience, I might share one or two of the stories as part of a live presentation. I could focus my talk on one aspect of owning cats: living with a feral cat, how to prepare your home for a new kitten, personalities of cats, why we are either attracted to cats or not, the importance of spay/neuter, what cats give us, quirky cat stories, sad stories with happy endings, stories featuring workplace and library cats, what prompted me to write this book, and how I went about compiling it. There are probably as many presentation possibilities as there are cats.

- Develop interesting topics from your novel. Let's say that your novel features a lifelong love story between two professors beginning in the late 1890s and covering a sixty-year period, and it is set in the south. You could dress in period clothes while telling parts of the story. You could talk about what went into writing the story. You could create an interesting talk wherein you analyze the mindset of various lovers in classic stories over time. Compare life in the south during this period to life elsewhere on this planet.

Talk about how some well-known fictional characters (or one of your characters) would approach the technology age.

There are numerous ways to promote your book through presentations—you can teach, inform, educate, entertain, or all of the above. Your primary goal should be to give your audience something of value—to leave them with something that makes their life better or, perhaps, that simply makes them feel better.

Be clear as to why people have come out to hear you. What do they expect to gain from your presentation? Remember that they came for their own benefit, not yours. Try to fulfill their needs and desires. If your book is nonfiction, and you've advertised that you'll be speaking on a particular topic, you probably have a pretty good idea about what your audience members hope to gain from the experience. Make sure that you give them the benefit they have come for.

I've attended talks that did not live up to the author hype. Even though there were supposed to be "secrets revealed," "lessons learned," "a window to greater understanding," "keys to instant success," audience members walked away with nothing more than a weak concept of the topic. In fact, some well-known speakers within the publishing field offer nothing more than a canned speech illustrated by clever PowerPoint slides. So what's missing? Content, believe it or not. The information is there, but it is not presented in a user-friendly way. There is no audience interaction. In fact, some of these speakers do not initiate questions and they slip out of the meeting hall and back to their hotel room (or the airport) as soon as their program is over.

People come out to hear a novelist speak for different reasons than they do a nonfiction author. They may show up out of curiosity. They want to learn more about you—the author. Some of them might be interested in the type of book you've written—they're fascinated by the period in which your story takes place, they love humor and came to be entertained, or they also write and want to pick up some tips.

Certainly, nonfiction books seem easier to promote through live presentations. Still, authors are stymied as to how to create interesting, entertaining programs around their books. Here are some additional tips that might help both fiction and nonfiction authors:

- Use visuals. This might include unique or common props or a slide show/PowerPoint presentation.
- Do something surprising such as sing, play a musical instrument, do a magic trick, or dance. I attended a Jewish memorial service recently and enjoyed a surprise when the Rabbi began to shimmy down the aisle singing, "If I were a rich man . . ." This is not something I will soon forget.
- Present a demonstration. There are many books that are conducive to demonstrations—for example, cooking, craft, gardening, marketing, and many other how-to books. For a fantasy novel, demonstrate now to use a fencing foil or apply stage make-up.
- Hire an actor or radio announcer to read from your book while you narrate.
- Don't try to give away too much from your book. Choose one aspect of one topic or expand on three points.
- Involve the audience! Ask everyone to stand. Then begin a series of questions designed to eliminate some of the people. Award a prize to the last man or woman standing. Encourage a few people from the audience to participate in a brief reenactment of the story, or get them involved in accompanying your rap or singing demonstration by repeating a series of words on command, for example.

- Get someone to assist you by creating little surprises while you're on stage. They could walk across the stage behind you with a dog, a sign, or a crazy costume, for example. Or have them bring you a hamburger or a big gulp of soda. Of course, you will work these things into your presentation in some way so they get a laugh.
- Attend other presentations. Pay close attention to how other speakers handle themselves before an audience. Adopt those elements that work and stay far away from those that don't.

How to Create Presentation Topics Based on Your Book

When you schedule a speaking engagement designed to promote your book, can you provide a list of possible speech topics? In the case of a club or organization related to a specific topic or a certain period in history, for example, members might hear a dozen or so speakers every year. Program chairpersons appreciate having a choice of topics so they can stay away from those that have been covered within the last few months. It would behoove you to create a list.

Post the list at your website to demonstrate your range of possible programs for those who are seeking speakers or for those you have contacted and who want more information about you. Here's an example from my list of presentations:

- Two Simple Steps to Successful Authorship
- How to Write a Killer Book Proposal
- Book Promotion for the Bold and the Bashful
- How to Get Your Book Reviewed Many Times Over
- Promote Your Book Through Magazine Articles
- Platform-Building Tips and Techniques for the Author

- How to Write the After-Publication Book Proposal
- The Psychology of a Book Proposal
- How to Use Your Personality to Sell More Books

For a book on selling real estate, your list of presentations might look like this:

- How to Establish Curb Appeal for Your Home or Office Building
- Tips for Choosing the Right Real Estate Agent
- Understanding Today's Real Estate Market
- Just What Can You Expect From Your Agent?
- Simple Steps to Selling Your Home
- Insider Information for Home Sellers
- When to Buy and When to Sell Locally

For a historical fiction novel, your list of speech topics might include:

- From Banker to Novelist in Five Years (Your story.)
- Fascinating Things I Discovered During My Research
- Little Known Historical Facts About New England
- Little Known Facts About Your Favorite Authors
- The Real Story of Self-Publishing
- So You Want to Be a Novelist

For nonfiction, your chapter titles and subheadings might be appropriate titles and topics for presentations. For fiction, you might tell the story of one particular character—perhaps offering some back-story that is not included in the book. Get into the psychology of why someone would behave in a certain way, as depicted in your story, for example.

Sometimes the process of researching and writing a book can be a life-changing experience. This might be something worth sharing with your audiences.

Presentation Tips for the Nonfiction Book Author

When you commit to a speaking engagement, you do so primarily to sell books, right? Even though your decisions are based on practical matters, such as your profit potential, your audience should never, ever feel as though you are giving them a sales pitch. You may be poised to sell books, but the last thing you want to do is appear as though you are there primarily to sell your books or services. This is the same concept as writing articles for publication around the topic/theme of your book or using social media for exposure. Keep the fact that you want to sell books to yourself. It's your secret. What you want to get across to your audience is that you are there to help them solve a problem, become more skilled or competent, learn or put to practice a new concept, for example. In more concrete terms, you want to offer audience members solutions to a problem they're having and/or information to help them over a hurdle or to successfully meet a challenge. They are coming to you to learn more about something that interests them or for help, answers, clarification, or resolutions.

Certainly, you want everyone in your audience to know that you have a book for sale. This fact was pointed up in the promo for your presentation. It was mentioned in your introduction. There is a display of your books somewhere in the room and probably one with you at the lectern, which you can hold up a time or two and reference. Audience members were each handed a postcard or bookmark with the cover of the book on it. But the last thing you want to do when speaking on behalf of your nonfiction book is to shamelessly pitch it throughout the presentation. Your speech or workshop is not a sales pitch. It is an opportunity to demonstrate the value of the message and information in your book. It's about giving and sharing. It's a soft-sell. If you do it right and if you are speaking to the right audience, they will recognize the benefits in your presentation and realize the value of the book. Some of them will purchase it now. Some will buy it later. Some will never get around to it.

Are you aware of your responsibility as the author of a nonfiction book? When you write a how-to, informational, reference, or self-help book, for example, and then you launch out to present programs on the theme of your book, you are taking on a measure of responsibility. Like it or not, people will start looking to you for the answers they seek on this topic. If you are striving to get all of the exposure you can through appearances, published articles, additional books, etc., you'll soon be considered an authority on your subject and your responsibility grows. Remember that you started it! You put yourself out there and you owe it to your readers to give them what they require and desire from you.

How do you approach your live audiences? Do you give them what they expect? What do they expect when they come to listen to you speak about your book? Most likely, you spend a lot of time thinking about your presentations and hoping that you will come across okay. But do you consider your presentations from the point of view of your audience? Can you put yourself in their place?

Victoria Cobb expends quite a bit of energy thinking about her audiences. She is a TaiChi and QiGong instructor who teaches at retreats and in corporate settings. She found a way early on in her workshop presentations to get the attention of her audiences. She says,

> I evaluate each engagement. Getting a handle on age and careers is vital to a successful speech. My purpose is to help

others feel better about themselves and to move forward in life with a healthy attitude. It is important for me to be flexible as everything can change at a moment's notice. For example, one of my first groups was at the Jet Propulsion Lab in the San Fernando Valley, California. I was a bit nervous, especially since I needed to be patted down by security. The group was late coming in and they were tired. Everyone looked like they were coming down with the flu or had colds.

She says,

I asked, "How is everyone?" There was nothing but dead air. Then the group began talking among themselves. This was a company event and attendance was mandatory. Quietly I said, "Doing these exercises will give you a better sexual experience!!!" I laughed and the group laughed. For the next forty-five minutes we had a wonderful time playing QiGong and I sold about thirty books.

As Cobb points out, it is important to get into the heads of your audience—to know what they want from you and to be willing to give it. Let's say that you've arranged to speak to a group of armchair travelers or quilters, businessmen/women, animal lovers, gardeners, hopeful authors, artists, etc. Here are my suggestions for a successful author presentation:

- Give, give, give. Some authors are afraid that if they give too much, people won't buy their books. Actually, if your book is so shallow that you can tell all there is to know about it fully within even a ninety-minute speech, it probably isn't worth much to start with.

- Try to stick to a theme throughout your talk. Find ways to expand on a few topics in your book—offering anecdotes and material that you didn't flesh out in the text. Share a generous helping of tips, techniques, statistics, anecdotes, and resources on just a few aspects of your book, while letting your audience know there is still much for them to learn by reading the book. Because I am an authority on my subject, there's a lot I can offer audiences aside from what's in any one of my books. This is what you want to strive to accomplish. The more you know about your topic, the more value you will bring to your presentations. By value, I mean take-away benefits—information and concepts audience members can use. You want them to understand the what, why, when, where, and how of the topic you are presenting. That's the keyword—"understand." Because if they don't "get it," they won't be inclined to or able to use it.

- Become an authority figure—the go-to person on this topic. How? By being everywhere. Remember, speaking is just a portion of your book marketing repertoire. Not every potential reader will attend your presentations, but more of them will if they know about you and trust you. You also need to blog regularly; submit articles to magazines, newsletters, and e-zines; get involved in high-profile organizations related to your topic; be interviewed for podcasts and radio; use your social media pages, and show up at book festivals, conferences, and trade shows (where appropriate).

- Make it entertaining. While it is important, when you're promoting a nonfiction book, to provide information and resources and offer up some new ideas, don't neglect the emotional value of what you offer. Decisions to purchase are often made at an emotional level. Cause audience members to think, but also cause them to laugh, chuckle, roll their eyes, applaud, tear up, etc. The how-to aspect of your book might be what sells it, but emotions may clinch the deal. In the case of a nonfiction informational or reference book, for example, the emotional aspect might be in convincing the potential customer that he or she will have a better chance of meeting their goals if they educate themselves on the topic of your book. If the customer believes that he will become healthier or more financially successful, have better sex, or fulfill another dream if he buys your book, he is more apt to do so. And this, folks, is the basis for emotions selling books.

Customers and clients want to know, "What's in it for me? How will I benefit if I buy into this concept and purchase this book?" So your job is to *demonstrate* the value of your product (your book) through your presentation.

So often when authors are invited to speak or to write an article based on their books, they describe their books. They don't know the difference between a feature and a benefit. It is important that, as a speaker, you do. Know when to talk about the features and when to share the benefits. FYI, a feature is about the book, a benefit is the direct effect the material in the book can afford the reader. When you think of benefits, think of how to answer this audience question: "What's in it for me?" Consider, is the reader interested in the fact that the book has a lovely cover, that it has expert quotes intermingled with information and statistics, or are they interested in the fact that the book will guide them in reaching a goal or teach them a new skill that will give them more confidence or more wealth, for example?

A good author performance might include a mention of the book maybe once or twice. The person who introduces the author might hold it up and pitch it. It might be displayed in the front of the room where you stand to speak. You may mention the book a couple of times briefly in your presentation. Additionally, you will announce at the end of the program that you are available to sign books in the back of the room or that the book is for sale for $19.95 at the conference bookstore.

During the course of your presentation, you might hold your book up when you say, "That's why I decided to write this book," or "I wrote this book for all of those people who have come to me with questions over the years on this topic."

Sure, point it up, use it as emphasis, but just don't make the book the focus of your talk in a way that resembles a pitch. That is a huge no-no.

What Can You Say About Your Book of Fiction?

It is common for nonfiction authors to go out and speak on the subject of their books. Children's book writers promote their books by doing readings where children congregate. But what about novelists? How can you promote your mystery or your historical, fantasy, period, adventure, etc. novel by doing speaking gigs?

Use some of that imagination that you poured into your story. Yes, book promotion is serious business, but the activities you choose in order to get your book known do not have to be rigid and boring. Likewise, your venue doesn't have to be ordinary.

As you've noticed, we have done our best to discourage you from reading from your book. You can do readings, but only if you can pull this off really, really expertly. If you cannot read well out loud or you do not have a nice voice, do not attempt this in front of your audiences. It will not be effective. Either have an actor do the reading for you or take steps to improve your speaking voice and your reading skills.

Here are a few tips for a more successful reading:

- Memorize the sections of the book you wish to read. If you know the material well enough, you will be able to spend more time making eye contact with your audience—and engaging your audience is of primary importance.

- Hold your book up high enough while reading so that audience members can see your face. Glance down only to remind yourself of the next few sentences. Recite most of this material while facing the audience.

- Consider narrating between portions of the story you're reading. Stop to tell the story behind the plot or to explain how you developed your main character, for example.

- Learn how to effectively use pauses, vocal variety, and honest emotion in your reading.

- Hand out copies of the portion you will be reading. Sometimes it is easier for audience members to grasp the intent of the author when they can read along.

Where can you do readings? At writer's conferences, writer's group meetings, book clubs, bookstores, specialty shops, public or private/specialty libraries, home parties featuring local authors or just you, coffee and tea houses, and just about any place where people gather. I heard authors reading from their books while I was eating pizza on an outdoor patio at a local gourmet Italian restaurant last summer. (Unfortunately, the authors were not good readers and their performances were not very effective.)

Fiction authors can present programs just like their nonfiction counterparts do. You can talk about the story in your book or your personal story of becoming an author. But there are many other ways to present your book to audiences.

Let's say that your novel features an adventuring woman who meets up with some interesting characters while chasing a lifelong dream and it is set in the 1890s in New York. You could tell parts of the story. You could talk about what went into writing the story. How about comparing your characters with some famous characters from the classics? Give a lesson in character development or storytelling ability.

Margaret Brownley often goes out and talks about her novels. She says,

> If you don't know what to talk about to a general audience, simply tell your story. How did you become a writer? What difficulties did you have to overcome? What advice can you give for following a dream? Talk about why you wrote the book and the research required. For example, a heroine in a forthcoming book of mine is a dime novelist. The history behind dime novels is fascinating and would appeal to members of book groups and librarians. I also spoke to a mixed crowd (men and women) on old west myths and started things off with an old west trivia quiz. Everyone had fun and learned a lot. Readers usually want to know where I get my story ideas, so I always try to include something on that.

Use seasonal prompts for your speech themes. If we are nearing an election, discuss how your character and or other well-known characters would handle being president—what would they bring to the position? If you are promoting a Christian novel in March or April, you might use Easter as a theme in your presentation. Maybe your story features a strong father figure, you should be able to focus on that aspect of your book when speaking to a group around Father's Day.

What are some other themes you could use when planning presentations around your novel? Consider world events, disasters, legends from the past. How does your modern-day adventurer or rebel compare with the activities or the characters of Billy the kid or Butch Cassidy? What would Princess Geneva in your young adult fantasy text to the grizzly wolfman in your book if they had cell phones in that era?

You don't have to stick solely to the story you tell in your book. You can dissect your story and create a larger picture, get into your characters' heads, discuss your characters' life choices and the "what ifs" that could have occurred instead. As you can see, you could get creative with your presentations related to your novel no matter the genre or theme.

Raven West likes the idea of talking about your characters. She speaks frequently to get exposure for her novels, and she suggests,

> If you can't talk about your fictional characters as if they are real, then how do you expect your readers to perceive them as real? You've spent months, or maybe years, alone at the keyboard with these people. You probably know them better than you know some of your flesh and blood friends or relatives, and I'm certain you could tell stories about those people with no problem!
>
> When you speak about your book, you don't need to come up with a topic. All you need to do is start talking about your characters as if they were sitting in the room with your audience, because, if you've written a great character, that's exactly what they're going to be doing.

According to West,

> This is one time that I would say, "read from the book." Before you start reading, you could say, "You're not going to believe what Johnny said after she told him she loved him!" Then read what he said, exactly the way you think he would say it. Make your characters real people and your audience will want to get to know them better.

She says, "I always get a thrill when a reader writes a review that says they really 'hated' one of my characters who are only alive in my mind. Even if they hated someone I liked, they're making a comment on a totally imaginary person who I made up. Getting a reaction—any reaction, good or bad—is exactly what I'm looking to accomplish as a writer!"

West advises fiction authors,

> Remember, you're not selling yourself, you're selling your imaginary world and the people who live there. Make your audience want to go to that place and meet the people there. If you really want them to love what you've written, you have got to make them believe you love it, as well; or how much you hate the villain. Show them the entrance to a ride of a lifetime (through your presentation), then make them buy the ticket!

Intriguing and Outrageous Venues for Novelists

Where can you go to talk about your novel? Just about anyplace. Use your imagination. Of course, there are major, independent, and specialty bookstores; all sorts of specialty shops; churches; museums (for a historical novel); pet stores (for a story about an animal hoarder or therapy pet); kitchen stores (for a novel featuring a chef or a serial killer who always smells like grilled steak); purse and accessory shops (for a book set within the fashion district in some big city); a bait shop (for a book featuring commercial fishermen); a motorcycle shop (for a novel focusing on a businesswoman who rides a Harley on weekends); or a hobby shop (for a story featuring a man obsessed with building model cars). If you are donating a portion of the proceeds from your book to a charity, you might arrange to be part of a fundraising event where you can sign books for your readers. Get the idea?

Wendy Dager once did a signing in a cupcake bakery because, in her novel, *I Murdered the PTA*, her main character refers to the PTA members as "cupcakes" and there is a big cupcake on the cover of the book.

I've also known novelists to speak and/or sign books at a winery, an animal shelter, an airport, senior centers, and even a haunted house.

Have Fun Talking About Your Children's Book

Here's one type of book that most experts will allow authors to read in public, but please make sure you know how to grab and hold children's attention. Develop the skills needed to read to children. Use some of the tips and techniques outlined in chapter five and consider attending a storytelling festival and a couple of storytelling group meetings. Also sit in on story time at your local library and pick up some tips from watching the librarian read to children. It is important that a children's author be able to relate well to children and is understood when they read to them. It takes a knack. If it doesn't come to you naturally, you really do need to go out and gain some skills.

Ned Rauch-Mannino promotes his book, *Fingertip Island,* to second through fifth graders (ages seven through twelve). He says,

> As a children's author, most of my speaking experiences take place where children are found: in schools. I like to work

with teachers who use my book in the classroom to explore components of children's literature, themes, and character development. Rarely are students in the classrooms I visit unfamiliar with my work, as cooperative teachers prepare students with in-class readings and related assignments before I arrive. This makes for an active class, eager to learn more and share their thoughts. Of course, my audiences are found to be wildly unpredictable. It's impossible to guess what an eight-year-old will say, ask, or do next. For example, a third grade student once asked me to autograph everything in his possession, including his desk. Flattered, I had to decline. But young students' inquisitive nature leads to some excellent questions, as well as ideas for future books.

According to Rauch-Mannino, "I'll also visit book fairs, libraries, and literary events. But the captive, prepared audiences the classrooms present are by far favored." He says,

My audiences are more than readers: they're believers. At the middle grade age, so many readers readily take to heart the dialogue from speaking experiences. If I say a specific character's favorite food is mint chocolate chip ice cream, they won't only accept it and move on, they will develop that trait and expand the character without any further assistance from me. Children really invest themselves in stories they love. And I am delighted when I can add to that experience—that passion. It's encouraging to see my readers, young as they are, respond to and advance the story with their own imaginations.

Rauch-Mannino says he has to be cognizant of his young audience when he presents a program for school children. He says,

Children make for a great audience. But to do the audience justice, I need to have a solid understanding of what children really want to hear. If I talked for forty-five minutes, well, my audience would lose interest and become antsy. So to engage this audience, I really have to be *engaging*. Inquisitive by nature, children want the opportunity to ask questions. I never hesitate to give it to them. However, I am sure to ask the audience questions, too. For example, I like to ask what might happen if my readers found themselves in the story. How would they react? What problems might their first reaction cause? Sometimes these questions are asked in advance, by collaborating with teachers who present the questions in exercises. Last winter I visited a fourth grade class, arriving to find each student had completed an art project as to what they would do on FingerTip Island. With much credit to teachers, I can find a number of ways to involve the students. At a combination fourth and fifth grade assembly, we had students chosen to represent characters. Again, before I arrived, the class had built a make-shift FingerTip Island set out of construction paper and cardboard. So my reading turned out to be a live-action play. I've even seen FingerTip Island-shaped cookies, with other themed-foods for a "meet the author" snack time.

Rauch-Mannino points out that,

It's key to remember that children must be approached differently. I have to join them on their level. I need to be interactive, and understanding, and patient. I also have to be ready for my own imagination to be challenged.

During every event, though, I need to be aware of the energy level. Too little during a reading, and I'll have to pick up the tempo to avoid boredom. Too much can be worse. During one visit to a classroom, I was handing out bookmarks during the post-event snack. The teacher stepped out to take a phone call, and the students, sensing the missing supervision, went wild trying to collect autographs, tell stories, trade characters, or simply get my attention. Twenty-three nine year-olds clamoring after you, freshly-energized with juice and cookies, can be really scary.

Aside from local schools, children's book authors can also generally set up readings at libraries, children's bookstores, Christian bookstores, toy stores, churches, preschools, and parks. Book festivals often have a children's area where authors can read from their books.

Karen Lee Stevens, author of *Animals Have Feelings, Too!*, also finds her audiences in schools. She says,

We give several humane education presentations each month (through All for Animals in Santa Barbara, California) at local preschools, elementary schools, and children's organizations. Since our book is designed as an A–Z guide of feelings, it not only teaches children that animals and people share many of the same feelings, but they also learn some cool vocabulary words along the way! It's been easy to set up events; often, parents or teachers will hear about our program and ask us to do a school presentation. Other times, a business owner will approach us because their child or grandchild attends a particular school and they want a presentation in that child's classroom. If I hear about a new school program or event, I will call the principal and offer to do a presentation and give away books. For instance, recently there was an obituary in the local newspaper for a beloved bird at a preschool who had just passed away. I contacted the school to offer my condolences and to ask if they'd like a presentation. They eagerly accepted and the school ended up being one of my favorite places to visit again and again. We do not charge the families or schools for our presentations and book giveaways. That cost is covered by our sponsors and grants.

The Awkward Truth in Your Writing and Speaking

There are a few things that are like fingernails on a blackboard to me. One of them is when speakers or writers profess the truth in their statements.

Honestly (pun intended), when someone prefaces a statement by saying, "I have to be honest here," "To tell you the truth," "Truthfully," "In all honesty," "To be completely honest," "Do you want the truth?" and so forth, I have to wonder if everything they said before that were lies.

Why do people point out that they're being truthful only now and then during a talk? What are they thinking? What message are they trying to leave with their audience? It seems as though they're saying, "Hey, I'm a blatant liar except that now I'm going to be honest."

I guess people who do this are trying to make a point of honesty with regard to something that one could easily lie about. Maybe it is a sticky topic and they want to preface the comment by letting their audience know they are being painfully honest at some cost. I would advise those folks to be careful with their "honesty" prefaces, because I'm sure there are others besides myself who hear those statements and wonder, "Okay, what has this guy/gal been lying about up until now?"

Does this bug you? It probably will now that I have pointed it out.

On the other hand, I want to give you something to think about as you write or talk about your memoir, a true story about your cat or dog, for example, or an account of something you witnessed. While it's not okay to fabricate to the point that some authors in the news have done in past years—to write blatant lies—it is okay to ignore some of the details of your stories. In fact, I tell authors that it is sometimes okay not to tell the entire, complete truth. Many times, it's best that you don't.

If a detail is not pertinent to the story, it doesn't move the story forward, or it isn't entertaining, for example, don't include it. Who cares whether you stepped into the car using your right foot or your left one? If it doesn't matter, don't mention it. Give your reader the information he needs in order to visualize the story—to help him to be a part of the story—but not so much detail that he becomes distracted or overwhelmed by it.

Maybe, in reality, you had to cross two streets and walk around the other side of a green Honda with a dangling license plate and a child's car seat inside to reach the dry cleaners where you picked up your linen table cloth for your intimate dinner that night. But is all of this detail necessary to the story you are telling? If not, drop it. Say, instead, that you walked around the corner to the dry cleaners and picked up the linen.

Sometimes keeping to the order of things rudely interrupts a story. Maybe it happened that John came to your door and walked right in. But it may make a better story if he hesitates at the door before knocking and reconsiders what he's going to say. Instead of writing the true account—that Jayne called the doctor three times before she got an answer—if this isn't important to the story, just have Jayne dial the phone and speak to the doctor.

In other words, stick to your story, of course, but don't be so truthful that it hurts your readers.

How to Entice People to Attend Your Presentations

In a perfect world, once you set up a speaking gig, you can go back to your writing and someone else will start advertising your presentation far and wide. In most cases, however, this is a fantasy. In fact, once you become a published author and begin the time-consuming, energy-draining job of promoting your book, you will have scant little time to write anything meaningful ever again.

Oh, maybe that's a bit of an exaggeration, but if you hope to sell more than a few copies of your wonderful book, you will need to do a lot of promotion. This includes promoting your speaking engagements and workshops.

Sure, some program chairpersons, bookstore managers, and conference organizers will do an incredible job of publicizing your event. If you get one that falls down on the job, however, and you have not done any promotion, you'll be mighty unhappy when you arrive at the event site and discover that no one has shown up to hear you.

Most author-speakers have learned: never count on someone else to promote your presentations. The first thing you want to do when you book an event is have a conversation with the person in charge of publicity. Exactly what will they do to publicize the event? Discuss what this person generally does to bring in a crowd and how effective it has been in the past. Express a willingness to take up any slack. Stay in contact with this person to make sure he or she is following through in a timely manner. Well-intended people sometimes drop the ball, and you want to be sure to pick it up in time to salvage your event in case this happens.

I've seen the results of neglectful promoters. One sticks in my mind. It was a lovely day in a beautiful California city. The book festival had just begun, but where were the visitors? After an hour of the occasional straggler walking by and visits from other vendors, along came a bubbly and slightly frazzled young woman carrying an armload of beautifully-designed brochures. Come to find out, they had picked up the advertising materials for the book festival from the printer that morning and were just now distributing them to downtown merchants. Obviously, this is something that should have been done at least a week prior to the event. Someone goofed, and everyone involved paid the price. The minimal news coverage brought only a few browsers. The bulk of the sparse attendees were attracted by signs along the main street half-block away, which had been put up that morning.

Here are some publicity activities that should be considered when you plan a speaking engagement.

Things you can and should do:

- Announce the presentation at your website. Create an appearances or calendar section at your site and keep it updated. I like to also keep past appearances listed as a sort of resumé for site visitors (in particular program directors and conference organizers who might be interested in booking me to speak).
- Post the announcement at your blog site several times during the weeks leading up to the event.

- Follow up by posting links to your blog on your Twitter page.
- Place an announcement in your newsletter.
- Where appropriate, prepare a bio for the program chairperson, store manager, or librarian to include in their newsletter, club bulletin, or in the newspaper press release.
- Send press releases to local newspapers and other appropriate newsletters and websites (only after checking to make sure the organizer didn't already cover this base).
- Use your social media accounts to promote your presentation.
- Send notices and then reminders to those on your email list who reside in or near the city where you will be speaking. I prefer receiving personal invitations from friends and colleagues as opposed to high tech, professional-looking, graphic-heavy advertisements. Keep it simple, light, and genuine.
- Call key people and try to get a commitment from them. This might be some of your more supportive and influential friends.
- Do a radio gig prior to the event and announce your pending appearance. (If you don't have connections, ask the program chair, conference organizer, or bookseller to help you get booked.)
- Post flyers on bulletin boards at your local library and bookstores or send flyers to the library and bookstores in the city where you will be speaking. If your book (and your talk) are on a subject represented by local businesses—say, gardening, pet care, spirituality, acupuncture, herb remedies, or car repair—ask to post notices where appropriate. This might be at garden centers, pet stores, churches/Christian bookstores, health food stores/spiritual centers, or mechanic shops/car lots, etc.
- Contact bookstore owners in the area where you will be speaking to let them know there might be requests for your book. Suggest they order extra copies.

- Where appropriate, schedule a book signing at a bookstore or other venue in that city the same week. Some authors always try to schedule a book signing in a city where they have a book festival or conference.
- If this is a book signing at a retail store, create fliers announcing your event and ask the manager to have clerks tuck one in with each purchase during the two weeks prior to the signing.
- Make a poster for the store (or library) window.

Again, follow-up, follow-up, follow-up. Don't let anyone drop the ball on your parade.

Wendy Dager says she never leaves publicity entirely to bookstores and other organizers. (Many of us have learned this lesson in the most disappointing ways.) She says, "Social networking and professional-looking press releases sent well in advance to newspapers and other venues are extremely important. However, authors should be aware that you can promote like crazy and still not get the turnout you expected or hoped for."

Wendy is right. Sometimes, despite all of your publicity effort, you find yourself sitting alone in a bookstore or other location with a stack of books in front of you that nobody is buying—or even looking at. I once did a book signing where one person showed up. She bought a book. Another time, I entertained around seventy-five people at the same venue. What did I do differently? The first time I did nothing to promote the event. The bookstore manager placed a press release in the newspaper. Also, my book was for a fairly small niche audience—not the general public. Add to this fact that I was not, yet, a high profile figure in the community.

Five years later, I came out with *The Ojai Valley, An Illustrated History* and invited the community to celebrate with me. I arranged to be interviewed and photographed for the local newspaper and announced the event in conjunction with the article. I had done a lot of pre-publication promo and had taken orders for about 200 books by the time it was released. I did a huge mailing (no email back then) to customers and others whose names were in my Rolodex, those 100 or so I had interviewed for the book and their families, those associated with the agencies and associations I used during my research, local librarians, city hall staff, community leaders, friends, neighbors, etc. The event was a huge success and I sold dozens of books that day.

Here's another gem that can help you get better coverage for future events. Support other authors every chance you get and you may get their support when you need it.

- Attend signings and other events for authors in your community.
- Send congratulatory messages to authors with new books or who have won an award for their book. Locate their contact information at their websites by doing an Internet search using their name or the title of their book.
- Offer to review books in your genre or topic for your own newsletter, your organization newsletter, your blog, or another publication you typically write for. If none of this applies, at least review the book for Amazon.com and other sites where the book is offered for sale.

I have to tell you that "hometown gal writes book," isn't really news anymore. That's why I suggest using a hook to get publicity. Schedule your talk in conjunction with a world event or a holiday, for example. Newspaper reporters will be more apt to run a piece in February about an author who will be speaking on the topic of her book, *Internet Dating for Dummies* at a local meeting of relationship counselors on Valentine's Day. Or they might not hesitate running your piece announcing the signing for your humorous novel on fatherhood and fathering during the week of Father's Day.

Of course, if bigger news hits the wires that week, your press release might be reduced to a few lines or, worse yet, rejected. Newspaper editors are under no obligation to run press releases. That's why it is important to come up with a *wow* topic and a provocative headline.

Obscure and Outrageous Seasonal Prompts

Father's Day, Halloween, Christmas, and Thanksgiving are just a few of hundreds of seasonal prompts you could use in setting up speaking engagements and in designing publicity for your talks and for your book.

I have a book of cat stories—*Catscapades, True Cat Tales*. I often promote it around Valentine's Day, Easter, Mother's Day, and Christmas as a great little gift book for someone who enjoys cats. But I could also tie it into some of the many obscure seasonal prompts and possibly get publicity in local newspapers. For example, did you know that there is a Happy Mew Year for cats, Responsible Pet Owner's Month, Hug Your Cat Day, Adopt a Shelter Cat Month, World Animal Month, Adopt a Senior Pet Month, National Be Kind to Animals Week, Pet Appreciation Week, Take a Pet to Work Week, Sylvester the Cat's Birthday, and even Scoop the Poop Week?

Can't you just imagine the fun a reporter with a sense of humor would have helping me promote an event for Scoop the Poop Week?

I discovered these and many other fun and serious reasons to celebrate (and to promote) at three different seasonal/holiday sites (listed below). Here are some of the other great prompts you might be able to use in promoting your book: National Hugging Day, Thank Your Customer Week, National Ghostwriters Week, Celebrate Your Name

Week, National Words Matter Week, If Pets Had Thumbs Day, Read an E-Book Day, Family Reunion Month, Make a Difference to Children Month, National Tooth Fairy Day, and Read in the Bathtub Day.

Find more at these sites:

http://www.brownielocks.com
http://www.holidayinsights.com
http://www.gone-ta-pott.com

Write an Effective Press Release

For some—in fact, many—the prospect of writing a press release is daunting. If you don't feel intimidated when it comes to writing your first press release (also known as a news release), you might be a bit naïve. While I don't mean to frighten you, you should know that there are right and wrong ways to write and submit press releases. In fact, there are many, many right ways and even more wrong ways.

Among the wrong methods are: submitting the press release too early or too late for publication, directing it to the wrong department, neglecting to provide contact information, omitting pertinent information about the event, writing a bland account of the pending event, writing an over-the-top exaggerated and dramatic account of the pending event, writing an article and trying to pass it off as a press release, using the press release to promote yourself and your book instead of simply announcing the event, and so forth.

Among the correct methods are: submit the press release according to the newspaper standards (generally ten days to two-and-a-half weeks prior to an event), provide contact information in case a reporter wants to request an interview with you or additional information, and include all relevant information—who, what, why, where, when—in an interesting way. Here are some sample press releases for author events:

TALK UP YOUR BOOK

June 20, 2012   Contact: Jerry Jackson—xxx-xxx-xxxx

For publication between July 4 and 6, 2012

Subject: Pruning techniques for longer plant life

Are some of your plants suffering under your care? Most local residents are confused about when and how to prune their prize plants.
Jerry Jackson, author of *Is it Time to Prune? Facts and Fallacies for
California Gardeners*, will be on hand to answer your questions,
squelch your fears, and build your confidence about pruning your trees
and shrubs.

Stop in Saturday, July 7, at Galleria Garden Supply on Baker
Street between 1 and 4 p.m. for a demonstration and Q and A session.
Refreshments will be served. Free rosebush pruning guide for the first
twenty-five guests.

For an evaluation regarding one of your own plants, bring a picture
of your pruning nightmare or load up the real plant if it's in a pot.

September 3, 2013   Contact: Sandra Abbott—xxx-xxx-xxxx

For publication between September 15-17, 2012

Subject: Novelist brings classic authors to life

Have you ever wondered what Thoreau ate for lunch? What sort of relationship did Hemingway have with his cat? What inspired Stevenson to
write? And which famous literary artists had affairs during their lifetimes?

Join other literary buffs and readers of the classics for an evening
with the masters. Sandra Abbott, author of *The Women of Clementine
Lane*, a newly published modern-day novel with an old-fashioned
twist, will share some little-known truths about some of our favorite
dead authors.

Tuesday, September 18, at 7–9 p.m. in the Floral Room of the Seaside Circus Hotel on Haley Avenue.

Leslie Korenko offers this advice to authors who have a signing or other event planned, "Every venue manager has ideas for promotion, but you need to get familiar with your local newspaper and do a short press release at least two weeks before your presentation. Post your appearance on Facebook and then, afterward, boast about how well it went."

Post-Event Publicity

So true, Leslie. Get all of the publicity you can before the event. Bring family and friends along to fill seats—just in case attendance is sparse. If you get a crowd, put your support group to work bringing in extra chairs, distributing handouts, serving refreshments, and so forth. Be sure to have someone take photos throughout the evening so you can use them for publicity purposes afterward.

Depending on the size of your city and your newspaper, and what else comprises the news for that week, you might even get a photographer or reporter from the paper to attend.

Invite local celebrities to your author event. This might include the mayor, city council members, or another political figure. If you work for a large company in town, maybe you can entice the CEO and several co-workers to show up. Does a well-known author or actor live in your city? If you've been making connections as a way to establish and build on your author's platform, you may have made friends with some of these high-profile people. If so, give them an enticement to appear at your author gathering.

I know a young adult fantasy book author who often engages the services of magicians (who happen to be her friends) when she does book signings.

I once connected with a very well-known actor who lives in our community. He and I were interested in the same youth organization. I noticed his letter to the editor on a topic close to my heart, and, the next time I saw him at an event, I asked if he would agree to an interview for an article on that subject, should I get a magazine editor interested. Without hesitation, he said, "Yes." I think that you will find most high-profile people willing to help out when it involves a charity, project, or subject of their interest.

Keep in mind that a reporter is more apt to show up at an event where there is a celebrity. Also consider that a celebrity is more apt to attend if the activity has a fund-raising aspect to it—a percentage of proceeds from the book are going to his/her favorite charity, for example.

It's one of those win-win situations. You get great exposure, the celeb gets great exposure, and a charity benefits, as well. It follows that people will buy more books if they know they are supporting a charity.

No matter how the evening shapes up—as a hugely successful gala affair of the season or a fun evening for a dozen or so people—if there was no reporter in sight, be proactive and submit a photo and a short story to the newspaper yourself. Probably the best you can do is a photo with a three-line or so caption.

Make sure to post an enthusiastic recap of the event on your social media pages, at your blog, and in your newsletter. Send thank you notes to the event host and all who attended. You might even send friendly emails to those on your email list who weren't able to attend.

Perhaps some of them live in another city and would be willing to help you plan a similar event close to their home.

Let the World Know You Are a Speaker

Do you want to be found? If you have a book to promote, the answer should be *yes*. But I can't tell you how many professionals, authors, and experts I have trouble locating online. When I finally discover their websites, often there is no easy way to contact them. In some cases, I might eventually stumble across an email form in some obscure place at their website. Sometimes, believe it or not, it is no longer viable.

As an author, you should have a website and it should appear immediately when your name is typed into the search prompt at any of the major search engines. Unfortunately, with the advent of Facebook, LinkedIn, etc., your social media pages might appear first—even ahead of your website, unless your website URL includes your name. My Matilija Press website used to show up on the first page of any search using "Patricia Fry" as the keyword. Now this site doesn't appear until the second page. This is a shame, because I showcase my books here.

I have since established a second website using my name. Now, at least, that website appears on the first page of a search and it is linked to my Matilija Press website.

Be sure to search your name occasionally so you are aware of how easy or how difficult it is for your readers and fans to find you. Make sure your contact information at your website is up to date.

You should be promoting your book in all of the most prominent places at your site. If you want to get out and speak, present workshops, and get involved in appropriate conferences, you should be advertising that fact, too.

- Post a page on your website listing your speaking and signing schedule. You can enhance this by offering a list of your speech topics, providing a few photos of you speaking to groups, and listing testimonials from program organizers and audience members.

Peter Bowerman suggests:

> Create a link on your site dedicated to your speaking. It doesn't have to be fancy, but include the topics you can speak on, your bio/credentials, and last, but absolutely not least, testimonials from both attendees and conference organizers, which means you should be proactive about gathering those testimonials. I'd hand out short questionnaires at the end of a workshop, asking for feedback on your talk, suggestions for improvement, and specifically ask if they'd be willing to share a testimonial about your speaking that you can put on your website (and give them the option to just use initials if they want).

- Post a notice prominently on your home page announcing that you are a speaker—available for invitations. Link it to your speaker page.
- Announce the fact that you are a speaker on your business cards and brochures. Encourage people to take some to hand out to others who schedule speakers.
- Talk to people you meet in passing or at bookselling events such as book festivals about the programs you present.
- Blog frequently about your speaking events and mention them on your social media pages and in your newsletters. Also create articles and essays on the topic of public speaking to bring attention to yourself and the fact that you have some experience and expertise on the topic.
- Seek out opportunities to be interviewed at other blog sites, newspapers, newsletters, magazines, etc. and always mention the fact that you speak on behalf of your book.

- Have several topics you can speak on and keep coming up with more.

In this day of strong competition for authors, it is still ever so important to get out and meet your public—to develop a personal relationship with them. I urge you to be proactive. Use the tips and techniques in this book to groom yourself as a public speaker, to locate appropriate speaking opportunities, and to publicize them. Also continually advertise the fact that you are available as a public speaker through every means at your disposal.

The Successful Author Book Signing

One of the most common and popular methods of book promotion is the traditional bookstore book signing. Some of us can recall attending book signings with our favorite authors and standing in line for hours eager for a chance to get that revered autograph. We read about signings where authors sell hundreds of books. When we become authors, we dream of filling mega-bookstores everywhere with our fans waiting patiently for autographed copies of our books. Unfortunately, that dream soon dies.

You Are *Not* J. K. Rowling

If you've published a book and arranged for a signing or two, you know that the experience for a relatively unknown, like you and me, is way different than a signing for a well-known, such as J. K. Rowling, John Grisham, or celebs like Shirley MacLaine, Betty White, or Hillary Clinton. We have fans, friends, and family members, but not to the extent the celebrities do.

So the first thing a new author needs to do is to lower his/her expectations with regard to any book signings they schedule.

Does this mean that you should forget about doing any signings? Absolutely not. Even rather disappointing signings come with gifts. What are the benefits of a signing beyond selling boxes and boxes of books?

- You become acquainted with booksellers in your area. Bookstore managers and their clerks can be great advocates for your book. Make friends with them and encourage them to read your book. You may have to give away a copy or two. If they like your book, they are more apt to recommend it to their customers.

- You get great exposure for your book through ads, promo posters, newspaper articles, fliers, etc. which are circulated, posted, and published prior to (and sometimes after) the event.

- You get experience talking about your book. If you are astute, you will quickly learn which lines, words, and phrases create interest in potential customers and which don't. Experience and experimentation are the best ways to fine-tune your sales pitch.

- You meet a few new potential customers you can add to your mailing list. Someone who purchases your book might be a good candidate for others you may produce. Even those who don't buy your book on the spot may eventually become customers. But if there was no book signing, they would not have found out about your book and they may never become a customer.

- This opportunity might lead to others. Authors often meet people at book signings who invite them to speak to their groups, participate in a library event, share a booth at a book festival, participate in a conference, be a guest blogger at their blog site, etc.

I suggest to authors that they look at every experience as an opportunity and at every opportunity as exposure for their books. The many signings I've done have resulted in a wide variety of sales scenarios—some over-the-top successful and some rather dismal. But several of them opened doors that I did not expect.

It was at that very first signing, for example, that I got the idea for writing the local history book. The bookseller suggested that someone needed to compile the vast amount of local historical material in our museums and libraries under one cover for tourists and residents. I went right to work on that project and became the first person to produce a comprehensive history of the Ojai Valley, California. This turned out to be a lucrative project. It afforded me recognition within the community that I would not otherwise have earned. I established my own publishing company in order to produce that book and this led to many additional self-published books. It also opened numerous other doors that I ultimately walked through.

I have made some great contacts while signing books. I've met some of my best clients at book signings. I've landed interesting speaking engagements. I've come up with new article ideas while signing books. I've met other writers who wanted to write about me. I've learned something each time about bookselling and promotion. Oh yes, and I've also sold books.

This can be your story, too, but only if you get out there and set up some book signing events. Get past the prejudices against doing book signings. You'll hear some of your writer's group or online forum members say that book signings are not worth your time. Consider how worthwhile your evening would be if you sat at home, instead. How many books would you sell from your living room sitting in front of the TV? How many contacts would you make? Could you write off the expenses for your evening meal and the electricity it takes to run the TV?

Wouldn't it make more sense to spend the evening out at a bookstore talking to potential customers about your book, meeting people, possibly making a few (or a lot of) sales, and maybe even falling into some great opportunities? Plus, you can write off your expenses for mileage while distributing promotional materials, for the materials themselves, for refreshments, and so forth. Even if you sell five books and make around $50 (after the bookstore's cut), it's more than you would have made staying home. And what about the exposure?

While you are out schmoozing with people and pitching your book, you are being noticed in ways that you can't yet imagine. You may feel as though your book signing failed or you didn't get through to your audience while speaking, but sometimes there is an opportunity lurking in the background, which came about because of this exposure.

The Festive and Fun Book Launch Party

Some authors, before doing a signing or presentation, throw a book launch party. They invite everyone they know, including, in some cases, the general public, to a gala or a casual event designed to celebrate the publication of their book.

My three daughters spearheaded a book launch event when I published the first edition of my local history book. It was quite a nice dress-up affair held on the patio of our world-famous outdoor bookstore, Bart's Books in Ojai, California. We hosted around seventy-five friends, supporters, contributors to the book, and community leaders, since the book was such a welcome addition to this community. They had a cake frosted with the cover of the book, and we served punch. The bookseller sold around fifty copies of the book that day. (Most of the guests had already purchased copies by then.)

There are many scenarios for book launch parties. Some people are not comfortable selling books at parties, especially if it is held in a private home. Others find ways to get around the discomfort of making a book launch party commercial by donating proceeds from the sale of their books to a charity.

Karen Lee Stevens, a Certified Humane Education Specialist and founder and president of All for Animals, is the author of two books designed to foster compassion for animals. Her latest, a children's book, was funded through donations and all proceeds go back into her organization, All for Animals.

When this book came out in 2011, Stevens threw a party, which, because of the nature of the book, she called a "pawty." She says,

> We decided to hold a book launch "pawty" for our children's book, *Animals Have Feelings, Too!* at a local dog spa, which was the perfect, animal-friendly venue for such an event. Because All for Animals (the book's publisher) is a nonprofit organization, the spa owners hosted the pawty at no charge. It was really a win-win for everyone—we held an event without worrying about the cost of renting a facility (which can be expensive) and the spa received lots of free publicity as well as potential new customers who may have been visiting the facility for the first time.

> Our book's illustrator, Teri Rider, is very dedicated to our mission of creating a compassionate world through humane education, and she drove four hours from her home in San Diego to Santa Barbara to attend the event. She stayed for the weekend to help out and to give a speech at the "pawty." Again, since All for Animals is a nonprofit, we were able to negotiate a complimentary, two-night stay at a nice hotel for Teri while she was in town, which helped keep our costs down.

> In order to sell as many books as possible, we asked guests to purchase copies of our book for themselves, but we also encouraged them to purchase an extra copy, which we could donate to a local elementary school. Some people purchased as many as ten books to donate, which resulted in the sale of

almost 200 books that day; nearly half of which we donated to school children throughout the community!

The only thing I would have done differently is to have the event catered. We ended up spending a lot of time and effort renting a truck, transporting tables, chairs, and canopies, shopping for all the food, in addition to setting up and cleaning up. Being able to walk into an event that was all set up by the caterer would have been a lot more relaxing.

Bobbie Christmas describes her most successful launch party. She says,

It was for a book I coauthored with an author in Bermuda. The author planned and promoted a big event, complete with music and free food. He cooked the food himself, and friends volunteered to dish it out. When we opened the doors, people were already lined up outside. To reap the benefits of his investment, he set up a book-signing table right beside the only exit. Everyone who attended had to walk past the two of us, and there we sat with a huge pile of books. Most people wanted to thank him for a nice evening, but to get to him, they had to buy a book, because of the line of people waiting for him to sign books. As a result, most of the attendees bought at least one book before they left. We sold more than one hundred books that evening.

Speak at Book Signings

I believe there are three elements that make a book signing successful—well, four, if you consider one's expectations. What one author considers successful, another might deem a complete failure. It's all in one's perspective. Strive to maintain realistic expectations based on all aspects of the planned event, how well you are known, etc.

The first element of a successful book signing is a good book—one that is of interest to a large segment of people or a strong niche audience. It must be relevant, well-written, well-organized, easy and pleasant to read and comprehend, and professionally edited.

The second ingredient is effective advertising. This is discussed in more detail in chapter ten.

Third, I recommend adding a speaking and/or demonstration element to your signing. People are more apt to come out to hear an author speak on what led to her writing this rather provocative novel, for example. Create a brief talk around the theme of your nonfiction book. Give a cooking demonstration or a lesson in writing poetry. Here, you are providing benefits your readers might respond to.

Additionally, there will be browsers in the bookstore (or specialty store) who are oblivious to the fact that you are there promoting your book. They, too, might be drawn to your presentation, if they realize you are talking about something they're interested in or you're conducting an interesting demonstration. Get to the event site early and walk around with your book. Greet shoppers and invite them to come to your program.

I also recommend that you walk around and engage store customers when you have lulls between visitors to your signing table. Introduce yourself and hand your book to them to hold and look at as you talk briefly about it. Someone who handles the product is more likely to purchase it.

Raven West believes in insurance. When she goes out to speak, she sometimes stacks the deck. She says, "One little trick I learned was to have my own 'entourage' accompany me to these events. I have three to five friends there with cameras creating a real buzz when I walk into the bookstore." This tactic can certainly get the attention of shoppers who might not otherwise pay any attention to someone sitting alone with a stack of books to sign.

Here are two ways you can enhance your book signings. Get gigs locally at appropriate book and specialty stores within a forty-mile radius of your home. But also plan trips throughout your state and beyond, visiting bookstores and setting up signings. As this book indicates, the personal touch is most effective for authors. So you may want to plan two trips—one to personally introduce your book to book buyers throughout your state (and beyond) and another to do the book signings you set up. I find that contacting bookstore owners via email or by phone or letter sometimes falls flat. They are generally so jammed with books that they don't even want to consider another one, unless they see it and like it and like the author. You might want to check out the bookstores in person to determine which ones are most conducive to a signing. This will also give you the opportunity to show the bookseller press releases and other clips illustrating previous book signing successes.

A personal meeting with the bookseller will also give you the opportunity to discuss some of your ideas for promotion in the area—methods you have in mind for enticing customers into the bookstore. This might include radio interviews, visits to corporate lunchrooms where you'll chat with employees and hand out discount coupons for your book, book reviews in local publications, and so forth

Not every author has a heart for the traditional book signing. Here's what Bobbie Christmas says about them:

> Signings seem to me like a pitiful plea for people to come buy your book. In the past, I had to comply when publishers set up a book signing. I saw how people averted their gaze when they spotted me at a table with my books. I'm sure they feared they would be lured in and pressured to buy a book.

I learned to bring candies and goodies to give out, so people would feel comfortable coming close. Most walked away with a quick "thank-you," but some people later drifted back to converse, once they saw I was not a high-pressure salesperson; and some even bought books. At any book signing, however, my highest sales come from people I already know and to whom I promoted my appearance. If an author does not have an email list of potential buyers, sales can be abysmal at signings.

She offers this advice:

Rather than static signings or sitting at a booth at a festival, I recommend offering something free. To promote *Write In Style,* I give brief seminars on creative writing. During my talk, I refer to my book but I do not turn my talk into a sales pitch. Instead, I look things up in the book or tell stories about how I wrote or sold it. I'm sure this promotion method works best for nonfiction, though.

Major Bookstores Versus Independent Bookstores

We all know that the reign of the bookstore, as far as being book-selling king, is all but over. I am one of several who doesn't believe the Main Street bookstore concept is dead. But bookselling through bookstores, the structure of the stores and the way they purchase and present books, is certainly in transition. Even though we've all watched our favorite independent bookstores fold these past years, some remain and there are new ones coming into being.

If your book is with a traditional publisher, it may be stocked in bookstores nationwide. If you have self-published, or you've gone with a pay-to-publish company, it is beyond difficult to get your book into a major bookstore. Consider that we are producing hundreds of thousands of print books each year and even the largest mega bookstore can carry only around 150,000 titles total. Which ones will they choose? Those for which large publishers are paying for space and those that are selling, of course.

So if you are doing the right kind of promotion that is bringing people into the bookstores to purchase your book by the truckloads, sure booksellers will carry your book. In the meantime, if your book is listed in *Books in Print*, booksellers have access to ordering it if a customer makes such a request. Some bookstores are also dealing in digital books—Barnes and Noble, for example, has the Nook. A few other stores are using the Espresso Book Machine to produce books on the spot.

While the machine doesn't seem to be serving the purpose some thought it would, and there aren't as many of them in use as expected by now, the idea hasn't died. In fact, there are around forty machines in use worldwide and over thirty of them are in public and university bookstores as well as libraries throughout the US and Canada. You'll find these machines in Denver, New York, Pittsburgh, Seattle, Washington DC, Sacramento, Ann Arbor, Tucson, Montreal, Vancouver, and Toronto, for example.

As you can imagine, independent booksellers can make snap decisions about the books they carry. But the mega bookstore manager does not have that luxury. They must get clearance from top management and, I can tell you, this can sometimes be a rigorous, time-consuming, and disappointing process. Getting paid for your shipment of books can be a nightmare. But that's another story.

Mega bookstore managers will sometimes do book signings with local authors, however. Some of them even have shelves dedicated to books by local authors. Many self-published and pay-to-publish authors I know have managed to get book signing gigs at some of the major bookstores in their hometowns. I can't say that these have been any more lucrative than those held in independent bookstores and other venues. Smaller bookstore and independent business owners can generally be more flexible and creative in planning these events. Remember that there are many stores other than bookstores that carry books related to their inventory. This includes pharmacies, grocery stores, gift shops, craft stores, hobby shops, nurseries, auto parts stores, wine shops, children's stores, kitchen stores, pet stores, and so forth. We no longer have a new book store in our city, so the proprietor of Made in Ojai (a store carrying wares of all kinds made by locals) has created a section for books by local authors.

Okay, so the first step is introducing yourself and your book to booksellers and, as I indicated, this is most effectively done in person.

How to Get Invited to Do a Book Signing

Once you discover the contact person for the bookstore, specialty store, or other venue where you'd like to do a signing, present him/her with information about your book—perhaps a press kit. This would include your bio, a description of your book, a few testimonials or excerpts from reviews for the book, maybe a clip or a press release either announcing or describing a successful signing, your website or your publisher's website address so the bookseller can get additional information, and, of course, your contact information.

Explain who your audience is for this book (presumably this store's customers) and how you expect to entice them to attend your signing. Maybe you present an interesting program or you have gifts for all who attend. Discuss your plans for publicity and your expectations with regard to the promotion the store manager will do.

Be prepared to offer facts and figures and references (related to former successful signings).

Retailers often get busy and forget to return calls, respond to emails, or contact the newspaper, for example. It is up to you to stay on top of all phases of the potential event. Follow-up, follow-up, follow-up.

Book Signing Tips

Before you leap out and start planning book signings to promote your newly published book, here are a few ideas that will help make these events more successful. (While we're on the topic—let me say that it's possible to get book signing gigs for an older book, too. It may not matter to the bookseller/retailer or your customers that your charming, informative, or interesting book is one, three, or even five years old.)

Three weeks or a month before the event

1. Take charge and initiate invitations to do book signings. Using the suggested approach outlined above (under "How to Get Invited to Do a Book Signing"), actively promote yourself and your book to all of the right people—bookstore and specialty shop managers, for example.

2. At the time that you arrange for the book signing, discuss publicity and designate who will do what aspects of promotion for the event. Agree on a timeline and note the results of your discussion in writing.

3. Consider sharing the book signing table with one or more other authors. A group of authors might attract more people. Not only do they each have a separate array of friends and other supporters who might show up, the theme of their books

might bring in additional customers for your book. For a more appropriate gathering of potential customers, choose someone with a book similar to yours or that compliments it. You want to make sure that the people he or she attracts would be interested in your book, as well.

4.   Discuss publicity with the other author(s) and give clear assignments. For example, each of you should post the event at your websites, in your blogs, at your LISTSERVs and on other social media pages, in your newsletters, and in other appropriate publications.

5.   If your book is with a traditional publisher, make sure there are plenty of copies on hand for the signing. If not, place an order now. Or make sure the bookseller does.

Two and a half weeks before the event:

6.   Send press releases with a photograph of yourself and/or your book cover to all newspapers within a forty-mile radius. (See sample press releases in chapter ten.) If the bookseller has agreed to submit a press release, make sure he has the information he needs and follow through with him until the press release is submitted. (Note: if this is a multi-author event, submit information for and photos of the other authors, as well.)

7.   Contact everyone you know and invite them to your book signing/presentation. Even those who have already bought a copy of the book (or received a complimentary copy) might enjoy attending and may even purchase a book as a gift for someone else.

8.   If this is a shared experience, remind the other authors to make their contacts.

Ten days in advance of the event:

9. Discuss publicity again. Will the bookseller design posters and flyers to advertise your signing? If not, do this yourself and deliver them to the store a week in advance of the event. Ask the bookseller to include fliers with each purchase during the week.

10. Post fliers and posters at appropriate places throughout your city.

11. Make sure there is a poster or two in the store window and offer to design a store display of your books.

One week in advance of the event:

12. Send a reminder email to everyone you have previously invited to attend.

13. Know ahead of time what to expect: Will you have a microphone? Lectern? Table at which to sit for signing? Or will you have to arrange for these things yourself?

14. Check the store stock. Will you need to bring additional books to sell?

The day of the event:

15. Be prompt. Arriving a little early won't hurt and will give you time to settle in.

16. Bring handouts such as a related article, report, or a sample chapter. When I'm signing *Quest For Truth*, I hand out my article on meditation walking. When the event features *The Mainland Luau*, I give out a recipe that isn't in the book. Bring business cards, brochures, promotional bookmarks, and plenty of pens.

17. Reach out to people—don't wait for them to come to you. Hand copies of your book to folks in the audience or those

who visit your signing table. Walk around the store and chat with customers.

18. Keep track of the number of books you autograph in case there is a discrepancy.

After the event:

19. Send a note of thanks to the store manager and staff.

20. Post a "brag" at all of your social media sites, in your blog and newsletter, etc.

21. Email everyone who showed up and thank them for coming. Email those who couldn't make it and tell them what a nice event it was. Repeat comments you heard and announce connections you made. For example, you might say, "The city librarian was there. She purchased copies for the new young adult section at the main library." Or "I overheard one gentleman say, 'I wish I had access to a book like this when I was a youngster.'" Or "I bought this a few weeks ago for my grandfather and he loved it—said it kept him laughing."

22. Attend other signings in order to support fellow authors, but also to find out more about what works and what doesn't.

23. Realize that signings and presentations will rarely exceed your expectations and hardly ever meet your highest goals. But *any time* you are given the opportunity to have this sort of free publicity, you are making headway in your promotional effort.

The Demonstration Presentation

People love the demonstration book signing or presentation. They get the opportunity to learn a new skill or concept. Most of us pick things up easier when we watch or participate in a demonstration.

I have watched authors make crème brulee on stage (and serve samples to the audience), create a live herb and flower wreath in the backroom of a nursery, show how to work with a PowerPoint program, and demonstrate how to properly wash your hands. I gave a demonstration at a Toastmasters meeting once showing how to start an African violet from a leaf. I also did one featuring how to travel with your cat. (Don't worry, no cats were harmed in the process.)

Just imagine the sort of demonstration you could present related to your nonfiction book or novel. How about designing a large photo or art display to accentuate a historical novel or a biography or memoir, for example? For a book on how to create curb appeal, show before and after photos of several homes. Show how to bind a book, do some creative gift-wrapping, do close-up photography, film a book trailer, do self-hypnosis, prepare elegant and easy hors d'oeuvres, etc. Get creative—think outside the box.

Author Wendy Dager doesn't typically plan demonstrations to accentuate her novel, but she realizes that her style is somewhat a curiosity to some. She says,

> My first novel, *I Murdered the PTA,* came out in June of 2011. That's when I learned that bookstore owners usually want you to do a little talk or question and answer session prior to a book signing. I've always enjoyed public speaking and even won a few speech contests as a teenager. Because I have what might be described as a quirky personality, I'm able to hold people's interest with humor, my vintage wardrobe, my unusual choice in hair color—usually pink, purple, or red streaks—and most importantly, by scripting nearly every word down to the last joke or aside. It might sound spontaneous and fun, but it's generally quite calculated in

order to keep me from saying "um" or having awkward pauses. Naturally, this doesn't work for question and answer sessions. But after a while you learn what people are going to ask, so you already have an appropriate answer. It's also good to have a brief, funny anecdote or two to share.

Dager also has an ebook novella featuring a serial killer who loves vintage clothing. She could bring in some vintage purses from her own collection to display when discussing this book.

Speaking of ebooks, can you promote them through signings and other live presentations? Sure you can. Keep reading.

The Ebook Signing

Ebooks are definitely making news. We keep hearing how ebook sales are up. But this does not mean that the print book is obsolete.

What if your book is in ebook form only? Can you do signings (and for that matter, speeches) when you have an ebook? Sure you can. Only be prepared to make some adjustments.

Here are some tips for giving presentations on behalf of your ebook.

- Keep in mind that it is still a viable book with a purpose—to educate, inform, teach, and/or entertain your target audience. Talking about or presenting a program around an ebook is the same as if you were talking about a print book. The only difference is that you don't have a hard copy to show.
- So why not make a prototype? Create one or more bound books to pass around. You may have to keep reminding your audience members, however, that the book is actually only in ebook form. They can download it and enjoy it on their iPad,

Nook, Kindle, etc. You might even pass around an iPad with the book loaded onto it.

- Develop a book trailer and show it on a computer or TV screen so everyone can view it. A book trailer is a brief film designed to advertise/promote a book, and this is a great way to introduce an ebook. It makes it more tangible, somehow.
- Run the trailer or display the book cover on a couple of digital picture frames situated prominently around the room or on the signing table.
- Print out a sample chapter to give to each attendee.
- Have plenty of quality promotional postcards or bookmarks to hand out. Offer to sign those for attendees.

If you are set up to do so, you can take orders on the spot for your ebook. If your signing is at a bookstore, the manager may be able to take customer orders. Otherwise, give coupons with a percentage off the ebook, if you are generating the download from your site. If you are suggesting that attendees order the book for their Kindle, Nook, or iPad, for example, offer a gift to those who send you a copy of their order confirmation. The gift might be a report on the topic of the book or one of your short stories.

Be sure to get the names and email addresses for everyone who attends your book signings and demonstrations and add them to your email list for future signings, any workshops you'll be offering, to notify of new books you've produced, and so forth.

Speak at Conferences on Your Book Topic

As you may know, there are conferences held in many locations worldwide on numerous topics including travel, arts and crafts, writing, publishing, computer technology, agriculture, ecology, animals, photography, health, real estate, finance, business management, education, sports, spirituality, paranormal, and more.

A conference might be a one-day event or run for ten days. Most are two and three-day events, usually over a weekend. Conferences generally consist of anywhere from five to thirty-five (or more) workshops running throughout the duration of the conference. Often, they'll have two or three (sometimes more) sessions running simultaneously. At some point during the conference, everyone will come together to hear the keynote speaker—generally in conjunction with a formal dinner. Sometimes the keynote address is given early on the first day of the conference as an opening to the event.

If you have written a nonfiction how-to, informational, or reference book, you may be considered an expert—or at least very knowledgeable—on that topic, and you may be able to get a speaking gig at an appropriate conference. If you hope to do more than one or two conferences per year, you will probably be required to do some traveling.

So what can a conference presenter expect as far as expenses and fees? There are nearly as many scenarios as there are conferences, across the United States. Some conference organizers are authorized to pay all expenses for their presenters. Some pay for your hotel stay, all meals associated with the conference, and free admittance to the conference. Others may give you the conference admission and meals only and pay you a small stipend.

Why should you pursue the opportunity to speak at conferences on topics related to your book? Because this is where you'll find your audience. If you have a book featuring tips and resources for artists and crafters who want to sell their work, many of your readers might gather at a conference on the business of arts and crafts. Maybe your book is a primer for families who want to go green or a step-by-step guide to installing solar power. You might find your audience at conferences related to green living.

Being a writer, you are probably already familiar with writer's conferences. Perhaps you've attended a few of them. If you are promoting a novel, you may be inclined to seek speaking opportunities within these familiar territories.

You may recall listening to novelists speak at writer's conferences on character development, how to promote a novel, writing a dynamite opening, tips for a more descriptive way of writing, how to show and not tell, how to use dialog, and so forth. Perhaps you've heard novelists talk about their writing journeys. I sat in on a session with a former police officer once who talked about how to accurately describe the appropriate guns and ammo one could use in their stories. I enjoyed a presentation at a conference not too long ago where a novelist shared her research techniques. So, yes, you could, conceivably, get a speaking or workshop slot at a writer's conference or even at a writer's retreat. This may be satisfying and enjoyable, but is this sort of exposure lucrative for a novelist?

Margaret Brownley speaks successfully at conferences, and she has developed a fairly versatile repertoire. She says,

> I gear my talks toward the audience. Writers like "how-to" information and readers enjoy an entertaining look at the life of a writer. Since I write westerns, I also give talks on women of the old west. I've spoken at the Romance Writers of America and American Christian Fiction Writers national conferences. Even though the audiences are mostly writers, my novels sell out at conference bookstores.

So how do you land a speaking gig at the conferences of your choice?

- Research conferences in your field and in your region and select a few. (See links to conference directories on page 198.)
- Do a Google search to locate conferences in specific areas. Use keywords, "health conference Nashville," "spring pet events New York," for example.
- If at all possible, attend a couple of conferences to find out what sort of programs they present. You can do this while you are compiling or writing your book and receive the added benefit of additional knowledge and perspective in your field or genre. (A small conference might cost around $50 to $100 for the weekend. A more prestigious, longer-running one might come with a fee of $800 or more, depending on what they offer. If you're not ready to be a presenter, but you want to attend in order to learn, consider asking for a volunteer position.)
- Study the list of programs and workshops at conference websites. What topics are covered? What could you bring to the table for this audience that relates to your book?

- Create a handful of unique, yet potentially popular programs you could present to your particular audience. Certainly, you could recycle some of your former presentations.

- Contact the organizers per the requirements at their websites. If there are no submission guidelines at the website, simply introduce yourself and your potential programs through an email to the appropriate person, include a brief bio, and ask them to contact you for additional information and/or an invitation to speak.

When I locate an event of interest, I study the information presented at the website and, if it seems appropriate, I submit a proposal or I send an email of introduction, based on their submission guidelines. If there are no guidelines posted, I will email or call the director and ask how to apply to be a speaker or a workshop leader. I have a résumé prepared listing my qualifications as an industry professional, an author of books in this field, as well as a speaker, and I'm always ready to make workshop or speech topic suggestions. Tip: I sometimes alter my résumé depending on the type of event or program I am applying for.

Sandra Beckwith often speaks at conferences. She says,

My book, *Publicity for Nonprofits*, was published in 2006. During the first eighteen months after the book came out, I spoke at several national and regional conferences. This was no coincidence; I submitted many proposals to appropriate organizations well in advance of the book's release and did a few teleseminars, as well. I was paid for all of them with the exception of one teleseminar, which led to a follow-up in-person paid speaking gig for the organization. I earned almost as much in speaking fees for that book as I did for the advance.

QiGong expert Victoria Cobb says,

> Last summer I was invited to teach at a retreat in Michigan. It is a wonderful long-running, spiritual retreat. For over forty years, these like-minded people have gathered. There are many classes and about 300 people who attend. I was their energy teacher and one of many massage therapists.
>
> I sold books and DVDs in the bookstore and made bottles of flower remedies, gave massages, and taught what I have learned as a student, teacher, and healer. This was a remarkable and memorable event! Last year at the event I sold twenty-five DVDs, fifty-three books, and all thirty remedies. I have been invited back for this July . . . a rare thing since no one has ever been invited twice in a row.

It's true, conference directors like to invite new people with fresh ideas and unique presentations. If you want a repeat invitation, look around while you're at the conference and come up with something appropriate but unique to suggest for the following year.

While some conference organizers are still selecting speakers a month prior to the event, many of them have their programs set practically a year in advance. I've discovered that, if you want a speaking gig at a particular conference, you'd better be proactive. Early in 2011, I contacted the director of a writer's conference I wanted to participate in. She told me, "Contact us in October." When I did, I was told that all of the speaking slots were filled and the event wasn't until spring. In this case, I should have checked in earlier than I was told to.

Here's what I recommend: Research conferences that occurred one to four months ago. Contact the organizers of those events. If they suggest you reconnect in six or seven months, make a note on your calendar to contact them in three. They may put you off for another three months, but that's okay—they know you are interested. Besides, there is always a chance that they are beginning to interview possible speakers for their program next year.

Nancy Barnes presents workshops and speaks on how to write your life story or memoir. She says,

> It's easy to research conferences now that their information is all online. When I started out I wanted to establish myself as a speaker, so I "paid my dues" by renting an exhibit booth at an expo. While I was there, I closely examined the expo program and dropped in to watch many other speakers. Then I put together a better presentation—a better PowerPoint, a livelier description, and a great title—one that ensured the expo organizers allowed me to speak at the next conference. (Since they'd met me already as a paying exhibitor, they were inclined to give me a chance.) Once I had my foot in the door at that expo, it gave me credibility when I applied to speak at other events. Now I keep a spreadsheet of ten conferences, and about ten book festivals, with dates a year and a half out, and I monitor their application deadlines using Google alerts to be sure I'm applying for each one.

Some books are conducive to sell at tradeshows. There are differences between conferences and tradeshows, however. Conferences are generally learning opportunities. People attend conferences in order to gain more knowledge, information, and resources on a particular topic. Typically, during the day, attendees sit in on presentations and workshops by professionals, experts, and others with experience in various aspects of the topic or field. There are often casual mixers and/or elegant dinners in the evening, sometimes accompanied by an awards program or an entertaining keynote address. There is generally a bookstore set up where attendees can purchase books by the speakers and workshop leaders. As an alternative, speakers will be provided a signing table separate from the bookstore for an hour or so after their presentations.

The Typical Tradeshow

Tradeshows, on the other hand, are more commercial than educational. This is where company representatives come to exhibit their products before the public. BookExpo America is the most well-known tradeshow for publishers and authors. You'll also find tradeshows related to health and fitness, agriculture, beauty, equestrians, gems, science, technology, the library industry, business, manufacturing, and travel. I have a client who might be able to sell copies of her travel memoir at a travel tradeshow. A book on inventors and inventions might do well at a manufacturing, technology, or business tradeshow. Another friend with a book on the best fishing spots in the west could benefit by attending a trade show related to fishing or outdoor sports.

Some tradeshows have a conference element to coincide with the show where educational opportunities take place. Most of the information about the products and services are promoted at the booths where hosts hand out materials and demonstrate their products. A tradeshow is similar to a book festival in that exhibitors spend the day either in their booths talking to visitors or walking around chatting it up with other exhibitors. Booth space is generally quite expensive at a tradeshow, depending on the size of the event. If you are an author of one or two books, you could save money and still have a great opportunity to showcase your book by sharing a booth with a related company.

My client with the travel memoir might get a spot in a booth with a major travel agency, an airline that flies to the destination of her story, or she might secure a booth with several other travel writers. How would a company owner benefit by allowing her space in the booth? She might attract potential customers that the reps aren't engaging. Someone is in the booth when the reps are out schmoozing.

An astute author will find out which booth would be most likely to attract her audience and which company reps could most use her assistance in their booth—handing out brochures and sample items, for example.

So how do you locate tradeshows? If you have a health and fitness book to promote, for example, do an Internet search using keywords: "health fair Montana," "health and fitness conference-Los Angeles," or "Phoenix health tradeshow."

Also, use these sites to search out appropriate speaking and exhibiting opportunities at conferences and tradeshows:

http://www.shawguides.com

http://www.allconferences.com

http://www.tsnn.com

http://www.eventseye.com

http://www.eventsinamerica.com

What Can You Expect as a Conference Presenter?

The application and acceptance process for conferences can vary. Most likely it will start with your email to the conference director. You'll include the following:

- Your name.
- Any of your affiliations related to the theme of the conference. For writer's conferences, I typically let the organizer know that I am the executive director of SPAWN.
- Your background in this industry/field, including information about your book(s).

- A couple of presentation ideas (based on the type of presentations they've offered in the past, what you can find out about their attendees, your expertise, etc.).
- A list of previous conferences in which you've participated.
- Your fee, if you typically get paid.
- Contact information.

You will receive one of the following: nothing in return (rude, isn't it?); an email putting you off—"We'll get back to you . . . "; a request for additional information; or (this is the one I love to receive) a gushing acceptance—"We are absolutely thrilled to have found out about you and would love, love, love to have you be one of our speakers." (Note, this response generally means, "We are rather desperate for speakers with any sort of credentials and we don't pay our speakers." However, it's awfully nice to receive such a welcome. It always makes me feel all warm and fuzzy.)

Nancy Barnes points out that every conference and expo is different. She says,

> They are competing to stand out. They need to keep their offerings fresh from year to year. So the more you have to offer, the more likely you are to be selected as a speaker. One conference organizer I contacted wanted to see up to ten proposals. I knew some competing speakers would be there, so I wanted to propose topics they couldn't cover. I submitted seven 100-word summaries (two were classes I hadn't even created yet) and guess which they chose? So, now I will develop those new classes, and I am sure I'll learn something new in the course of preparing! Good for me. All of my class proposals are squarely in my niche, which is self-publishing family history books and memoirs, so I am developing my

brand, no matter the topic. And these conferences give me good audiences—people who will be more likely to hire me, buy from me, and refer customers to me, as compared to people who meet me in other settings. It's worth developing new seminars to develop these kinds of contacts.

The next step in the process is the negotiation period. This could consist of their pronouncement that they do not pay their speakers and then silence while they wait for you to decide if you still want to do the gig.

They may offer you a free ride—all expenses paid, only the conference for free, or anything in between. In the world of writer's conferences, while I fall into a sweet, all-expenses or most-expenses paid deal once in a while, generally, I pay my way, get the conference and meals for free, and earn a small stipend ($100 to $300). (Read more about getting paid to speak in chapter 17.)

Keep in mind that I also sell books, get great exposure for myself, my books and my editorial business, and have the opportunity to meet potential clients. When I figure my conference expenses at the end of the year against fees I've collected for resulting client work and book sales, I always come out ahead. Plus, I enjoy the conference experience and working with new clients.

Beckwith agrees that conferences are a great way to get exposure. She says, "For me, it's never about book sales—it's always about exposure to a key audience that I'd like to help." However, she does have her standards. She explains,

> I evaluate each speaking invitation according to the time involved (travel to the west coast requires two extra days outside the speaking engagement), the estimated audience size, the audience itself, the financial offer from the organizers (do they pay for travel? a speaking fee? just waive the

conference registration?), and the income potential. I am less likely to travel across the country to do one workshop for thirty people than I am to be the keynote speaker for 500 or more—especially if the workshop invitation requires me to pay for my own travel. I could never sell enough books to make it worth my while to travel a great distance at my own expense, which is why book sales is not the motivator for me.

She adds, "I'm also influenced by the destination and whether it presents an opportunity to visit friends, and my projected workload at the time of the event."

According to Beckwith, "When I speak at writer's conferences, I am usually reimbursed for my travel expenses, don't have to pay the conference/event registration fee, and am often paid a speaking fee. For my humor book on men and my publicity books, I have nearly always received a speaking fee and been reimbursed for my travel expenses."

Some conferences operate on a shoestring and cannot afford to pay anyone except, perhaps, the keynote speaker. Others get generous donations from the business community and higher entrance fees and they can reimburse their presenters for travel expenses.

If you want to get paid or have your expenses paid, you need to seek out those conferences that operate on larger budgets. You'll also need to provide quality presentations. No conference organizer will hire someone with poor speaking skills to come and read passages from his novel. However, a conference director who is authorized to pay speakers might invite an author with unique qualifications, who has devised a meaningful and/or entertaining program for their proposed audience, to come and speak; but they have to know how to find you.

The third thing the conference organizer will ask you to do, once you have agreed on the particulars, is to send a brief bio they can use in promoting the conference and a description of your workshop or presentation. It is important to keep to their space requirements when writing your bio. If they want three lines, provide three lines offering the information most pertinent to those who will be attending this conference. Don't forget to include your contact information. I can't tell you how often I have asked for a bio for various reasons and the author neglects to include an email or website address.

The next step is to make arrangements for the trip and to secure a hotel room. If you will be flying, ask the organizer where the nearest airport is and what the shuttle accommodations are. Often, conference organizers will arrange for someone to pick you up at the airport. It's kind of cool to step off a plane and see someone standing there holding up a sign with your name on it. This is especially fun when you also see a chauffeur in full uniform standing there next to your guy, holding up a sign with the name of a celebrity. Then you go outside and watch that person slide into the backseat of a limo while you crawl into a dirty, dented Volkswagen with paperwork and sticky candy wrappers all over the floorboards.

It's incredibly more convenient if you can stay in the hotel where the conference is being held or within walking distance of the conference center. Generally, the organizers get a special rate for a block of rooms at the hotel where the conference is held or one nearby. Still, you can often locate a cheaper place to stay somewhere in the neighborhood. Depending on the transportation situation in this city, however, you could end up spending more than if you had stayed at the conference hotel. I goofed myself up one time by booking a cheaper motel a few miles away from the conference. The only transportation was a taxi service and it wasn't very reliable. I sorely missed having the luxury of running up to my room between sessions to freshen up or to pick up more handouts for the next workshop.

After you've been commissioned to speak at a conference, check the website every few weeks or so—more often, closer to the event.

You want to make sure your bio and workshop description are up and accurate. Find out something about the other speakers and their presentations. In some cases, this continues to change up until a few weeks of the conference. Contact the organizer with questions. One question you'll want to ask when you are a week to ten days ahead of the event is, "How many people do you expect?"

Sometimes the only figure they can give you is the total number of sign-ups for the conference. Attendees don't decide which sessions to attend until they arrive at the event. They can even bounce from one session to the other throughout the day. Other times, attendees make their workshop choices when they register, so the admissions person knows how many people signed up for each session.

A Workshop Versus a Speech

Some conferences are made up of all ninety-minute workshops. Others feature forty-five-minute sessions. What is the difference between a workshop, a presentation, and a keynote speech?

Typically, a workshop runs anywhere from one to four hours and involves audience participation. A workshop leader strives to teach a concept, skill, or process.

If you are asked to present a twenty to forty-five minute speech, there may be little time for much audience interaction beyond asking for a show of hands on certain points you will discuss. A speech might be informational, educational, inspirational, or simply entertaining.

The keynote speech is generally presented to the entire conference after an elegant dinner meal or to open the conference on the first day. A keynote address is usually entertaining, often humorous, and contains some poignant and/or otherwise meaningful stories and concepts. When I deliver a keynote address as the opener for a conference, I try to inspire the audience and encourage them to unite in their quest for information and material throughout the conference. I always offer a couple of tidbits and tips to help them enjoy and benefit from the event. I particularly want to instill in this audience that the success of the conference for the individual depends on what he or she is willing to put into it. I think this is an important point, but I don't dwell on it. If the conference has a slogan or a theme, I will work that into my talk and expand on it a bit so it resonates with the audience.

If it is the after-dinner keynote, the conference is usually half over. So I concentrate more on inspiring the audience to hold onto the feelings of excitement and encouragement that have been generated by the conference presenters and activities once they get back home to their writing projects. My goal is to inspire, entertain, and, of course, create a sense of unity.

I've listened to many keynote speakers, and one thing I appreciate in their delivery is their ability to bond with the audience. To know that the speaker understands our concerns and challenges and can relate to our situation is bonding and comforting. From this base, the speaker can generally motivate his or her audience through his or her message.

Some keynote speakers share stories from their own experiences. If they have a knack for storytelling, this can be wonderfully entertaining.

Many conferences have book festivals in conjunction with them. Sometimes it is a book festival with a conference aspect. Either way, if you get a speaking assignment at one of these conferences, be sure to ask if you can have a free booth to display your book(s).

How to Get Your Materials to the Site

It is cumbersome to travel by air with books in your suitcase. I did it once—never again. Do you know how much those things weigh? Handouts and books that are not packed securely can get scratched, scuffed, dented, and creased. There's always the lost-luggage concern. So what is an author to do?

If you're flying to the conference, ship your books ahead and catch up with them later. Generally, you can send books to the bookstore in charge of sales for the event, the hotel that is hosting the event, or an individual—the organizer, for example. Send handouts ahead as well. I would probably not send the handouts to the bookseller, but package them up separately and ship them to the hotel or to an individual.

Some organizers will copy your handouts and have them fresh and ready for you when you arrive. Just be courteous enough to send your computer file for the handouts in plenty of time so as not to inconvenience the conference staff. Once I was charged a fee for copies. Typically, the staff will do this gratis.

If your book is with a publishing house, arrange for the publisher to ship books to the site. Now, I've heard horror stories about books not arriving in time for important events, thus selling opportunities lost. So request the shipment far enough in advance and then follow up to make sure it goes out on time.

Carry with you one or two copies of your book and a copy of each of your handouts. Bring a thumb drive with the handouts on it just in case there were any problems with the handouts arriving or with getting copies made.

I usually pack my business cards and brochures in my travel bag. But you could send them ahead, as well.

What if your books don't sell out at the conference? If your publisher arranged for the shipment of books to the conference bookstore, the bookseller will handle returns. If you delivered or shipped the books, most likely, the bookseller will require that you pick up unsold books at the close of the conference. Sometimes you can convince the bookseller to take the books on consignment—especially if the book sold well at the conference. As an enticement, promise to do some additional promotion in the area to bring customers in.

If there are just a few books left, I will put them in a tote bag or in my luggage for the flight home. Sometimes, I make arrangements to donate leftover books to a local library. On a few occasions, when I had quite a few books left over, I was able to pack up the books, leave a check with the conference organizer or a volunteer, and have them shipped back to me at a later date.

You may wonder how book sales are handled at conferences. There are several scenarios. A local bookstore owner might come in and handle all book sales. Anyone wanting an autograph will come seek you out to get it. In some cases, you are provided a table in a separate room or a hallway where you can sign books for thirty minutes or so following your presentation. Some conferences are held in conjunction with a book festival or an expo and you can either rent or you are issued a booth from which you can sell books throughout the day when you are not presenting.

Your Amazing Handouts

Handouts are an important part of a conference workshop or other presentation. They afford you (the presenter) the opportunity to connect on another, more tangible level with your audience members. Conference attendees generally expect handouts, and you should want to offer them. Why? In order to give additional information, to reiterate some of the material you shared during your workshop, and to provide your contact information.

Margaret Brownley is a fan of using handouts when she speaks on behalf of her novels. She says,

> I read somewhere that people judge a speech by the quality of the handouts. For this reason I always provide a professional

handout with valuable information." In case you're wondering what sort of information an author of fiction might compile, here's how she does it: "The type of handouts depend on the audience. For readers, I often pass out a list of little-known facts involving the town and/or time period of my current book. I did a fun one on Tombstone, for example. The heroine of my March release is a dime novelist and I'm currently working on a dime novel fact sheet. Readers love to learn something and a handout helps them remember you and your books.

She says that for teens, "I might include places that accept poems, short stories, or run contests for teens. For high school career day, I passed out a list of writer-related fields and colleges. For writers, my handouts might include my favorite research sites. If I'm giving a talk on, say, dialogue I might include examples of dialogue from my book."

What is your ultimate goal as a conference speaker or workshop leader? Most likely, you want to sell books. But you also want to gain more name recognition as you continue to establish yourself as an expert in your field. Perhaps you also offer consulting services or some other business related to the theme of your book—you're an accountant, dog groomer, virtual landscaper, psychic, editor, or financial advisor, for example. Add this information to your handouts.

Handouts might include your name, contact information, website address, bio, title and brief description of your book, and description of your services. Also provide information and resources for your students/audience members. Including resources in your handouts will save time during the presentation. Instead of having to repeat pertinent information and key websites and wait for people to write them down, you can just say, "This information is on your handout."

I like to provide examples for my students/attendees. If I talk about query letters, book proposals, pitch letters, tip sheets, or press releases, I might offer samples of these documents as part of my hand-out material.

I recommend that you offer audience members an open email policy. I do and I remind my audiences and customers frequently that if they have a question or concern, they can email me at any time. Unfortunately for them, few do.

That's why I further suggest that you pass around a sign-up sheet during your session. People sometimes balk at randomly giving out their email addresses. So make sure to have a good reason for them to sign up—you are offering something they want in return, for example. It might be a subscription to your newsletter, a digital booklet on the topic of your presentation, a directory of resources that are meaningful to this audience, or a report. I also mention that I will let them all know when my next book is out.

Send the gifts out as soon as you return home and then file away the email addresses (or put them in your address book) and use them when you have something to announce related to the topic or a new product to sell.

Carol Dean Schreiner suggests this: "When speaking, have people drop their business cards into a basket. Before your session is over, draw a card and give one of your books away to the winner. Now you have the contact information for all of those people in your audience."

Sample Contact Letter

Your initial contact letter is generally in email form. Here's basically what I send as an introduction:

Dear Ms. (or Mr.) Conference Organizer:

I'd like to inquire about a speaking position at your conference next year in October. As you can see from my résumé (attached), I am a working writer and have been involved in writing and publishing for nearly forty years. In fact, I've supported myself through writing/publishing endeavors for the last twenty-five years. I have been presenting workshops, speaking, and delivering the keynote speech at conferences and other writers' events since the mid 1990s. (View a partial list of conferences in the attached résumé.)

Having established my own freelance writing business in 1973, and my publishing company in 1983, my expertise is in the business side of writing. I typically work with authors and freelance writers who want to publish their works as opposed to those who are writing for fun.

I am the author of thirty-six books and the executive director of SPAWN (Small Publishers, Artists, and Writers Network), a sixteen-year-old networking organization for anyone who is interested in publishing.

Please review the attached bio and let me know if you're interested in one of my programs (listed below) or if you have any questions.

Sincerely,
Patricia Fry
www.patriciafry.com
www.matilijapress.com
www.spawn.org

Sample Résumé or Bio

Patricia Fry has been writing for publication since 1973, having contributed over a thousand articles to about 300 different magazines.

She has 36 books to her credit, including *Publish Your Book, Proven Strategies and Resources for the Enterprising Author; Promote Your Book, Over 250 Proven, Low-Cost Tips and Techniques for the Enterprising Author; How to Write a Successful Book Proposal in 8 Days or Less; A Writer's Guide to Magazine Articles*, and *The Author's Repair Kit*.

Her articles have appeared in *Writer's Digest Magazine, Entrepreneur, Woman's Life, Authorship, Freelance Writer's Report, Canadian Author, IBPA Independent, Writer's Journal, Cat Fancy, Your Health,* and many, many others.

Patricia is the Executive Director of SPAWN (Small Publishers, Artists, and Writers Network), a sixteen-year-old networking organization for anyone interested in the publishing business. (http://www.spawn.org.) She also writes the popular monthly *SPAWN Market Update*.

On behalf of SPAWN and her own publishing pursuits, she attends approximately a half dozen book festivals each year and she's guest speaker/workshop leader or keynote speaker at anywhere from 5 to 10 writing/publishing-related conferences and other events annually. Past venues include the Much Ado About Books event in Jacksonville, FL; a National Association of Women Writers (NAWW) conference in Arlington, TX; the St. Louis Writers Guild Conference and Book Festival in St. Louis, MO (two consecutive years); the Pen Women Conference in Honolulu; the PNWA Conference in Seattle; the Wisconsin Regional Writers Association Conference in Janesville, WI; Spring Book Show and Writers Conference in Atlanta (two consecutive years); the San Diego State University Writers' Conference (several consecutive years); and several others throughout the U.S. She was the lead speaker at the SPAN Publishing Conference in 2006. In May of that year, she was the first woman ever to be invited to give the keynote speech at a Toastmasters Convention in the Middle East. She spoke before 800 Toastmasters in Dubai.

While some of her books have been published by traditional publishers, Patricia established her own publishing company, Matilija Press, in 1983, before self-publishing was fashionable.

She is a full-time freelance writer and author and she also provides editorial services such as editing, as well as assistance writing book proposals, self-publishing, and book promotion. Learn more about her books and services at http://www.matilijapress.com and http://www.patriciafry.com. Visit her informative publishing blog daily: http://www.matiljapress.com/publishingblog.

Speaking/Workshop topics include:

- Two Steps to Successful Publishing
- How to Write a Killer Book Proposal
- Publishing is Not an Extension of Your Writing
- Book Promotion for the Bold and the Bashful
- How to Get Your Book Reviewed Many Times Over
- How to Promote Your Book Through Magazine Articles
- The Anatomy of a Nonfiction Magazine Article
- How to Break into Magazine Article Writing
- Platform-Building Techniques and Tips

Appropriate conferences and tradeshows provide great venues for reaching and teaching your book's audience. If you want to gain more credibility in your field or become more well-known in your genre, consider addressing your potential readers where they congregate with like-minded people. If the topic of your book is timely and pertinent, you'll surely benefit at least as much as they will.

Use Your Personality to Sell Books at Book Festivals

Have you ever sat in a booth behind a display of your very own books at a book festival, greeting visitors in hopes that they will make a purchase? How many times have you walked away after a book festival despondent because you are toting most of the books you came with? Did you vow never to pay for space at a book festival again? It doesn't have to end this way.

Book festivals present exceptional opportunities for authors, but you have to do your part. For many of you, this means changing your outlook and your approach.

What is your main objective when you reserve space at a book festival? Most authors say, "To sell enough books to make it worth my while." They want to break even financially and then some. And that pretty much sums it up.

Have you ever considered the side-benefits to participating in a book festival? There's exposure, of course. If you stay in the game and continue promoting your book to your audience for the long-term, exposure can lead to sales. Exposure is more valuable than many authors know. There are people who purchase books on the spot. But there are many others who don't buy a book they actually want until they've seen it, heard about it, and/or read about it numbers of times.

Exposure can garner other advantages, as well—some that the author may not consider as such even in the face of the opportunity. Let's say that your book features unusual gifts you can make for under $25. You might meet a stringer for a home and garden, country, or craft magazine who would love to interview you for an article. A librarian might want to include your children's book in her summer reading program. A small business owner might see your book on office organization and hire you as a consultant. Likewise, an organization or corporate leader might take your card and call you several weeks or months after the event to order two boxes of your business management book for her employees.

Exposure is not typically a one-shot opportunity. Very often, there are ongoing and far-reaching effects resulting from exposure. Authors often say to me, "I did a book festival once. Didn't sell many books. Won't be doing that again."

I will sometimes ask the author, "Did you meet anyone interesting at the book festival?"

She might say, "Not really."

I'll say, "I almost always meet someone who offers me an opportunity of some sort."

The author might then reply, "Oh yes—there was this guy who came by my booth. He gave me his card—what did I do with that? He said that he was in charge of buying goodie-bag gifts for conventions and he wanted me to give him a bulk discount price. I guess I forgot to contact him."

Hellllooooo! That's called an opportunity.

Some authors recognize the opportunities that occur at book festivals and still don't consider book festivals worth attending. I know one author who met the producer of a syndicated radio show who wanted to put him on the air with his book. Another one met a man who later filmed a documentary around the theme of his book. That documentary still airs regularly on the military channel.

New authors ask me what to expect at a book festival. I have attended around sixty or seventy book festivals over the years—large ones like the Los Angeles Times Festival of Books and small, local book fairs. Each of them seems to have a personality of its own. The thing is, you just don't know what to expect at a book festival. One year, you might sell numbers of books and meet up with many opportunities, and the next year at the same event, you may sit alone for most of the day and sell nothing.

I've seen authors turn what could have been "nothing" days into good days. How?

- The author engages people as they walk past her booth. If she has a children's book, she might say, "Do you know a child who likes to read?" She may also ask parents with children, "May I read a short story to your child?" Try this and you *will* sell copies of your charming children's book.

- When someone seems interested in a book, the author talks to the visitor about benefits not features. (What can the book do for the potential reader?) This often means reaching out to the potential customer to learn more about his experience related to the theme of your book or his level of expertise or interest. I often ask, "Are you a writer?" Then I learn something about where this individual is in the process of writing a book or considering writing a book or promoting a book, for example. I am better able to address his particular needs when I know something about him and his current challenges.

- The author knows how to listen. Sometimes the visitor just wants to tell his story or rant about his experiences related to the theme of your book. If your book addresses some of the issues he brings up, let him know this and he may become a customer.

- If there is nothing happening—it's a really slow day—the author might walk around the event with his book and show it to other book festival participants. I often sell copies of my publishing/book promotion-related books to other authors at book festivals.

- Authors who maintain a good attitude even when things seem slow will sell more books than those who appear disgruntled. This is so true. I've "womanned" the SPAWN booth at various book festivals for over fifteen years and I've watched many members pitch their books. I've noticed that when an author becomes discouraged and allows it to show in his or her demeanor, people lose interest in his or her books rather quickly.

Book festivals (sometimes referred to as *book fairs*) are held generally in the spring and fall. However, I've also attended book festivals in the summer and winter months. While most book festivals are held out-of-doors, those occurring during possible bad weather are sometimes held inside large auditoriums, hotels, church halls, or convention centers.

A booth at a book festival will cost anywhere from $50 to $1,000. The larger the fee, generally, the more people in attendance. There's always the possibility that you can share a booth with one or more other authors. This can be fun and, when the booth fee is high, a bit more lucrative.

It has been my observation that people are more inclined to stop at a booth where there are a variety of books to browse through. Many are attracted by books with great covers, which is something you should consider way before you publish. People do judge a book by its cover. This doesn't mean that everyone who expresses an interest in a pretty book will purchase it, but they certainly will not buy a book they don't even notice.

I've watched authors sit behind books with dull, uninteresting covers all day long at book festivals, and not get one iota of interest from the public. Some books attract people like magnets, make them smile or even laugh out loud. Sometimes it's the title that creates interest. However, those books most inclined to attract people have covers that are colorful, pleasing to the eye, touching, eye-catching, beautiful, creative, or simply *wow*. The book festival isn't the only venue where the cover matters. Keep this in mind if you are currently in the planning stages of a book. Some book covers are so bad that I would advise the authors to rip them off of all remaining books and have the books rebound with a more professional cover.

Tips for a More Successful Book Festival Experience

Perhaps you've had a bad experience at a book festival. Consider the information in this chapter, reevaluate the situation, and maybe you'll gain important insight into what went wrong. You may be inclined to blame the location of your booth or a lack of appropriate advertising for the event. Certainly these things can be factors; but don't give up on book festivals altogether. I want you to consider more seriously what you could have done to make lemonade out of lemons.

Start by choosing a book festival that will attract your readers. If your book features the history of a small community in Connecticut, you probably won't find many customers in Texas. But you'll definitely want to exhibit your book at local book fairs and flea markets.

If you partner with one or more other authors, make sure your books are compatible. I once shared a booth with the author of children's books and mysteries. The signage on the front of the booth and the description that went into the festival program reported that this booth had children's books and mysteries. No one came into our booth in search of a metaphysical adventure or a book on how to establish a freelance writing career. Thus, I sold no books that year at the Los Angeles Times Festival of Books.

Typically, I sell dozens of my books on publishing and book promotion from the SPAWN booth at this book festival and many others because the SPAWN booth attracts authors and hopeful authors.

Some authors lack people skills. If you aren't naturally outgoing and you hate the thought of hawking or pitching your book, either forget about participating in any but, perhaps, small hometown book fairs and flea markets, or get some help. The theme of this book is that personality sells books, and this is especially true at book festivals.

Yes, you can quit, if you want. But, I would much rather encourage you to learn how to use that personality of yours to reach out and engage your potential customers. You don't have to become unnaturally flamboyant. Just be friendly and real. If you have a passion for the theme of your book, let it show.

What will you gain if you hang in there and try a few more book festivals using a more sociable persona? You'll meet like-minded people; you'll learn something more about your field or genre; you'll possibly receive some amazing opportunities; and, oh yes, you'll sell books.

Have I told you about Toastmasters? Another very good reason to join, and the reason why many people join every year, is to learn how to communicate more effectively in everyday situations. Toastmasters (as well as other speaker training programs) can help you to do a better job of pitching your book. What you'll learn is that it isn't a matter of pushing your book on people; it's a matter of communicating with them and engaging them in conversation that can lead to book sales.

I watched a woman in the SPAWN booth at a major book festival last year way outsell everyone else in the booth. The premise of her children's book is to encourage kids to eat their vegetables. First, she had a colorful, attractive book with a charming dog as the main character. She was creative in decorating her booth space. She greeted everyone who came by, paying particular attention to children and their parents. She was friendly, enthusiastic, and never seemed to tire of expressing enormous passion for her book. Her excitement spilled over onto booth visitors. Sometimes families would be standing three deep listening to her chat about the story in her book, the dog, character, or the reason why she wrote the book. She was naturally and charmingly energetic. She may have been displaying the personality she was born with, but I believe a better, brighter personality can be developed when someone is highly motivated.

So what do I suggest? Speaker training, of course. But also attend book festivals, trade shows, and flea markets. Notice the displays and the demeanor of the people in the booths, and key in on what seems to draw people to certain booths.

How to Prepare for a Book Festival

As for the mundane details: bring change, credit card slips (or a credit card reader for your iPhone, iPad, or Android), pencils/pens, posters, brochures/advertising, postcards/business cards, tape, book bags, sign-up sheets, a clipboard, book stands, table cloth, handouts, give-aways, decorations (some people bring a vase of flowers), chairs, and plenty of books to sell. Find out if there will be food booths. Bring water and snacks, just in case you have trouble getting away from your booth to eat.

Before hauling all of this stuff to the event, check to see what is being provided. Often it is tables, a booth cover or umbrella (for outdoor events), tablecloth, and two chairs. Sometimes you can pay extra for electricity. In this case, you might want to bring a digital picture frame or laptop on which to show your book trailer or photos from the book. We like to bring an extra fold-up camp table to go in the back of a large booth and a tablecloth to cover it. Once, on a very hot weekend, the day was saved when the husband of a booth-mate brought us an electric fan.

If you plan to do book festivals and speaking engagements, you might want to invest in a small hand truck (dolly) or a small suitcase on wheels. A light-weight, fold-up hand truck will cost you anywhere from $30 to $150.

Book bags (tote bags) are also a nice touch. Order a quantity with your publishing company name, logo, or image of your book on them. You can also buy plastic or paper bags for purchases.

As far as the number of books to bring: I would carry in fifteen or twenty books, leaving another twenty-five or so in the car. The number of books you sell will depend on the type of book you have and, of course, the nature and interests of the attendees. You might sell zero books or 100.

If your book isn't a huge draw, consider bringing in something that will create more interest. I've seen authors post a large paint-by-number picture and invite people to add to it with colored markers. One author I know had a crossword puzzle enlarged to an enormous size and passersby took turns working on it. Of course, while these things are going on, the author is chatting with the visitors and, when appropriate, telling them about his book.

Have a jar full of pennies or candies and ask people to guess how many there are. The winner takes all. Have a drawing for a book or something else of value to readers—a light or a book for their Kindle or Nook, for example.

Provide a sign-up sheet. Promise a free ebook to those who sign up.

Advertise your book as a great gift for Father's Day, Valentine's Day, or whatever holiday is near. Have a sign indicating that you will discount your book for the festival, offer a free gift with each purchase, and/or gift-wrap the book.

These are what I call icebreakers, and they provide a good opening for conversation. But you need to train yourself to continue onward toward a sales pitch. For example, say, "I'm running a special today, the book is discounted by twenty percent and I will gift wrap it for free." Or, "You get a chance to win this book bag (book light, gift certificate, etc.) with each purchase."

Come up with something that will invite a response. As I said, when I see someone pick up one of my books, I often ask, "Are you a writer?"

The potential customer then tells me, "I'm thinking about writing a book," "I just finished writing a book," or "I am trying to promote a book . . ."

Upon hearing this, the ball is in my court. I might say, "Tell me about your project." The conversation moves forward from there. Often, the booth visitor reveals a problem, concern, or challenge he can't overcome—finding a publisher, choosing a publishing option, selling books, getting his book into bookstores, etc. If he doesn't mention a problem, I will ask, "How are things going?" Most authors, especially if they have stopped to review one of my self-help books for authors, are facing some sort of publishing or book promotion challenge. I usually have an answer for him. I give what I can on the spot and then refer to a section in one of my books that covers the topic in more detail. I've sold many, many books using this method. In case you missed the point of it, let me give you the condensed version.

1. I notice someone picking up or thumbing through one of my books.

2. I wait for a few seconds and, if he doesn't ask me a question, I ask, "Are you a writer?"

3. I listen to his response and then I express an interest in his project.

4. If he asks a question or reveals a problem he is having, I offer a generous amount of information and maybe some resources or, at least, some direction.

5. I then point out the large amount of information and resources in my book on that and other topics he will need to study.

In other words, engage the booth visitor, express an interest in his work, detect a problem, respond generously to the problem, and then pitch your book, which promises to provide even more information and solutions.

I've observed that novels and poetry books by unknown authors (such as you and me) are more difficult to sell in a book festival setting. I've seen novelists and poets sit behind their books for two days straight and never sell one. I've also watched as unknown novelists and poets autographed a dozen books for booth visitors within a few hours. What made the difference?

Authors who sell more copies of their novels have a couple of things going for them. They have an enticing title, an attractive cover, and their book is in a popular genre. Plus, they know how to talk with people about their books. They're friendly and engaging.

One poetry book author stands out in my memory. She shared the SPAWN booth with us at the Los Angeles Times Festival of Books several years ago. She didn't sell many books all morning. Around noon, however, she began reaching out to visitors. She drew their attention to her book and began engaging them in conversation about poetry.

Many of them agreed to either read a poem or listen while the author read from her book. By one-thirty, she had sold a dozen copies.

About that time, her husband showed up and they began working in tandem. He would attract customers and lead them over to where she was sitting, and she would clinch the sale. By the end of the day, she had autographed thirty copies of her poetry book. And remember, poetry is one of the hardest types of books to sell.

I don't remember what their sales pitch was, but I'm pretty sure they had a one- or two-sentence spiel that they used to get potential customers' attention.

I recommend to authors of all types of books that, early on, they come up with a one-or two-sentence description of their book. Not only will this help them to write their synopsis and their introduction, it will go a long way toward helping them discuss their book with others. I further suggest that authors create a thirty-second "commercial" to use in pitching their book to agents, publishers, and potential readers.

This may take some practice. Authors sometimes require the assistance of an editor or someone practiced in book promotion to put something coherent and descriptive together. How can you use the descriptive sentences and the elevator speech? It may help you design more effective back cover, press release, and website copy. But it is also valuable in pitching your book to potential customers such as those you meet at a book festival. (Read more about the thirty-second commercial in chapter sixteen.)

There's a lot you can do to entice sales, but your main asset is your personality and your communication skills. So, again, I suggest that if you are lacking in these areas—get help.

When You Go on the
Airwaves—Radio and TV

Do you listen to talk radio? Have you noticed that practically all of the guests on every show, no matter their topic, have books? A book has become as common to a professional as a business card used to be, and it is used as casually.

Whether I am listening to a talk radio program or watching one on TV related to spirituality, religion, parenting, politics, relationships, health, hoarding, the economy, or some aspect of self-help, every guest seems to be promoting a book on the subject. In most cases, however, these individuals did not speak on the topic until they came out with their books. They were not considered experts in their fields until they became authors. Now the former bank associate is doing radio interviews and TV appearances to talk about her book on childhood abuse, the chef shares his book of kitchen tips, the retired accountant travels around talking about his novel, and the factory worker is promoting her true crime book.

Yes, there seems to be a real flood of authors guesting on every talk show around. Do you wonder how they get the invitations? Even more importantly, do these appearances on radio and TV sell books?

Most authors, when they're planning a book, expect to appear on TV shows like *Good Morning America, Live With Kelly, The Talk, Ellen DeGeneres Show, The Daily Show, The View,* and some of the popular talk radio programs. Some of you will make it happen. These opportunities, however, are generally out of reach for most of us. Remember, we're the unknown authors.

Please don't let this discourage you from ever trying to get the major publicity available. You might have written the book of the century—one that is of great interest to a large viewing audience. Sure you already believe this describes your book, but only a scant few of you are correct in your evaluation. The rest of us are delusional. This doesn't exempt you from getting publicity via radio and TV, however. Not at all. Most cities of any size support one or more radio stations and often they have at least some talk shows scheduled throughout the day and night. You probably don't have to travel too far to locate a TV station with shows that host authors at least occasionally; and don't discount public radio and TV stations.

I write within a strict niche, as many of you do. Yet, I've appeared on TV in Alaska and California. I've been interviewed numerous times on regular and public radio in many cities and blog talk radio (on the Internet). I have to tell you that being interviewed for radio or TV is a different experience from standing up and speaking to a group of people. In fact, most often (for radio) you give the interview from your home office (or wherever you happen to be) by phone. I've heard authors being interviewed while waiting for a flight, vacationing with family, recuperating from surgery, and I'm sure some of them were still in their jammies. We've all seen people appear remotely on TV programs, as well. Skype is one technology that makes it possible for guests to appear on a TV station in Los Angeles from a remote location in another city or country.

Raven West has done a few radio interviews with regard to her nonfiction book, but says, "Fiction is a totally different animal. Unless you're a 'name,' it's very difficult to book yourself." But she adds, "I do know that after I've done a radio interview, either in studio or over the phone, sales of my books do increase. I'll do pretty much whatever I need to in order to promote book sales and increase my fan base."

Speaking to a radio audience is different because you can't see or hear them. If you are accustomed to receiving feedback by way of facial expressions, applause, and body language, keep in mind that this medium does not afford these benefits.

How do you locate radio and TV interview opportunities? You're probably familiar with some of the talk shows in your region. This is a good place to start. Check their websites for instructions for becoming a guest and follow the guidelines. Call and talk to the program director. If you speak to someone by phone, I suggest standing tall during the conversation, speaking clearly and as animated and friendly as your book topic dictates. The program director may be evaluating your voice and manner even during your initial contact. So put your best foot (or speaking voice) forward.

Do an Internet search for additional radio and TV stations. Study directories such as *Gale Directory of Publications and Broadcast Media* or *Literary Market Place,* and books such as Fran Silverman's *Talk Radio Wants You, An Intimate Guide to 700 Shows and How to Get Invited.* Also, consider getting listed with GuestFinder (http://www.guestfinder. com) or *Radio-TV Interview Report* or *The Radio Book* (see the Resource List in chapter 18).

Kim Dower is a literary publicist and media coach. She runs an agency called Kim-from-L.A. She says,

> I work with a variety of authors and all kinds of books, getting them exposure through various types of media from radio, television, and print interviews to social and viral media outlets. I offer whatever they need in order to help prepare them for speeches, presentations, book signings—any situation where they find themselves in front of a camera, a microphone, or an audience.

Dower is in agreement that "An author's presentation is key to promoting their book. Successful authors know how to promote their books, and this is a skill that can be learned. The key is to get readers/listeners/viewers turned on and excited by the ideas in the book and the passion and enthusiasm of the author." She says, however, that,

> with hundreds of thousands of books coming out each year and only so many media spaces available, you can imagine the odds aren't in the author's favor. The first category of people to get booked on shows is always celebrities. Always was and always will be.
>
> The next is breaking news and politics. What's the latest disaster and what talking head can address it? "Softer" topics—biographies, self-help, fiction—come way, way down on the list. And we need a valuable "hook" to get these authors booked. How does their topic fit into what's going on the world today—now? What makes this author or their topic relevant? If the topic is strong and timely and the author is a great presenter and the book is provocative, we have half a chance of getting on the show.

According to Dower,

> Getting on smaller radio and TV shows is more realistic, but still difficult. An author needs a good, short pitch—one paragraph to describe the topic and why the author has the credentials or expertise to talk about it. And why is this topic important?" She also likes to challenge authors to "offer three provocative or newsworthy questions that they will answer during the interview.

Dower says,

> Besides an author preparing his/her bullet points—the things they will say no matter what—it's also really important to know the show/host/station and the demographic of the audience. Who is listening/watching? You will give a different kind of interview to an audience of eighteen to twenty-five year olds than you would to those thirty-five to sixty. What is the host like? Do they do a fast banter type of morning drive show or is it more thoughtful? So, 1) know your audience, 2) know the three things you want to say no matter what is asked, and 3) know how to control the interview. The worst things you can do," according to Dower, "is either give one-word answers (yes, no), stop talking or not know how to engage and be engaging. Talking, nonstop is also frowned upon. It's boring and puts everyone to sleep.

So what makes for a successful media appearance? Dower says, "Enthusiasm and passion and energy; delivering a few 'take-aways'—some real tangible information that is new and interesting; leaving the audience with enough to make them like you and be interested in your book." But she cautions, "Don't give so much away that they have no reason to purchase it."

Dower suggests using the Internet to find radio stations across the country that have talk shows. She says, "Research and listen to the show. Don't try to get on a show you know nothing about."

Prepare for Your Author Appearances *Now*

As I said earlier, it is possible to conduct an interview from home in your robe and bunny slippers or bathing suit and flip flops. I recommend dressing, however, and standing tall—no slouching. If you look professional, you will feel and act more professional. When you stand, or at least sit up, you will come across sounding more alert. Smile—it will come through in your voice.

Barbara Florio-Graham suggests preparing for a telephone interview with a radio or blog talk radio show host this way:

> Don't use a cell phone during the interview. If you do telephone interviews often, invest in a headset. Make sure pets are comfortable in another room. I use post-it notes or other page tabs to mark the pages of my book that I might want to refer to and I print out the table of contents for easy reference. I have a page of notes based on the questions sent by the host earlier and I continually make notes so I will remember things I want to comment on."

I work along the same lines as Florio-Graham. I never ever use a cell phone, unless I happen to be traveling and there is no other way. I always request the host's list of questions or the topics he/she hopes to cover with me. I might also offer to send the host my suggested questions or line of questioning. They often appreciate that gesture.

During the interview, I make a lot of notes. Sometimes radio show hosts get involved in long narratives. By the time they finally come up with a question for you, you may have forgotten some of the things you wanted to comment on.

Jot down one- or two-word reminders. Don't get so involved in writing notes that you neglect to listen to the host. You never know when a question will come up and your full attention is required. Have a bottle or glass of water nearby in case your throat gets dry.

While I suggest preparing thoroughly, there are simply some things that you cannot prepare for. Here is a story from my radio show history file. I was contacted by an Internet radio show host who wanted me to "appear" on his show. Of course, I agreed. Remember, I learned a long time ago to always say, "yes."

The day of the show, I realized I hadn't heard from the host for a few weeks and I wanted to make sure we were still on. I emailed him. A few hours later, he responded by saying, "Yes, we're on for 12:30 this afternoon." (In a scant twenty minutes.) That's when he told me the agenda. He said, "I will introduce you and then you take it from there. At exactly 1:15, I will break in and sign off." What? I was supposed to just speak without a host asking me any questions? And I had twenty minutes to prepare?

Believe it or not, I nailed it. I managed to give a coherent presentation with a beginning, middle, and end that I felt was extremely useful and informative to my audience. If someone had measured my stress level during the first few minutes of that "interview," it would have been off the charts. Once I got in the groove, however, I did just fine. How does one succeed when given such a test?

When you are prepared—you know your material and you're comfortable presenting it under normal circumstances—the rest is all attitude. If you're thrown a curve like this—you're expected to perform at a moment's notice, for example—just adopt your best "can-do" attitude and meet the challenge head on.

Brian Jud is quite familiar with the concept of using TV to promote books. He says,

> When I published my first title, *Job Search 101*, I wanted to promote it as a guest on television shows. However, I knew nothing about performing on TV. So I took some media training and then went to my local cable television system with the idea that I would host a show for thirteen weeks (the minimum they allowed) to practice.
>
> The name of my first show was *Job Search 101*. I chose that name to get the word out about my book. Since it was public access television, I was not permitted to be commercial. So I used the name of the show and used my books as props to get as much exposure as I could.

According to Jud,

> getting your own TV show on cable television is not difficult. I created a storyboard for thirteen shows and took a three-week mandatory course offered for free by the cable network. Once completed, I arranged for a director, sound engineer, and a person to operate the character generator and camera operators, all through the cable network.
>
> I was responsible for finding guests to appear on the show. That was not difficult. I always had a waiting list. After a few years of hosting *Job Search 101*, I changed the name of my show to *The Book Authority* and began interviewing authors, publishers, designers, etc.—all people

in the publishing industry. In total, I have produced/hosted about 750 shows. In fact, it remains the longest continuously running cable TV show in Connecticut.

Additionally, I have been a guest on over 1,200 television and radio shows.

Karen Stevens is no stranger to local radio and television, either. She was the host for the *Pet of the Week* program on KEYT Channel Three in Santa Barbara, California for several years. Each week, she'd pick up a different cat, dog, or bunny from a local animal shelter, bring the animal to the show, and introduce him or her to her audience. She says,

> I felt that the exposure on local television and radio was invaluable to me as an author as it increased my visibility and credibility in the community. Many news people approached me for stories they were working on about animals because I had written a book about animals and they considered me an "expert." During my *Pet of the Week* segments, I would occasionally get to plug my book and we would have a book giveaway from time to time, which always resulted in a lot of calls to the station.

It's hard to predict which books will be of interest to radio and television show hosts and what sort of connections you might make as you continue your quest for exposure. But knowing the potential for book sales through radio and TV, it seems reasonable that you would pursue this avenue of book promotion with some gusto.

Viable Virtual Speaking Opps

Most authors will be interviewed for Blog Talk Radio, podcasts, webinars, teleseminars, and so forth at some point during their promotional efforts.

The first thing you'll want to know is, are these forms of promotion worthwhile? It depends on who you talk to. The problem is that sales and other benefits from some of these publicity methods are difficult or impossible to track. According to Margaret Brownley, "I've done a couple of webinars and teleseminars, but I don't think these necessarily result in book sales, perhaps because they tend to be less personal. They do, however, increase name recognition, the importance of which can't be discounted."

There you go; again with the *exposure* routine. Name recognition is certainly a benefit to any author who wants to sell books.

I recommend to authors: even before your book is a book, become acquainted with and known through appropriate websites. I've been saying this since before the popularity and ease of doing podcasts, webinars, etc. I continue to advise authors to seek out book reviews and interview opportunities throughout the Internet. So what is actually available, and how can authors benefit?

First, study websites related to your topic or genre and discover how you can become involved. Remember, their visitors are your readers. Is there a newsletter that you can contribute to or place announcements in? Do they review books, interview authors, feature recommended books, or run a speakers bureau? Perhaps they record interviews with authors and post them at their sites. Once you have taken advantage of book promotion opportunities at some of the more obvious and even obscure websites in your field or genre, shift your attention to the world of social media.

Basic Social Media

Everyone is using social media today for personal and business purposes. While social media connections are generally made in writing (except for, perhaps, YouTube) I thought it useful to mention this extremely popular medium. You can, as a matter of fact, incorporate photographs and even videos into your social media messages and at your own web-site. (More about this in a moment.)

Most of you reading this are set up to communicate with your readers through Facebook, LinkedIn, Twitter, and so forth. You may (and should) have a blog. For those of you who don't know, a blog is a web log that you can use to share information, stories, snippets from your life as an author, and announcements for new books, scheduled speeches, and so forth. It is a way to communicate with your readers. Not only can you have your own blog, but you can comment at or be interviewed on other blogs related to your book theme or genre. This puts you before a whole new group of potential customers.

When you become a nonfiction author, you are also considered an expert in your field. People want to read what you write and hear what you have to say. Why not add to your professional credibility by seeking interview opportunities at websites that feature podcasts, webinars, Blog Talk Radio, and so forth?

Carol Sanford, author and public speaker, actively uses social media to help land her speaking gigs. She says,

> My contrarian but positive spirit is one of my two greatest assets in the social media space, as well as bringing a truly unique perspective and doing so boldly. The other is my very unique offerings on very important subjects which intrigue people immediately and draw them to me. I make these offerings evident in all of my tweets. I also have a blog where I promote others, who then tend to come see who I am and do the same in return. One of those led to a speaking gig. I have a YouTube channel and it has gotten me some speaking opportunities. People can see and "feel" me when they can hear and see me. My Amazon Author's page has a video for the same reason.

Sanford is also active in landing radio interviews. She says,

> I follow the people with radio blogs related to my topic and who do interviews with authors. I retweet their stuff and make myself useful to them. I also follow a lot of journalists who write in my field. Journalists were a great strategy for me. I get lots of press as a result of putting key ones on a Twitter List and staying connected to what they are writing, by tweeting it and commenting on their blogs and posts with links on my blog and Facebook pages." According to Sanford, "Journalists are a good route for authors, since they are always looking for content." But she cautions, "You have to give generously and be useful to them, if you are to receive from them."

Children's book author Renay Daniels also likes social media. She says, "What really works is to have your friends rave about your book on their Facebook pages or in chat room forums." She also suggests that the author express their passion for their project in all of the most public places. She says, "If an author is enthusiastic about their book, it makes it easier to sell."

Karen Lee Stevens is accustomed to being in the public eye through several mediums. But she says,

> I realize that many authors are naturally shy and I understand their reluctance to go out and speak on behalf of their books. I do think that for books to gain valuable media exposure, authors need to make public appearances to promote their books. With that said, authors who are shy have many new technologies at their disposal that can get them in front of large audiences without having to leave their homes. Creating a video about their book, which they post on their website or Facebook page, is a great way to promote a book. For me, I created a three-minute video of my shipment of books being delivered to my home and posted it on YouTube! It gave potential book buyers a behind-the-scenes look at the excitement an author experiences even before the book hits bookstores, and it allows readers to feel a connection to an author without ever meeting him or her in person.

The Teleseminar

A teleseminar is a program—often an interview, a workshop, or seminar—presented through a conference telephone call. People can call in and listen in real time (and in some cases, ask questions) and the seminar is generally recorded so people can go to a website and download the seminar or listen to it streamed from the website.

Susan Daffron has been presenting teleseminars, webinars, and podcasts for several years as part of her work with authors and with animal rescue. As the president of SPAWN, she interviewed dozens of publishing and book promotion professionals and recorded about two year's worth of monthly teleseminars on topics relevant to our members. The recordings are available for download by our members. She says,

> A teleseminar is done through a conference telephone call line. People call into a phone number or listen through their computer. People can either listen live during the call or get the recording later, if it is available. The recording is an MP3 file, which can be played on any MP3 player or a computer. This would include an iPod.

The Webinar

According to Stacy Harp, founder and president of Active Christian Media,

> "A webinar is simply a seminar that you hold on the Internet. Some webinars are listened to via the phone, and others you can watch by logging into the webinar using Skype or another computer phone interface. Webinars are becoming more and more popular. Because the technology has advanced so much, many businesses are no longer traveling to meet with their customers. Instead, these companies use webinars to train people and educate their customers.
>
> Webinars are also a great marketing tool for authors, although, I don't see many authors using webinars, yet. But they should,

because they can sell more books this way. For example, if you have a book already published, a webinar would be a great way to have a virtual book club. You can even charge for the club if you want to make it exclusive, and the author can offer a special one-on-one time with their readers as a benefit.

Harp explains additional ways authors can benefit financially. "Authors can give discounts to people who attend their webinars, or even an advanced credit if they are planning another book and they already have raving fans who want to buy all of their books. Really, the opportunities are endless."

Harp explains that the process of setting up a webinar isn't all that difficult. She says,

Anyone who can talk and record what they are saying can technically create a webinar. What makes it a webinar is uploading it to the Internet and making it available on the web. Most people think "live event" when they hear the term *webinar*, because that's how most people come to know about them. What's cool about doing a live webinar is that you can sell it afterwards as a product. Most of the Internet marketers I follow do just that. They have a webinar about something they want to sell you, and then they try to sell you their products at the end. Most of the marketers also send a follow-up email to their email list and allow people to listen to their webinar free for a short period of time.

According to Harp,

I think webinars are better when the presenter uses either video or at the very minimum PowerPoint or Key Note to make slides so that they can convey information visually, and not just via audio. One service I found recently is called Screencast-o-matic, which you can use to record what's on your computer, including showing a PowerPoint slideshow, and then you can edit it and upload it as a video. You can also use it as a webinar if you'd like, but it would not be a live presentation; it would have to be prerecorded. You can learn more at www.screencastomatic.com.

Daffron offers this:

Some teleconference services now help you create webinars, such as the one I use (Instant Teleseminar). There are also companies that are specific to webinars such as GoToWebinar. com. You still call into a conference line or listen via your computer. With a webinar, you do have to be sitting at a computer to see the slides, though. Some webinar-specific software, such as GoToWebinar, forces you to install software on your computer to see the slides. Others are completely web-based, so you only need a regular web browser.

The Podcast

A podcast is a type of digital media that can be presented in both audio and video. Podcasts can be listened to or watched on portable media players. There is special software available to be used in creating podcasts, or you can use Skype.

Daffron describes a podcast. She says, "A podcast is an MP3 file that has been loaded up to a syndication service like iTunes. For example, the podcast I do (www.petliferadio.com/takeme.html) is just an MP3 file. But it's syndicated to other sites. Podcast syndication works like an RSS feed for audio." Daffron points out that we've all seen the RSS feed button at most blog sites. She offers this article to those of you who would like more information about this concept: www.thebookconsultant.com/LMPArticle.asp?ID=130.

According to Daffron, "The term podcast is sometimes used to include video. I think that's confusing. I've also seen the term *videocast*, which makes a little more sense. I usually think of something like that as video."

Skype

Harp gives us a lesson in Skype technology. She explains it this way:

> Skype is the most popular voiceover Internet protocol service. Put simply, Skype is what most people use when they make Internet phone calls. All you need is a computer and a microphone and you can literally call anyone in the world using Skype's platform. Generally, Skype is not used to do podcasting, as the actual term *podcasting* has nothing to do with recording a call or a video. However, what you record using Skype can be *turned into* a podcast. With Skype, you can make computer-to-computer calls with other Skype users, anywhere in the world, and it's free. You can talk to these people with just your computer microphone or using your webcam.

She says,

> Skype also offers other features like your own phone number, text messaging services, and the availability to use Skype to call someone who does not use Skype. For an author, I would highly recommend using Skype, especially if they want to be a guest at a book club, host their own book club, or even lead their own book club. If the people interested in hearing the

author have a computer, it's very easy to set up in a big or even a small venue, and "broadcast" the event that way.

Harp continues. "As for using Skype on an iPad or iPod, that is possible if the iPad or iPod has video capability and they can stream video. Most of the older iPods aren't compatible with Skype, but the newer ones are. Skype is also available on many of our newer smart phones."

The Roundup

Some of you will eagerly become involved with these technologies. You'll run webinars and podcasts at your website and social media pages and maybe do a few remote seminars and other presentations using Skype. Others will simply be a part of these technologies through the expertise of others. You'll seek out interview opportunities with those who are creating webinars, teleseminars, and podcasts. When you do, be sure to get the links and promote these to your list, subscribers, readers, and followers as well as program and conference organizers.

Don't allow a podcast or teleseminar to be a one-shot thing. Make as much of the opportunity as you can by spreading the word—passing along the link. There are probably a whole lot of people who get your newsletter, who follow your blog, who have read your books and articles, but who have never heard you speak. Pitch this concept to your lists, followers, and readers. If your presentations are useful and entertaining, you should be able to further endear some of your fans to you through these videos and recordings. (Learn more about how to participate in interviews through these mediums below.)

Blog Talk Radio

There is also what's known as Blog Talk Radio. Stacy Harp has her own Blog Talk Radio program called On the Wall Radio.

She says,

> In 2005, I had an idea to bring advertising for books to the Christian publishing world. After attending a National Religious Broadcasters EXPO, I opened my company, Active Christian Media, and included in my marketing package an interview with the author of the books I was promoting. The overwhelming majority of the authors I have interviewed are Christians and/or conservatives.

According to Harp,

> The people I like to interview most are those who are passionate about their subjects. I've had the opportunity to talk to many unknown authors who have had the best stories and passion about their books. A person who is passionate about their work and not afraid to talk about it is always a great guest.
>
> I find most guests through press releases and publishing companies. Some people also like Help a Reporter Out, also known as HARO. I haven't been overly enthusiastic with the service because it generally doesn't address my audience.

She advises,

> I think the best things an author can do is make a press kit, blog, network online, and hire someone to do publicity for them if they can afford it. Be bold enough to hunt down talent you think would be a good fit for your book. Send show hosts information about your book: A press release with information about your blog and website, a .pdf file

of your book, or a review copy. But before you send any of that, know your host—listen to the show, know the audience. Don't take that platform for granted.

One thing that is annoying is having an author contact you and they have no clue who you are or who your audience is. The author should seek out the venue that they will fit into.

Harp will take the time to work with an author who isn't accustomed to this type of interview. She says,

I like to help newbies realize that a shorter answer is much better than a long-winded answer. One surefire way to know that a person is not media savvy is if they blather on and on and on about something and the interviewer only gets to ask one question. It rarely makes for a great interview, so I try to help them understand that in advance.

I first met Harp when she interviewed me for her Blog Talk Radio show related to my new release, *Promote Your Book*. She explains the concept:

Blog Talk Radio (BTR) is an Internet-based radio network that boasts over 100,000 programs. Every single show on BlogTalk Radio.com has a program that can automatically be downloaded to a person's computer either through iTunes or just their desktop. What makes Blog Talk Radio such a success is that this technology has made doing live on-air broadcasting very simple. When someone signs up to be a host on BTR, all they need is a phone and a computer. You don't even need a microphone to have a show on Blog Talk Radio.

The system allows hosts to record their programs via the phone and enter show content via their computer. Blog Talk Radio automatically includes within their system an available RSS feed that will allow listeners to subscribe to the show and download it automatically in iTunes.

Your Awesome Author Interview

So, you can create your own podcast or webinar. You can put on your own teleseminar. You can have your own Blog Talk Radio show. But most likely, at least in the beginning, you will be conducting interviews with people who use these methods of creating, preserving, and sharing information on topics of their interest for their own websites.

Someone with a pet rescue site might contact you for an interview related to your new book on feral cats and cat colonies. The owner of a site focusing on everything bird-related might want to interview you about your book on bird-watching. Certainly, if he hears about your book on serious Internet scams, the owner of Internet warning sites will want to interview you.

Or you might go in search of these opportunities. Scour sites on your topic. Here is a directory of Blog Talk Radio sites you will want to check out: www.blogtalkradio.com/categories.aspx.

Interviews and interviewers come in all shapes and styles. Some interviewers want you to respond to questions via email, and they post your interview as-is at their site or publish it in their magazine. Others prefer to conduct a telephone interview, which they will paraphrase in their publication. But the most popular interview processes today are the real-time podcast and the online radio show.

Not everyone is comfortable being interviewed. Yet, if you expect your book to reach a high level of popularity—if you hope to sell thousands of copies of your book—you really must learn to handle the interview.

I have been interviewed numerous times in a variety of ways. Personally, I love the email interview where I just respond at my leisure by typing my answers. I like having the time to think about my responses and to reread them before submitting. My worst interview experience occurred when the interviewee, in a real-time interview, began challenging my responses—playing the devil's advocate. I'm not a debater and I don't do well under that kind of pressure. I had to work hard so as not to come off sounding defensive. I hope I was able to carry that off. Book sales after that interview were up and that's always a good indication of a good interview.

You truly never know what to expect from an interview, and maybe that's one reason why the fear of the interview is so prevalent among authors.

If you would like to be interviewed on the topic of your book, here are some tips and techniques that could help:

- Locate interview opportunities through websites and publications related to your topic as well as those that feature general author interviews. If you spend some time exploring the site, you will soon discover whether or not they conduct interviews. If you see no indication of interview opportunities, post an email asking for the opportunity.
- Do a Google search to locate directories of websites and publications with general interview opportunities or those related to your expertise.
- Study this directory in order to locate Blog Talk Radio opportunities: www.blogtalkradio.com/categories.aspx.

- Once you've located interview opportunities, create a succinct but impressive bio to include with your inquiry. A potential interviewer will want to know that you are articulate (which should show through, at least to some degree, in your writing style), qualified, credible, knowledgeable, and interesting. A bio can help to portray this. A good interviewer who conducts live interviews will also want to hear your voice. So give your phone number, as well.

Handle yourself as a professional during any interview. Here are some tips:

- Think like your target audience. What do they want/need to know about your subject? Even if your interviewer gets off track with his line of questions, you can bring the discussion back to the issue at hand. Always keep in mind, "What information and resources can I offer my audience?"
- Don't be afraid to give. It's highly unlikely that you could ever give away too much during a thirty or sixty minute interview. Besides, the more you give, the more the listener will want. And it's that yearning for more that will sell copies of your book.
- Expand on each topic just enough, but don't overdo it. Respond fully to questions, but avoid going off on a tangent.
- Jot down several key phrases you'll want to remember. Work them in when you get the chance.
- Read and listen to other author interviews to get an idea of what works and what doesn't. Of course, you want to keep your own style of speaking, but there are also mistakes you'll want to avoid.

- Practice speaking off the cuff. You will definitely need this skill when doing a live interview.
- Have someone record or videotape you speaking and listen to/ watch the recording with a critical ear. Is there anything you need to work on? Do you use too many filler words?

Raven West is one author who is not a fan of webinars and teleseminars. Why? She says,

> Because I enjoy talking to people eye-to-eye and interacting with live human beings. All of this social media is so very anti-social in my opinion. I can certainly understand the convenience. I've conducted teleseminars and teleconferences many times on the phone because the board members were all over the country. And I'll admit, if a conference planner wants me to participate in one of these, I wouldn't hesitate because it is another opportunity to sell more books. But in general, I'd much rather have a reason to get dressed in the morning! Also, there is really no greater experience than signing a book and seeing that person's expression when you hand it back to them. You can't do that on-line, or even on a Kindle.

This is so true, but there are some potential customers we can't reach any other way except through recordings, videos, or e-readers. This is why most authors develop such a complete and full repertoire of promotional activities. As authors, we won't get far in our quest for success if we participate only in those activities we like best. Remember, authorship is a business just like being an insurance agent, a car dealer or manufacturer, an electrical contractor, or a merchant. And there are certain responsibilities and requirements for success.

Locate Internet Publicity Opportunities

We mentioned some methods of finding appropriate publicity opps in each of the previous sections. Brian Jud offers a few more:

> In order to find relevant blogs, etc. there are sites such as technorati.com, blogtoplist.com and stumbleupon.com that list many. If the author seeks relevant webinars, I suggest following experts in their field on Twitter or Facebook to learn when they will be hosting informative sessions.
>
> There are several companies that host webinars. I perform monthly webinars for SPAN (Small Publishers Association of North America) and Createspace in addition to conducting them for IBPA (Independent Book Publishers Association) affiliates. I use GoToWebinar.com. I can re-purpose some of the content, but it usually takes about ten hours to create the first version. I use them for exposure and to generate leads for my other services, as well as to generate leads for my newsletter.

According to Jud, "Once you get a webinar 'in the can' use it over and over for other audiences. With minor changes to customize your content, you can make it appear to various audiences that you created the session just for them."

Can you sell a lot of books through webinars and other Internet media? Jerry Waxler doesn't believe so. He says,

> For me, webinars have not had the same level of sales as do live presentations. Since people are not in the room with you, their sense of loyalty is less likely to develop enough to get them to buy a book, and there is less likelihood of impulse buys. I consider Internet work to be mainly about boosting

networks and building brands than selling books. I also love to speak, and webinars give me an opportunity to experiment with different venues, topics, and audiences.

Our experts conclude that, because webinars, etc. may not reach enough of your readers in a personal way, they may not be as effective as personal appearances. But most seem to indicate that they will keep doing them. Why not have your presentations do double or triple duty?

As Raven West says,

It helps a great deal if you can find someone who will tape your live presentations so you can post them on YouTube, which you can also link to your own website or blog. This is also the ideal way to showcase your speaking skills to program chairpersons and directors, as well as the operators of speakers bureaus, which may provide you with an increase in speaking engagements, which, in turn, will also give you increased opportunity to sell your books.

Communication Counts: Talk About Your Book Everywhere You Go

You can't sell a book that no one knows about. One way to spread the word is to go out and talk about it. And I don't mean restricting your communication to captive audiences or those who visit your booth at a book festival.

I tell authors, "Talk about your book everywhere you go." I've sold books out of the trunk of my car to people asking for directions, on airplanes, while out eating at a restaurant, at my class reunion, at my grandsons' football games, while waiting in a dentist's office, as a guest at a fundraising event, while shopping, and many times at various meetings I've attended. I even sold ten copies of my book on publishing to a blind man in the Middle East once. He said he was buying them for friends. Another interesting opportunity to sell a book came about when I was sitting in on a séance. (But that's for another book.)

Sometimes sales are made quite by chance, when someone introduces me as an author or I am recognized from a recent newspaper article, for example. But usually, sales come about after some chit chat with someone I meet or happen to run into. Making unexpected single sales probably isn't the most lucrative way to sell books. But don't discount the opportunities out there. If you can sell even a handful of books every few months during the course of your everyday activities—volunteering at your children's school, at your job, working out at the gym, when visiting an ill friend, and so forth, you are actually ahead of the game. At the end of the year, that could be thirty books or so that you wouldn't have sold if you'd kept your mouth shut, right?

Sure, sometimes you can spend more time than you'd like talking to someone who wants to bend your ear about the topic of your book. As you can imagine, this happens to me all the time. People would rather have me give them the secret to publishing success, provide them with the right publisher for their project, and guestimate how many books they can sell if they have it hardbound than stop to read the book. It takes me a few extra minutes to help them understand that publishing success is not an exact science with easy answers, but a study that they must pursue. Yes, it takes time, but this is all part of my pitch—what it takes to convince someone to purchase my books. It takes time and the right line of conversation.

Even if you don't sell a book on the spot, be content in the fact that you have planted a seed, perhaps created an ally, and you've gained a slice of that all-important concept—exposure.

Raven West understands the importance of getting exposure at every turn. She says,

> I speak on behalf of my books wherever and whenever possible! I talk about my latest novel to my bank teller, hair stylist, manicurist, and all the customers within earshot. When I'm in the grocery store, or waiting in line in the post office (especially the post office since my second novel's main character is a postmaster!), I'm talking about the story and the characters. I'll talk to the check-out person in any store, and even other members at my Weight Watchers meeting waiting to get on

the scale. (I sold two of my novels to one member and possibly came up with a plot idea for another novel.)

Rik Feeney also looks everywhere for opportunities to talk about his book. He says, "I have a magnetic badge made up of my book cover that I wear everywhere I go. While standing in lines, at restaurants, and other public places, people notice the badge and ask about my book."

So, while this book is a valuable tool for those authors who want to speak to large audiences, this chapter is devoted to the common and highly important one-on-one communication that we all engage in each and every day. As Sandra Beckwith says, "Communication skills are essential because we're all responsible for promoting our own books and we need to communicate well to do that."

You might ask, how does one open the door to a conversation about his or her book? Here are some ideas:

- Get out of the house. If you work at home or at a job downtown, and even if you're still raising children, don't neglect your social, spiritual, and charitable life. Join up, volunteer, and participate in interesting things with interesting people. Some of you already do so—that's a good start. Continue reading through these ideas. They may help you to get more out of your associations and experiences.

- Engage people. We talked about engaging your audiences. Use some of the same tactics and charms to engage individuals. Compliment someone. Bring up a subject related to something you have in common—you're wearing the same brand shoes, you just finished a marathon within the same time, you're both enjoying the glorious spring weather, or you're each sipping a cappuccino, for example.

- Express curiosity. If you are a writer, you are probably naturally curious. If you're not, start expanding on this trait. Ask the person in front of you in line at the movie theater what is the best movie they've seen this year. When you see someone getting out of a new car, ask him how he likes his Ford. Ask the woman standing next to you at the makeup counter where she got her handbag.

- Help someone out—open the door for a gentleman who is carrying packages or a young mother pushing a stroller. Stop and help someone pick up papers she dropped on a windy day.

- Ask for assistance. In a meeting situation, or at work, for example, ask someone you don't know if she would be your assistant on a project or if you could come by and get some copies made in his department.

- Sit with different people in church or at meetings.

- Strike up conversations with people you don't usually speak with. It really doesn't matter what you say—just find ways to break the ice. Sometimes conversations will go smoothly and naturally; other times the person isn't willing to or able to talk to you at that time.

When you begin a conversation with someone you've just been introduced to, or an employee in the lunch room, for example, then what? How do you bring the conversation around to your book? Ah ha, now there's the trick. What I'm going to tell you might cause you to say, "Well, duh!"

It is elementary. Primarily, you're going to wait for an opening. Wait until someone says, "What do you do?" for example. Or, how about this? Ask the other person what he or she does or (if he is a coworker) how he spends his off time. You can also just make conversation by saying something like, "I'm tired today—I stayed up late promoting my new novel." Bingo—there you go. You've said it. Now you hope for a response such as, "You're a writer?" or "Tell me about your book." Most people are pretty darn excited to meet a real author and will express interest. It is up to you to give your spiel without overdoing it.

I like to carry my latest book with me and, when I sit down to eat lunch, I'm riding on a bus or plane or waiting for a meeting to start, for example, I pull it out. I might lay it on the lunch table or start reading it. If no one around you mentions it or asks you about it, you can say something such as, "No matter how many times I read this book, I still get a kick out of this chapter," or ask the person sitting next to you, "Have you read this novel, yet?"

Your Elevator Speech

Develop a thirty-second commercial. The idea being that, when someone asks about your book, you have a ready-made response.

The thirty-second commercial consists of a description of your book—a canned speech that you can use when meeting with a publisher, chatting with someone at a class reunion or in a business setting, or when talking to potential customers at a book festival.

You might revise your "commercial" depending on who you're addressing. Let's say that your book features indoor activities and crafts for kids during hot summer and cold winter days. If you are talking to a teacher, your spiel would be somewhat different than if you were speaking to a parent or a daycare provider, for example. If you're talking to a long-distance grandparent who is considering your book as a gift—you would mold your pitch to fit his/her situation.

You might describe your adventure novel differently to women than you would men. You would represent your fitness book in a different way to sports-minded readers as opposed to those who are sedentary and need motivation to get moving. I described my local history book in different ways, depending on whether I was talking to locals, tourists, long-time residents, history buffs, museum docents, descendants of early pioneers, or school kids, for example.

When developing your thirty-second commercial, you'll want to describe the book or story, but also mention the benefits to your potential readers. Answer the question, "What's in it for me?" Consumers (including readers) buy benefits, not features.

Three samples of thirty-second commercials:

Purge Your Prose of Problems is a desk reference book for book editors and for authors who want to self-edit their books more effectively. *Purge Your Prose* teaches you how to resolve almost every editing issue involving grammar, punctuation, syntax, and style and save thousands of dollars in editing fees. It even includes creative writing tips. Trust me, this is the only reference book you'll need on your desk from now on. Author: Bobbie Christmas.

Undercover Reunion is a novel for Baby Boomers, fans of *The Man from U.N.C.L.E.*, and anyone who has ever attended a high school reunion! The story follows two average middle-aged women whose childhood game of playing spies becomes all too real when they attend their thirtieth high school reunion. The excitement and suspense begins when they're recruited by a secret organization to thwart a former schoolmate's evil plans for world domination. Author: Raven West.

Publish Your Book is your guide to successful publishing, whether you write fiction or nonfiction. It describes all of your publishing options and actually helps you to choose the one that's right for you and for your project. It walks you through each step of the writing, publishing, and book promotion process so that you understand what you must do, when it needs to be done, and why you're doing it.

No matter where you are in the process of writing or publishing, this book responds to your questions and concerns. Author: Patricia Fry.

Note: In the case of this elevator speech, I then talk about what I believe would resonate with the individual—depending on where they are in their publishing journey. I might talk up the fact that the reader will have access to complete instructions and a timeline for self-publishing a book (establishing your own publishing company), that I include a chapter on how to choose and approach pay-to-publish companies, that I walk them through the entire process of writing a book proposal and even offer detailed samples, or that they'll find three generous chapters addressing the challenges and realities of book promotion.

You will respond differently to casual inquiries, such as from the former coworker you run into at Starbucks, a new hairdresser at your salon, a fellow guest at a banquet, etc. When someone asks, "What do you do?" or "What are you working on these days?" you may use the same "commercial" for the novel, but you'll tweak those for the nonfiction books, unless you happen to be talking to a writer or an author, for example. In the case of my book, *Publish Your Book*, I might say to a non-author, "I just came out with a book for authors who need help understanding the publishing process and how to successfully navigate the shark-infested waters of publishing." Or I could just say I write books for other writers and authors. If this person knows a writer (so many people today do) or is thinking about writing a book herself, the information may resonate with her and she'll ask more questions.

When Bobbie Christmas is having a casual conversation with a non-author, non-writer, she might focus her spiel on the value of her book for anyone who ever needs editing help—students, businessmen/women, employees in many positions, and so forth.

When devising your thirty-second spiel, remember that you will be reciting it. Write it out, but then read it aloud several times. You'll likely need to massage it over and over until it sounds natural and not contrived or like a hard-hitting commercial.

Develop Better Communication Skills

We've talked a lot throughout this book about how to improve your public speaking skills and how to present yourself in interviews. But what about the most common aspect of human communication—the conversation? Are you also practicing better conversational skills?

The fact is that conversation is essential in all of our relationships. Whether we are trying to get along with a spouse, negotiate with a vendor, or pitch our books, our success depends on our ability to communicate.

It's ironic that we receive so little training to help us hone conversational skills when we rely on this ability everyday of our lives. If you're old enough to be part of the "old school," you probably remember your parents and grade school teachers saying, "Don't interrupt while I'm talking," "Look at me when I'm speaking to you," "Don't talk with your mouth full," and so forth. Today, we get a constant daily dose of disturbingly poor quality communication examples via our beloved television sets. Just look at the commercials, for instance. People talk over one another, they talk with their mouths full, they mumble, and some of them absolutely massacre the language. For the most part, our conversational style and habits weren't taught, but they developed over years of modeling others and receiving peer feedback.

Feedback is a powerful tool in helping someone change poor conversational habits. But a person has to first acknowledge that there is a problem, and they have to want to improve. Most people aren't going to criticize the communication habits of others unless they are asked to. How do you say to a coworker, "You talk like you have a mouth full of mush—can't you enunciate more clearly?" Or to a friend, "I hate talking to you because you never respond to what I say. You go off telling your own story all the time without ever acknowledging mine."

What if you were to say to the coworker, "I love the way you present your thoughts, Lydia. It's difficult for some of us to understand you, though, when you swallow your words. It would be to your professional benefit if you would practice speaking more clearly. I'd be happy to help."

I know a woman who often talks over others. I called her on this once. I said, "That's the third time this afternoon that you've asked me something and then started talking over me when I attempted to respond."

She was obviously shocked for a moment and then told me that she appreciated my pointing that out to her. She said that was a family trait. "Everyone in my family talks at once. It's a bad habit that I'm trying to break."

What are your habitual conversation blunders? Is there something specific that you're working on? Are you aware of a problem in your way of conversing, but chosen to ignore it because no one seems to notice or care? Maybe you have an annoying habit and don't know it.

The 1950 edition of *The World Book Encyclopedia* states, "The ability to engage in interesting conversation is one of the greatest personal assets a man or woman can have. It is a great aid to business and social success and also makes for greater enjoyment of the company of other persons." I think we'll agree that this is still true sixty-two years later.

It's elementary, but worth repeating—there are two parts to effective conversation: speaking and listening. And both parts take thought and skill. Here are some tips for becoming a better, more respected conversationalist, thus a more effective book marketer.

- **Make eye contact.** Looking directly at the other person is a courteous indication that you are listening.

- **Speak clearly and audibly.** It's inconsiderate to mumble or to speak so softly that you can't be heard, yet I frequently encounter people who do this. Most of us don't know how we sound to others. If people consistently ask you to speak up or to repeat yourself, you may have an audibility problem.

- **Speak at a good pace.** We've all been in conversations with people who talk so fast that you can't keep up or so slowly that, by the time they finish expressing their thought, you've forgotten the topic.

- **Use language and images familiar to the listener.** You probably notice that you get more out of a conversation with someone who speaks and thinks like you do, than someone who uses vocabulary differently.

- **Stick to the topic.** Some people listen to you just long enough to hear the topic and then they change the focus of the story to themselves or to a topic they know more about. As an example, I might want to tell a friend about having gone roller skating with my grandchildren over the weekend when she quickly says, "I remember the last time I went skating." Or, "I had a great weekend, too. I went shopping and we had tea with the Marleys. Did you know that Jim and Bev Marley bought the sporting goods store downtown?" It's difficult to retrain someone with this habit. Just be aware that you aren't guilty of it.

- **Know when to change the subject.** Whether you initiated the conversation or not, change the subject when there appears to be nothing new to say or when others begin to fidget or act bored. In other words, cease droning on about your book if you begin getting clues that others are no longer interested.

- **Know when to speak and when to listen.** Conversation should be give and take. Each person involved in a conversation needs to speak and each needs to listen. Participate but don't monopolize.

- **Express an interest in what's being said.** This seems like an elementary statement, but, if you're at all observant, you'll notice that not everyone follows this good advice. Face the speaker with unfolded arms. Lean forward slightly. Make eye contact. Acknowledge statements with a nod, comment, or question when appropriate. Some people spend the time that someone else is speaking not listening—but thinking of what they want to say next.

- **Ask open-ended questions to promote communication**—that is, questions that require more than a yes or no response. Start questions with *why, how,* or *what.* "Why did you write a book on African elephants?" "What caused you to enter the flower business?" "Tell me how you managed to stay in business in this economy." "How did you feel when your twins left for college?"

- **Be prepared.** A good conversationalist engages his/her listeners and stimulates conversation. Hone your conversational skills by keeping up with trends and current events. Live an interesting life. Try new things so you'll have something to talk about. Accept unusual invitations. See controversial plays. Do volunteer work. Begin a new hobby. Travel. Go back to school. Read. Change jobs or professions. Especially stay up on news, trends, and activities related to the theme or genre of your book.

- **Model someone whose conversational skills you admire.** Who do you most enjoy conversing with? We all know someone who gets a lot of attention at social events and business meetings. What makes this person stand out in a crowd? What are some of his most endearing qualities? How does he make you feel when you're conversing with him? Study his body language, his opening and closing statements, and his speaking style. Ask him about his philosophy regarding communication. Does his attitude about people in general reflect in his approach to conversation? To improve your conversational skills, mimic someone who you consider successful in this area. Generally, this person expresses a sincere interest in others.

According to Brian Jud,

> I believe communication skills are vital to successful book marketing. They are important for personal networking, telephone selling, conducting in-store events, performing grass-roots research, making sales presentations, and negotiating sales with corporate buyers where orders for 300,000 books could be at stake. If authors work at their computers all day and are not out "pressing the flesh" regularly, they are severely limiting their chances for success.

Good advice. However, some authors can't seem to get off of the ground to communicate with the folks who might be interested in their books. How many lost opportunities can you count because you neglected to carry your book with you, you didn't speak up when you had the chance, you opted out of a conversation in progress instead of getting involved, or you had a conversation with someone but didn't mention your book?

I know, I know, you don't want to seem like a pushy, neon light advertisement everywhere you go. You don't want people avoiding you when they see you coming for fear you will put the sales pitch on them. Let's strike a happy medium between keeping your book a secret and overpowering people with your spiel.

Open Up to Small Talk

Small talk is probably the most commonly executed form of human communication we use today. If we're out and about taking a walk, running errands, attending meetings, and so forth, we acknowledge others, ask how they are, respond to their questions about our world, etc. That's considered small talk. You might converse briefly with another parent at your child's soccer practice about how well the team is doing, who's bringing refreshments next week, or the weather, for example. As part of your job, you might work with the public—providing information or offering help—and casual conversation is usually a part of your communication.

Some people consider casual conversation to be a waste of time. They think of small talk as shallow, mechanical, meaningless chatter. But have you ever noticed where small talk can lead? I'm certain that most of you reading this book have gathered and/or shared some pretty interesting or valuable or entertaining information while engaged in what started out to be small talk. This is how people ease into meetings, get to know something about an individual, and even determine whether they want a more meaningful discussion with the person or not.

How often have you discovered, through small talk, that you have a connection to the person you are talking to—you went to school with his daughter, dated his sister, do business with his company, or you learn he has read your book and recommends it to others on a regular basis. Now this is good to know, isn't it?

Some of you are aware that small talk can easily lead to a book sale, if you approach it in the right manner. You may consider small talk a waste of time, but I can tell you that effective managers, dynamite marketing personnel, and other accomplished communicators often begin their more successful and productive conversations with small talk.

A period of small talk before giving a pitch helps you:

- Build confidence within a specific situation.
- Learn something about the other person.
- Establish a sense of unity.
- Set the mood for a discussion.
- Create a bridge to more meaningful dialogue.

Small talk is a natural prelude to any serious discussion. It provides you and everyone else involved the opportunity to size up and evaluate the situation. Even animals in the wild take this "look before you leap" approach before getting down to business. When an animal comes upon an unfamiliar situation, territory, or another animal, for example, it moves toward and around it very slowly—carefully checking things out before becoming involved.

Small talk is the human's way of sensing a situation before jumping in. But its effectiveness is not just in the words you use. Small talk is most effective when your other senses are also on alert.

Through small talk, you can:

- Put people at ease while creating a smooth transition from the initial greeting to the business at hand. Diving into a business discussion without a preamble makes people uncomfortable and results in a more strained interaction.
- Persuade people to be more receptive to your ideas.
- Encourage others to reveal aspects of themselves.
- Initiate professional opportunities in situations even outside the structure of the business setting.

When you're using small talk as a lead-in to a business discussion, it will be necessary at some point to draw it to a close and begin the pitch you want to give or to make your request for a speaking slot, for example. The best way to do this is through a purposeful transition. Learn to recognize good transitional points in the process of small talk by watching television talk-show hosts in action. Most of them have impeccable timing and great style in making transitions. Here are a few suggestions:

- Learn to lead. Although knowing how to follow is vital to successful small talk, leading is equally important, particularly when the transition depends on you.
- Recognize an opening and jump in. Say, "Let me tell you something about this book." Or "I'd like to apply for a speaking position at your upcoming conference."
- Stop monopolists in their tracks. If possible, wait for them to take a breath or to pause. Then break in with a comment about their topic, and immediately lead the conversation in the direction that you want it to go.

People who are good at engaging others generally also seem to care about others. They remember that you like egg salad sandwiches, that you were writing an article for a local publication the last time you spoke, that you mentioned once before that you visit a nearby spa occasionally. And they'll bring it up in their small talk.

Don't discount the power and validity of small talk. As you can see, it can be a catalyst for something larger—"big talk," if you will. Through small talk, you might learn about a new radio show host who is seeking guest authors, an organization related to the theme or some aspect of your book, a corporate leader seeking gift bag items for a major convention coming to town. Or you might just sell one book to the individual you chose to converse with that evening as you passed him on your way to the wine bar. One book sold in one day simply because you engaged in small talk? Seems worthwhile to me.

Get Paid to Speak

Authors have a built-in motivation for giving free presentations. We have books to promote. We are eager to greet our readers and recruit new ones. We know the value of getting exposure for ourselves and our books, and we're willing to go out and talk for that pleasure. There comes a point in many authors' careers, however, when they feel entitled to something more than an opportunity to speak, refreshments, and, perhaps, a small stipend to cover the cost of gasoline.

Some authors have created businesses out of public speaking. Others have come to the place where they simply accept only speaking engagements that pay. I know authors who don't necessarily care about collecting a fee, but they won't travel unless their expenses are paid.

It's common for authors to start out speaking for free. Some eventually go on to join speakers organizations, get professional speaker training, and ultimately sign with a speakers bureau, which gets them lucrative speaking assignments. The way I see it, when an author draws thousands of dollars to speak numerous times each year, he is no longer an author who speaks. He is a professional speaker who happens to be an author.

Carol Dean Schreiner charges, but she didn't start out doing so. She says,

> When I first started speaking, I spoke to anyone who had an audience, usually at noon meetings for my meal. But I always had my business cards available in case any of those in the audience might need someone to speak to their company or association. I still speak for free occasionally, when it is for a group I feel needs me as a speaker and I know they do not have money to pay me.

She gives a tip about how to handle the topic of pay, "When an author-speaker is approached about speaking for an event, they should ask what the occasion is, who they had to speak the last time, and what did they pay that speaker." She says,

> I started at a low fee and gradually went up to what the associations were paying. I also tell new speakers to choose a topic on which they are experts. Write that speech in four different time slots, fifteen, thirty, forty-five, and sixty minutes. When someone asks them to speak, they can ask how long is the speech to be, and they are covered.

Schreiner has given presentations in some unusual places. She even got free passage on a cruise ship in exchange for speaking on the topic of her book. But the sweet deal didn't last long. She says, "I contacted about twenty cruise lines and asked about speaking. One responded." According to Schreiner, she spoke on her topic twice before the line was sold.

Novelist Margaret Brownley did an impromptu talk on a cruise ship once. She says,

My husband and I were booked on a Caribbean cruise and I asked the person in charge of the tour if I could give a talk. (Rule number one, always look for opportunities to talk.) It just so happened that I had a new book out that month. The tour person handled the arrangements and I gave an informal talk about life as a writer. The audience consisted of around eighty people—mainly retirees, and they seemed to enjoy it. While I didn't get a discount nor did I get paid, this did come in handy at tax time because I, then, treated the trip as a business expense.

Yes, this is one of the perks of traveling to speak, isn't it? Your expenses are tax deductible. This is another excellent reason why you should do book signings and other activities when driving over to visit Grandma and why you should plan to sell books at a major book festival when flying out west for some R&R. I sometimes take a few extra days to tour an area after presenting workshops at a writer's conference. But I keep my personal fun-day expenses separate from those related to the event. My visit to the zoo has nothing to do with the reason I am in that city. If I choose to splurge on a new purse, that should not be counted as a business expense.

Daniel Hall has written a book for those who want to get free passage on Carnival, Royal Caribbean, or one of the other cruise lines. It's called, *Speak on Cruise Ships, Eight Easy Steps to a Lifetime of Free Luxury Cruises by Sharing Your Passions and Interests as an Onboard Lecturer*. The book is available at Amazon.com

I also found several sites related to cruising for free. Just do an Internet search using keywords, "speak on cruise ships."

Leslie Korenko typically charges anytime she has to drive a distance. She says, "I charge a small fee of $50 to cover my travel expenses. But if the location is close, a free speaker is even more attractive to the organization or club."

Hope Clark also charges in order to be reimbursed. She says, "Location means everything to me. If an event isn't such that I can drive there and back in twenty-four hours, I require compensation. Every speaking event is an opportunity, but when writing is your income and you've been asked to speak for free instead of earning your groceries back home writing, there comes a time to draw a line."

Peter Bowerman was one of those who started out charging for his presentations. He says,

> For me, it hasn't been about once speaking for free, and now only speaking for money. I charged for the first "talks" I ever did (how-to workshops based on my books). But I still do plenty of talks for free, if they're local or if I'm already going to be somewhere out of town for another reason. You've got to be flexible. If I can drive twenty minutes to speak to a group of twenty folks and sell my books, I'll probably do it for free (or encourage the sponsoring group to charge for it and keep the money).

He continues,

> I've actually done precious little free speaking at civic group meetings an d the like, preferring to focus on events where I can speak on the subject matter of my books and drive book sales. Ideal is a little of both, where I've been asked to do a keynote/plenary and a topic-specific breakout session or two. It's fun to be able to get into more abstract "umbrella" subjects rather than always doing nuts-and-bolts talks.

As far as advice to move from a newbie-speaker to an in-demand speaker, just hone your "product" (i.e., you). Put some thought into coming up with engaging, compelling subjects that'll grab your audience and keep them talking about you the next day. In my case, my books have driven my subject matter, and I've brought my own energy and personality to the delivery.

Always deliver more than expected. Tell conference organizers to "put you to work" while you're there. Like I say on the speaking link on my site (see below), my philosophy is this: If you've paid me to come talk to your group, workshop, or conference about freelance writing, marketing for writers, or self-publishing, I'm going to make sure I find out how best to "reach" your audience and will craft my program(s) for optimal relevance to them and their worlds. Since, obviously, I can't be anywhere else that day or weekend, then put me to work and maximize your investment. None of this "blow-in-do-my-talk-blow-out" prima donna nonsense.

Bowerman continues, "It blows my mind how many keynote speakers I've heard who, though being paid handsomely, will literally wing it. They'll show up, do a rambling, unfocused talk, as if all should just be in awe of them by virtue of their presence, and they owe the 'great unwashed' little more than that."

He advises,

By contrast, go out of your way to be a generous speaker. In addition to just talking to people who ask for a few minutes of your time, that can mean having me do one-on-ones with attendees (which sometimes you get paid for). If they don't have a formal system in place, you might encourage them to charge for those one-on-ones and keep the money. Nothing endears a speaker to an organization faster than one who suggests ways to make money from his/her presence. That kind of stuff gets you invited back.

Check out Bowerman's speaking page: wellfedwriter.com/need-aspeaker.shtml.

Can you be a professional speaker and still promote your book(s)? Sure you can. You don't even have to speak on the subject of your book. Give an inspirational or motivational presentation for a large fee of $1,000 to $5,000, all expenses paid, and you may not care if you sell books. However, you probably will sell books. While you aren't technically promoting your books through these speeches, you are still getting the sort of exposure that will lead to book sales. You will be billed as the author of such-and-such books. Your contact information will be prominent. If you make an impression on your audience, people will want to know more about you, will want to hear you again, and will want to read what you've written, even if it doesn't relate to the theme of your presentation.

Take every opportunity to speak and take every opportunity to promote your book through great-looking bookmarks, postcards, and posters. During the networking sessions, wear a t-shirt or a button with the image of your book. Walk around and greet folks by handing them pens, magnets, bookmarks, or some more clever item with the name and/or image of your book on it. Create some really classy handouts and include the title of your book and your contact information.

Some authors earn a little extra money teaching their subject through adult education programs. Even if you are a regular instructor—say you teach your two-week session to a class of thirty students four times per year—you won't get rich. But you are getting out of the house. You're putting yourself in a position to sell books. You're getting exposure. You're staying sharp on your topic. If you're paying attention, you're getting ideas for additional books and articles.

I teach a course on article-writing occasionally for our college district adult education program. I typically sell copies of my book, *A Writer's Guide to Article Writing*, to everyone as a text. And I earn anywhere from $30 to $60 for one three-hour session depending on the size of the class. Naturally, because I hand out materials with my contact information on it and because I let students know that I maintain an open-email policy, I sometimes get the opportunity to work with some of them on their projects, which I charge for.

Mary Ellen Warner taught organizing workshops through her community's school system. She says,

> Adult enrichment programs were offered in several local school districts. I wanted to get involved, so I sent proposals to all of the districts within twenty-five miles of my home office. I eventually did workshops in eleven different school districts. Pay depended on the number of students enrolled. Classes were one night, two-hour sessions. Twenty-five students was usually the limit due to the size of the classrooms. The pay was a percentage based on the number of students. The adult extension programs at the local college were a set fee (and not nearly as attractive).

Warner advises others, "Check out the local school districts and their adult enrichment programs. In our area, now just about everyone who has a class has a book. What is your expertise? Do people want to hear about it as well as read about it?"

For Warner, her workshops led to other paying gigs. The students seemed to enjoy her humorous way of presenting and some of them began asking her to entertain for their clubs and organizations. She describes what it's like to be a guest speaker for a dinner program. "When you arrive, everyone is delighted to meet the speaker. Meetings are held in lovely venues. I'm served a wonderful meal; and there is almost always chocolate for dessert. Plus, after having fun and laughing all evening, the meeting planner hands me a check. Life is grand."

If you are interested in speaking for pay, a first step would be to hone your speaking skills. This would be the time to get some professional speaker training. You might also want to join a speakers bureau. (More about this coming up.) In the meantime, let's focus on your pitch.

Laura Dobbins is the book publicist for Lucinda Sue Crosby. She doesn't have a standard pitch letter. She pitches her client according to the event's needs. She says, "Since Lucinda has such a varied background it is easy to find different hooks to promote her and her work. Sometimes I pitch her as a businesswoman who survives by the art of reinvention." According to Dobbins, "The key is research, follow-up, and never giving up, because those who said 'no' in 2010 and 2011 have said 'yes' to us in 2012."

Recently, she contacted the organizers of a prestigious writer's conference in Hawaii about booking Lucinda. She used the angle that Lucinda played in a popular movie that one of their speakers directed. Here's her pitch:

"I represent an author, Lucinda Sue Crosby, who made seven films with your special guest _____. She worked on *Pretty Woman, Beaches,* and *Overboard,* to name a few. My client has an interesting background. Not only is she a former Hollywood actress, but also a Nashville songwriter, Commissioned Poet, award-winning journalist, and award-winning author. She is currently promoting her book *Francesca of Lost Nation* and will be releasing a children's book about adoption in the next two months. You can contact Lucinda directly or call me here: xxx-xxx-xxxx." (Dobbins also provides website addresses where the organizer can learn more about her client.)

Here's another pitch letter:

"Carol Dean Schreiner will put laughter in your heart and knowledge in your mind because she talks about real life. She has authored four books, *Wonder Woman Doesn't Live Here Anymore*, *Laugh for the Health of It*, *Steps To Storytelling*, and *Fabulous at 50, Sexy at 60 and Sin-sational at 70.*

   "You will discover she is a forceful but gracious presence that is blessed with the kind of humor and down-home warmth that has rightfully had her referred to as the "Erma Bombeck of Oklahoma." She is the mother of five grown children and was a single mom for many of those years. Carol makes a living by what she gets out of life, but she makes a life by what she gives to others. She's real . . . she's funny . . . she's inspiring, she's motivating, she's exciting and energetic." (Contact information follows.)

Speakers Organizations and Bureaus

A speakers organization typically offers opportunities for individuals to develop better speaking and communication skills. A speakers bureau is generally an organization that has formed for the purpose of helping speakers to locate speaking opportunities and to help event planners to locate speakers. Speakers bureaus come in all sizes with a variety of standards and some of them have themes.

There are major speakers bureaus where organizations, corporations, and conference planners with large budgets can go and find highly skilled professional keynote speakers on a variety of inspirational and motivational topics. Some bureaus specialize in booking entertainers and comedians.

Some speakers bureaus are designed for speakers in certain specialties such as aviation, utilities, writing, historic preservation, and so forth. The National Coalition for the Homeless sponsors speakers to go out and educate the public on homelessness. This bureau is comprised of people who are or who have been homeless. If you present humorous, inspirational, motivational, political, or religious speeches, for example, you might seek out a bureau that specializes in finding this sort of opportunity for presenters.

Perhaps you can find a bureau related to the subject of your book or the region your book represents. This might be the Eastern Seaboard, the Great Lakes Area, business, spirituality, ecology, or any number of topics. The Ventura (California) Museum has a speakers bureau. I could have joined and put myself on tap for engagements where they wanted someone to speak on the Ojai Valley (the topic of one of my books). The Maine State Bar Association has a speakers bureau as does the Professional Women International organization, Southeastern Guide Dog Association, and the Colorado Society of CPAs. And then there are virtual speakers bureaus, where you can record your presentation as a podcast and people can download and listen to it.

Many publishing companies now have speakers bureaus through which they book their authors to speak. I was a member of a speakers bureau at Ligouri Publications.

There are requirements for most speakers bureaus—either that you can speak on their topic and/or that you pass certain criteria. You may be required to perform before a board, submit a video of you in action, and/or take some training before being accepted into a specific bureau.

How much can you earn as a paid speaker? Celebrities get as much as $10,000 to $30,000 per speech. Motivational speakers earn generally around $20–$33 hour or $42,000–$70,000 per year on the west coast. Less on the east coast. Of course, this depends on how often they speak and at what fee. Travel expenses are generally paid, as well.

If you want to become a paid speaker, Schreiner suggests, "Join a speaker's group to learn how to market and promote your books in the speaking field."

Or you can do as several of our contributors to this book have done—simply seek out speaking opportunities that pay. When you get an invitation to speak, ask what they pay. The more speaking you do for a fee, the more apt you are to land some of those lucrative speaking assignments you desire.

Here are some additional tips:

- Start now collecting testimonials and references from event organizers and program chairpersons as well as audience members. Post these at your website on your "speakers" page along with your pitch and your presentation topics.
- If you have a specific speaking fee in mind, post that at your site, as well. Most speakers starting out, however, negotiate fees based on each circumstance (size of group/organization, ability to pay, audience size, length of speech, etc.).
- Use the suggestions in chapter three to locate paying gigs.
- In order to connect with an appropriate speakers bureau, do an Internet search using keywords: "speakers bureau" + name of city or state or "speakers bureau" + "motivational" ("inspirational," "humor," "storyteller," "fiction/literary," "author").

- Use links provided in chapter twelve to locate conferences, trade shows, and other such speaking opportunities.
- Locate speakers bureaus and other resources in the Resource List in chapter eighteen.

Whether you groom yourself to speak for a fee or you prefer sharing what you know for free, keep this book close at hand as a reference guide and resource list for the duration of your book marketing journey. Remember, personality sells books. So don't leave home without yours.

Resources for Budding and Expert Author-Speakers

Clubs/Organizations/Websites for Speakers

Toastmasters International
http://www.toastmasters.org
714-858-8255

National Speakers Association
http://www.nsaspeaker.org

Dale Carnegie Training
http://www.dalecarnegie.com

Become a Better Presenter
http://betterpresenter.com

Advanced Public-Speaking Institute
http://www.public-speaking.org

Public Speaking Tips
http://speaking-tips.com

Get Paid to Speak System
Darren LaCroix
http://getpaidtospeakbynextweek.com
http://www.speakers.com

Paul Hartunian speaker training
http://bestspeakertraining.com

National Center for Speaker Training
http://www.nationalcenterspeakertraining.com

Speakers Bureaus

American Speakers Bureau
http://www.speakersbureau.com

The American Program Bureau
http://www.apbspeakers.com

Premiere Motivational Speakers Bureau
http://premierespeakers.com

Executive Motivational Speakers Bureau
http://executivespeakersbureau.com
Find additional speakers bureaus by doing an Internet search.

Books

101 Secrets of Highly Effective Speakers: Controlling Fear, Commanding Attention by Carl Rae Krannich (Impact Publications, 1998)

The Art of Public Speaking, by Stephen Lucas and Yesaya Zerenji Mwasi (McGraw-Hill, 2003)

Ten Days to More Confident Public Speaking by Lenny Laskowski (Grand Central Publishing, 2001)

The 7 Principles of Public Speaking by Richard Zeoli (Skyhorse Publishing, 2008)

A Pocket Guide to Public Speaking by O'Hair, Rubenstein and Stewart (Bedford/St. Martins, 2009)

Ultimate Guide to Professional Speaking by Tom Antion
http://www.antion.com/beaspeaker.htm

Speak on Cruise Ships, Eight Easy Steps to a Lifetime of Free Luxury Cruises by Sharing Your Passions and Interests as an Onboard Lecturer by Daniel Hall (Amazon.com)

Talk Radio Wants You, An Intimate Guide to 700 Shows and How to Get Invited by Fran Silverman http://www.bookpromotionnewsletter.com

The Radio Book, The Ultimate Radio Station Reference Tool
Lists over 17,000 stations in Canada and the US
http://www.theradiobook.com

Voice Coaches

To locate a voice coach near you, look under "music teachers" in the Yellow Pages of your phone book. Check with colleges and music stores for a recommendation.
Roger Love, voice coach
http://www.rogerlove.com

PR and Speaking Mentors

Kim-from-L.A.
Kim Dower does media training with authors in all genres.
http://www.kimfromla.com

Dallas Woodburn
Offers PR coaching on interview and public speaking skills.
dallaswoodburn@gmail.com

TJ Walker's Media Training Workshop
http://www.mediatrainingworkshop.com

Media Training
http://www.mediatrainingcrashcourse.com

Annie Jennings PR (for authors)
http://www.anniejenningspr.com

Conference Directories

http://shawguides.com
http://www.allconferneces.com
http://www.bvents.com
http://www.tsnn.com
http://www.eventsinamerica.com

Book Festival Directories

http://author-network.com/festivals.html
http://bookfestivals.com
Also do an Internet search using keywords "book festival" and name of city/state.

Webinar/Podcast Resources

http://www.screencastomatic.com

http://www.GoToWebinar.com

Blog Talk Radio sites directory:

http://www.blogtalkradio.com/categories.aspx

Miscellaneous Resources

Audio tape: "From Author to Speaker: How to Get Paid to Speak." By Sandra Beckwith ($29). http://buildbookbuzz.com/speaking-audio-program

GuestFinder
Online directory of authors, speakers, etc.
http://www.guestfinder.com

Radio-TV Interview Report
The magazine producers read for guests and show ideas.
http://www.rtir.com

Directories of seasonal prompts
http://www.brownielocks.com
http://www.holidayinsights.com
http://www.gone-ta-pott.com

Blog directories
http://technorati.com/blogs/directory
http://www.blogtoplist.com

Contributor Bios

Nancy Barnes is the author of *Stories To Tell: An Easy Guide to Self Publishing Memoirs and Family History Books*. She is the owner of Stories To Tell Books, which provides editing, book design, and self publishing services for authors. www.storiesto-tellbooks.com

Sandra Beckwith is an author, writer, and former national award-winning publicist who now teaches authors how to become their own book publicists. Sign up for her free bi-weekly e-newsletter at buildbookbuzz.com and subscribe to her blog at buildbookbuzz.com/blog.

Peter Bowerman, a veteran commercial freelancer (since 1994) and writing/publishing coach, is the author of the three award-winning *Well-Fed Writer* titles (www.wellfedwriter.com), the self-published how-to "standards" on lucrative commercial freelancing. He chronicled his self-publishing success (currently, 65,000 copies of his books in print and a full-time living for ten-plus years) in the award-winning 2007 release, *The Well-Fed Self-Publisher: How to Turn One Book into a Full-Time Living*. www.wellfedsp.com

New York Times bestselling author Margaret Brownley has more than twenty-five novels to her credit. In addition, Thomas

Nelson has published her first non-fiction book *Grieving God's Way: The Path to Hope and Healing*. A Romance of America RITA finalist and Readers' Choice winner, she's currently working on the third book in her *Brides of Last Chance Ranch* series. Margaret and her husband live in Southern California and have three grown children. www.margaretbrownley.com or Margaret@margaretbrownley.com

Bobbie Christmas, book editor and author of award-winning *Write In Style* and other books for writers, owns Zebra Communications, a book-editing service in metro Atlanta, Georgia. www.zebraeditor.com

C. Hope Clark is editor of Funds for Writers, a writing resource service recognized by *Writer's Digest Magazine* for over a decade in its 101 Best Websites for Writers (http://www.fundsforwriters.com). Hope is also the author of *Lowcountry Bribe*, the first in her Carolina Slade Mystery Series, published by Bell Bridge Books (www.bellbridgebooks. com), available in all bookstores and online.

Victoria Cobb is the author of *The Yin and Yang of it...a Simple Guide to Playing QiGong*. She is a TaiChi, QiGong, and Yoga instructor who teaches at retreats, onboard cruise ships, and in workshops. www.lightbodytherapy.com or lightbodytherapy@hotmail.com

Lucinda Sue Crosby has had a love affair with the written word since age three when she taught herself to read. Since then she has either made a living at or won awards in an array of writing disciplines: published and recorded Nashville songwriter; presentation poet; TV film script collaborator; journalist; novel author; environmentalist. Her first novel, *Francesca of Lost Nation,* has won four awards. www. LuckyCinda.com

Susan Daffron, aka "The Book Consultant" (www.TheBookConsultant.com), is the President of Logical Expressions, which is a book and software publishing company based in Sandpoint, Idaho. She is the president of SPAWN (Small Publishers, Artists, and Writers Network) and the author of twelve books, including award-winners *Publishize* and *Funds to the Rescue.*

Wendy Dager is a professional freelance writer and author of *I Murdered the PTA,* a Daphne Lee-Lee Misadventure. The second novel in the series, *I Murdered the Spelling Bee,* will be published mid-2012. www.wendydager. com

Renay Daniels is a realtor, publisher, and mom. She resides in Bellingham, Washington with her three children and two bulldogs. *Ten Little Bulldogs* is her first children's book. www.tenlittlebulldogs.com

Kim Dower is a literary publicist and media coach. Her company, Kim-from-L.A., is celebrating twenty-five years in business (www.kimfromla. com). Kim is also a poet and author of her first published collection: *Air Kissing on Mars* (Red Hen Press), www.airkissingonmars.com.

Rik Feeney is the author of *Writing Books for Fun, Fame & Fortune!* and the soon-to-be-released *Publishing for Penny-Pinchers,* as well as the upcoming memoir *What Are Little Boys Made of...?* Rik is a book coach, book cover designer, and publishing consultant. He is the leader of the Orlando Florida Writer's Association group and often speaks at writer's conferences and seminars. Rik@PublishingSuccessOnline.com or www.PublishingSuccessOnline.com

Barbara Florio Graham has spoken to hundreds of groups, from small workshops to large international conferences. She shares many tips in her book, *Five Fast Steps to Low-Cost Publicity,* as well as on her popular website, www.SimonTeakettle.com.

Stacy Harp is the founder and president of Active Christian Media, a company that offers Internet marketing services. She also hosts a daily online radio show with her husband Randall and writes internationally for numerous websites all over the Internet. Stacy can be reached at stacy@activechristianmedia.com or www.activechristianmedia.com.

Brian Jud is an author, book-marketing consultant, media trainer, seminar leader, television host, and president of Premium Book Company, selling books to non-bookstore buyers on a non-returnable, commission basis. Brian is the author of *How to Make Real Money Selling Books* (*Without Worrying About Returns*). He wrote *Beyond the Bookstore* (a *Publishers Weekly*® book) and the *Marketing Planning* CD-ROM. Brian has also written and published five books on career transition that are distributed internationally. www.premiumbookcompany.com or brianjud@bookmarketing.com

Leslie Korenko is the author of two (soon to be three) books on the history of Kelleys Island, a small island community in Lake Erie, Ohio. She began writing books quite by accident, when a small project she was working on rapidly got out of hand. She has done presentations at libraries, historical societies, schools, and, because this is an island, several yacht clubs. www.kelleysislandstory.com

Ned Rauch-Mannino of Philadelphia writes for children, teens, and adults. His imagination-driving series *FingerTip Island* explores key themes related to issues of bullying, self-confidence, trusting others, and faith for middle grade readers. http://www.nedrauch.com

Carol Sanford is a business innovator and consultant to innovative businesses and leaders, including Fortune 100 companies, new economy business models, and entrepreneurs in large scale change, business strategy, and design. She is also the author of many works, including *The Responsible Business: Reimagining Sustainability and Success* (Jossey Bass). Author-speaker and winner of the International Book Award in Business. www.carolsanford.com

Carol Dean Schreiner is a professional speaker, trainer, storyteller, and humorist. She is the author of four books, including *Wonder Woman Doesn't Live Here Anymore, Laugh for the Health of It, Steps to Storytelling,* and *Fabulous at 50, Sexy at 60 and Sin-sational at 70.* www.caroldean.com or cdspeaks@sbcglobal.net

Karen Lee Stevens is a Certified Humane Education Specialist and the founder and president of All for Animals, a nonprofit organization dedicated to creating a compassionate world through humane education. She is the author of two books focused on animals, including *Animals Have Feelings, Too!,* an enchanting and educational A–Z picture book that helps young readers to understand and express their feelings and to treat animals with kindness and respect. www.allfor-animals.com

Mary Ellen Warner is a natural born storyteller. Her entertaining, educational, and inspirational stories explore leading-edge boomer issues. Visit www.marbilwarner.com to learn more about Mary Ellen's universal themes.

Jerry Waxler, M.S. has written two books for writers and is the author of the blog *Memory Writers Network.* Jerry is a board member at the Philadelphia Writers' Conference and teaches writing at Northampton Community College in Bethlehem, Pennsylvania. www.jerrywaxler.com. or www.memorywritersnetwork.com/blog

Raven West is the author of *Red Wine for Breakfast* (Lighthouse Press, 1999), *First Class Male* (Lighthouse Press, 2001), and *Undercover Reunion* (Createspace, 2011). She's conducted marketing seminars for Learning Tree University, California Lutheran University, Book Expo America in Los Angeles and New York, and she has been a featured presenter at the Santa Barbara and Ventura County Book Fairs and the Ventura County Writers Club and Independent Writers of Southern California (IWOSC). ravenwest.net

Dallas Woodburn is the author of two collections of short stories and editor of *Dancing with the Pen: a collection of today's best youth writing*. Her writing has appeared in *Family Circle, Writer's Digest, The Los Angeles Times*, and more than two dozen literary magazines. Connect with her at www.dallaswoodburn.com and dallaswoodburn.blogspot.com.

Index

tradeshows, 197–198
travel expenses, 271–272
TV appearances, 225–233

Undercover Reunion, 258, 291
Ultimate Guide to Professional Speaking, 283

venues. *See* public speaking *and* workshops
vocal variety, 74, 99, 107, 125, 149
voice, 125
    improve, 16, 72–77, 100–101, 107
voice coach, 75–77, 100–101, 283

Warner, Mary Ellen, 17, 48, 91, 95, 97, 100, 116–117, 124–125, 137, 275–276, 291
Waxler, Jerry, 18–20, 23–24, 45, 63–64, 95, 101, 132–133, 250–251, 291
webinars, 239–241
Well-Fed Author, 7
Well-Fed Self-Publisher, 287
Well-Fed Writer, 287
West, Raven, 55, 90, 151–152, 179–180, 227, 249, 251, 254–255, 258, 291
Wonder Woman Doesn't Live Here Anymore, 291
Woodburn, Dallas, 8–9, 36–37, 67–68, 69, 108, 118, 283, 292
workshops, 22–23, 43, 86, 131
    benefits of, 23, 48, 49
    examples, 24–25, 49
    for novelists, 23
    how to create, 24–25
    set up your own, 47–49
    venues, 47, 48, 49
Write in Style, 14, 181, 288
Write On for Literacy, 37
write speech. *See* speech
Write Your Memoir in 4 Weeks, 18
Writer's Guide to Article-Writing (A), 25, 210, 275
Writing Books for Fun, Fame and Fortune, 289

Yin and Yang of It (The), 20, 288